MW00651919

Exploring The BUILDING BLOCKS of

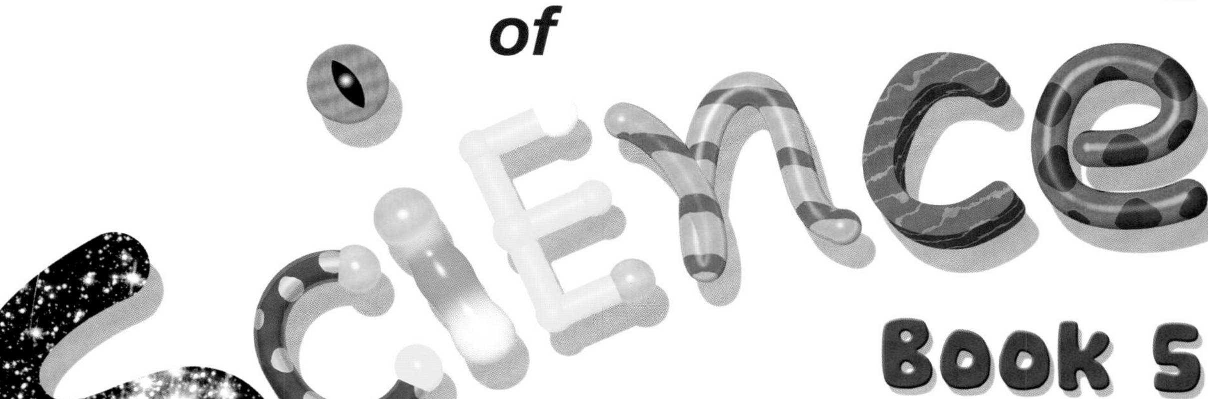

Book 5

STUDENT TEXTBOOK

REBECCA W. KELLER, PhD

REAL SCIENCE 4 Kids

Illustrations: Janet Moneymaker
Rebecca W. Keller, PhD
Marjie Bassler

Exploring the Building Blocks of Science Book 5 Student Textbook (hardcover)

ISBN 978-1-941181-08-9

Published by Gravitas Publications, Inc.
Real Science-4-Kids®
www.realscience4kids.com
www.gravitaspublications.com

Contents

Introduction

CHAPTER 1 What Is Science? 1

1.1 What Is Science? 2
1.2 The History of Science 4
1.3 The Philosophy of Science 5
1.4 The Scientific Method 7
1.5 Making Scientific Measurements 10
1.6 Interpreting Scientific Data 12
1.7 Summary 13

Chemistry

CHAPTER 2 What Is Chemistry? 14

2.1 Introduction 15
2.2 History of Matter 16
2.3 The Alchemists 20
2.4 Alchemy Meets Experiment 21
2.5 Summary 24

CHAPTER 3 Matter 25

3.1 The Atom Today 26
3.2 The Periodic Table of Elements 27
3.3 Using the Periodic Table 28
3.4 Summary 33

CHAPTER 4 Chemical Bonding 34

4.1 Introduction 35
4.2 The Role of Models in Chemistry 35
4.3 Models of the Atom 36
4.4 Models of the Chemical Bond 39
4.5 Types of Bonds 40
4.6 Shared Electron Bonds 41
4.7 Unshared Electron Bonds 42
4.8 Bonding Rules 43
4.9 Summary 44

CHAPTER 5 Chemical Reactions 45
5.1 Introduction 46
5.2 Chemical Reactions and the Atomic Theory 47
5.3 Types of Chemical Reactions 49
5.4 Combination Reaction 49
5.5 Decomposition Reaction 50
5.6 Displacement Reaction 50
5.7 Exchange Reaction 51
5.8 Spontaneous or Not? 51
5.9 Evidence of Chemical Reactions 52
5.10 Summary 53

Biology

CHAPTER 6 What Is Biology? 54
6.1 Introduction 55
6.2 What Is Life? 56
6.3 Philosophical Maps Help Us Interpret Science 60
6.4 Organizing Life 61
6.5 Summary 68

CHAPTER 7 The Chemistry of Life 69
7.1 Introduction 70
7.2 Types of Atoms Inside Cells 71
7.3 Types of Biological Molecules 71
7.4 Energy Molecules 72
7.5 Structural Molecules 73
7.6 Molecular Machines 75
7.7 Information Storage and Transfer 76
7.8 Chemical Reactions in Cells: Metabolism 77
7.9 Summary 78

CHAPTER 8 Cells—The Building Blocks of Life 79
8.1 Introduction 80
8.2 Types of Cells 81
8.3 Bacterial Prokaryotic Cells 82
8.4 Archaeal Prokaryotic Cells 84
8.5 Eukaryotic Cells 84
8.6 Cell Division 88
8.7 Prokaryotic and Archaeal Cell Division 88
8.8 The Eukaryotic Cell Cycle: Mitosis 89
8.9 Summary 90

CHAPTER 9 Viruses, Bacteria, and Archaea 91
9.1 Introduction 92
9.2 Viruses 92
9.3 Bacteria 94
9.4 Shapes of Bacteria 95
9.5 Archaea 97
9.6 Summary 99

Physics

CHAPTER 10 What Is Physics? 100
10.1 Introduction 101
10.2 The Basic Laws of Physics 101
10.3 How We Get Laws 102
10.4 Summary 104

CHAPTER 11 Force, Energy, and Work 105
11.1 Introduction 106
11.2 Force 106
11.3 Balanced Forces 107
11.4 Unbalanced Forces 108
11.5 Work 109
11.6 Energy 110
11.7 Summary 111

CHAPTER 12 Potential and Kinetic Energy 112
12.1 Potential Energy 113
12.2 A Note About Units 114
12.3 Types of Potential Energy 115
12.4 Energy Is Converted 116
12.5 Kinetic Energy 116
12.6 Kinetic Energy and Work 117
12.7 Summary 119

CHAPTER 13 Conservation of Energy 120
13.1 Introduction 121
13.2 Energy Is Conserved 121
13.3 Usable Energy 123
13.4 Energy Sources 123
13.5 Summary 128

Geology

CHAPTER 14 What Is Geology? 129
14.1 Introduction 130
14.2 What Is Geology? 130
14.3 Interpreting Geological Data 131
14.4 Why Study Earth? 133
14.5 What Do Geologists Study? 133
14.6 Geology and the Scientific Method 135
14.7 Summary 136

CHAPTER 15 Rocks, Minerals, and Soils 137
15.1 Introduction 138
15.2 Minerals 139
15.3 Rocks 142
15.4 Testing Rocks and Minerals 146
15.5 Soils 148
15.6 Summary 151

CHAPTER 16 Earth's Layers 152
16.1 Introduction 153
16.2 Inside the Earth 153
16.3 The Crust 154
16.4 The Mantle 155
16.5 The Lithosphere 156
16.6 The Asthenosphere 156
16.7 The Mesosphere 158
16.8 The Core 159
16.9 Summary 160

CHAPTER 17 Earth's Dynamics 161
17.1 Introduction 162
17.2 Plate Tectonics 162
17.3 Mountains 165
17.4 Volcanoes 166
17.5 Earthquakes 169
17.6 Summary 171

Astronomy

CHAPTER 18 What Is Astronomy? 172

18.1 Introduction 173
18.2 Early Astronomers 173
18.3 Modern Astronomers 175
18.4 Changing Views of the Cosmos 175
18.5 Summary 178

CHAPTER 19 Earth in Space 179

19.1 Introduction 180
19.2 The Earth in Space 180
19.3 The Earth and the Moon 183
19.4 The Earth and the Sun 186
19.5 Eclipses 188
19.6 Summary 189

CHAPTER 20 The Moon and the Sun 190

20.1 Introduction 191
20.2 The Moon 191
20.3 The Sun 194
20.4 Chemistry and Physics of Stars 195
20.5 Summary 197

CHAPTER 21 Planets 198

21.1 Introduction 199
21.2 Types of Planets 199
21.3 Earth-like Planets 200
21.4 Jupiter-like Planets 202
21.5 What Happened to Pluto? 205
21.6 Summary 207

Conclusion

CHAPTER 22 Putting It All Together 208

22.1 Science 209
22.2 Science and the Public 210
22.3 Science in the Movies 212
22.4 Real Scientists 213
22.5 Summary 214

Chapter 1 What Is Science?

1.1 What Is Science? 2

1.2 The History of Science 4

1.3 The Philosophy of Science 5

1.4 The Scientific Method 7

1.5 Making Scientific Mearurements 10

1.6 Interpreting Scientific Data 12

1.7 Summary 13

Introduction

1.1 What Is Science?

Have you ever wondered what science really is or what it is that scientists really do? Have you seen images of scientists in white lab coats working furiously with colored test tubes and looking for new discoveries? But is that all there is to science? Ask yourself, *What is science?* Ask your mom or dad and your teacher to give you a definition of science. What do they say? Do you get different answers?

If you are having trouble really putting your finger on a definition of science, don't feel bad. The term *science* is hard to define because science involves many different aspects of learning. It involves making observations about nature and designing experiments. It also involves making conclusions and trying to better understand the world we live in.

One definition of science is:

> *Science is a systematic way to study the world in which we live.*

The study of science uses a system. A system is an organized plan or method that can be followed. The method that scientists use includes observation and experimentation, collecting information, or data, and using this data to make conclusions and predictions about how the world works. In today's modern world, scientists also use instrumentation, or tools, to help them make observations that they can't make with their senses alone.

There are many ways to define science, but all definitions of science include several systematic steps for the process of scientific inquiry. These include: ❶ Making scientific observations, ❷ Proposing scientific questions, ❸ Designing scientific experiments, ❹ Collecting scientific information, ❺ Making scientific interpretations, ❻ Evaluating scientific assumptions, ❼ Discussing scientific implications, and ❽ Evaluating different points of view.

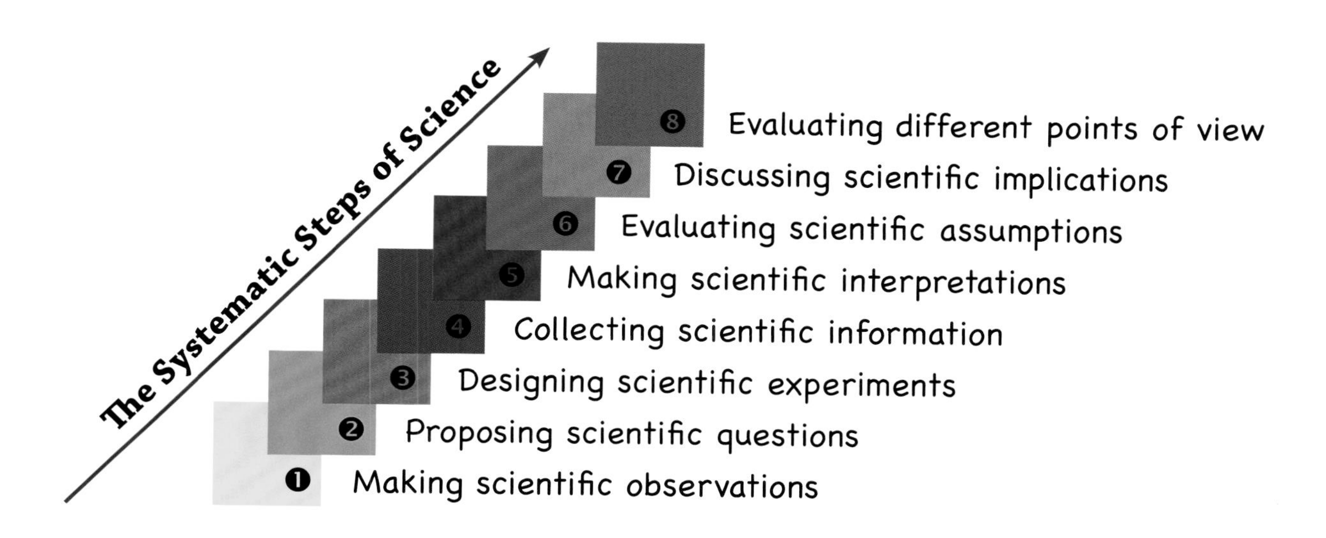

The word science is a relatively modern word. That is, you won't find the word science in any written documents before about 1400 CE. The word science comes to us from the Latin word *scire*, which means "to know." The word *scientist* was introduced in 1834 by a British scholar named William Whewell (1794–1866). Before this time, people who studied science were called natural philosophers.

Natural philosophers explored the world around them by coming up with and developing ideas about the world. Some natural philosophers further explored the world by observing what was around them and how these things work. By applying their ideas and observations, some created inventions to help them make new observations and discoveries.

Today, modern science is a combination of these different ways in which natural philosophers investigated the world around them. Modern science combines science as ideas, science as observation, and science as invention. Science as ideas is now called philosophy. Science as observation includes the various scientific disciplines, such as chemistry and biology. And science as invention is now called technology.

1.2 The History of Science

Who were the first scientists? Where did they live? What did they discover? How did they make discoveries? All of these questions explore the history of science. Because scientific thinking was developed over a long period of time by many different men and women, science has a rich and exciting history.

The word *history* comes from the Greek word *historia*, which means "a learning by inquiry." History is the study of events that happened in the past, and historians build narratives, or stories, about those events. Historians look for documents and artifacts and then use these documents and artifacts to piece together a story about what happened in the past and what it means.

Historians who study the history of science use different kinds of information to help them understand how modern science was developed. For example, historians of science look at the notebooks of Isaac Newton and other early scientists to understand how they thought. Historians of science look at writings from ancient philosophers and the languages that various peoples used to describe the natural world. Historians of science look at drawings people made about inventions that were used and other drawings that show what ancient people thought about the stars. By using different kinds of information, historians of science explore what happened in the past and how we know what we know today.

Historians of science do more than just look at the events of the past. They try to understand what the events mean. That is, they try to interpret the past in order to better understand how the past affects the present and how the present might impact the future. It is very important to have a solid understanding of how the history of science developed. When people forget their history and run into problems earlier people encountered, they may make the same mistakes because they haven't learned from their past.

Sometimes historians of science disagree about how to interpret the past. In the same way that scientists disagree about how to interpret data, historians of science disagree about how to interpret events. In history, like in science, it is always better to explore different interpretations of an event rather than just one. It is important in the study of science to view various viewpoints and then come to your own conclusions about what you think they mean.

1.3 The Philosophy of Science

As we just saw, science began as the philosophy of ideas about how the world works. When we talk about the philosophy of science, we are really referring to the ideas and ways of thinking that began in the area surrounding the Aegean Sea around 600 BCE. The word philosophy comes from the Greek words *philein*, which means "to love," and *sophia*, which means "wisdom." So "philosophy" literally means the "love of wisdom."

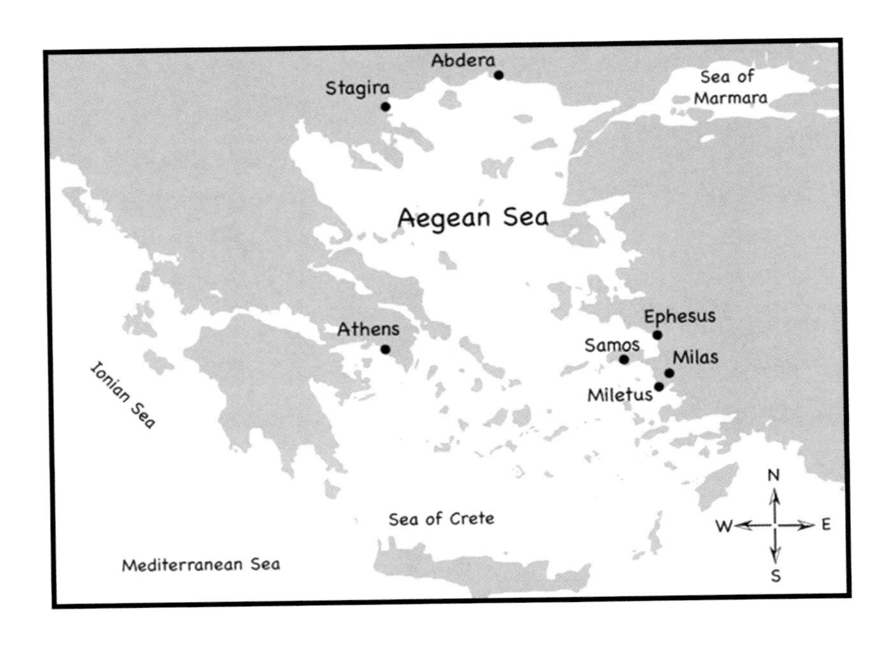

The earliest philosophers were clustered around the Mediterranean Sea, most notably ancient Greece. However, activities that we would today associate with modern science were happening all over the world. Ancient peoples, such as the Egyptians and native people of South America, were observing the sky and making mathematical calculations. The Chinese were doing primitive forms of chemistry with mercury and sulfur. And the Native North Americans were experimenting with plants in order to discover which were capable of healing disease and sickness. Today we associate all of these activities, or technologies, with science.

Before the 15th century, ideas about science (philosophy) and scientific inventions (technology) were largely separate from each other. Philosophers didn't much care for the crafts of inventors, and inventors didn't much care for the lofty ideas of philosophers. These two aspects of modern science did not really overlap in ancient times. Also, science as observation (particularly chemistry) was largely performed by alchemists whose work didn't overlap with that of either the philosophers or the inventors. We'll learn more about the alchemists in Chapter 2.

After the 15th century, the philosophical ideas that started in Greece began to merge with the technological discoveries being made by people all over the world, and discoveries made by alchemists began to play a role in both invention and philosophy.

From this time forward, modern science exploded as new discoveries and inventions were put together with philosophical ideas. Science as ideas, science as observation, and science as invention began to merge together, giving us what we know today as modern science.

1.4 The Scientific Method

Scientists ask a lot of questions. They see things around them and ask questions like: How does this work? Why does this happen? What would happen if I did this?

To find answers to their questions, scientists use the scientific method. There are essentially five steps in the scientific method: making observations, forming a hypothesis, performing an experiment, collecting data, and drawing conclusions.

Scientists observe how things behave and look for patterns that are similar from day to day. For example, you may notice that each time it snows, people in big trucks spread salt on the roads. You may also notice that cars have less trouble traveling on these salted roads than on roads without salt.

These are observations and are the first step in the scientific method. From these observations, you might think of a general statement that tells something about what you have observed. This is the second step in the scientific method and is called forming a hypothesis. A hypothesis is really just a guess. It is something that you think might be true about your observations but that hasn't been proven. For example, you might make the following statements about why salt is put on roads:

The salt melts the ice on the road.
The salt makes rubber tires sticky.
The salt makes the snow stop falling.

All of these statements are *hypotheses*. That is, they are hypothetical, meaning they haven't been proven.

The third step is to test the hypothesis by using experimentation. By designing an experiment to test the hypothesis, you can find out if the hypothesis is correct.

For example, you may decide to do an experiment to test the hypothesis that "salt makes rubber tires sticky." You might take two pieces of rubber and add salt to one and not to the other. The one you don't add salt to would be a control. A control tells you what you would expect without salt so that you can tell if the salt makes any difference. Next, you would compare the two pieces of rubber to see if the one with salt is stickier than the one without salt.

This brings you to the fourth step in the scientific method, collecting results. As a scientist, you should always record the results of your experiment exactly as you see them. If the salty rubber is "stickier" than the regular rubber, then you should record that. If the rubber is not stickier with salt, then that is what must be recorded. At this point, you should not let what you *think* might happen affect how you record your results. This is very important. Also, *everything* you observe should be written down. Even your mistakes should be recorded.

Finally, the last step of the scientific method is to draw conclusions based on what your results show. Here again, your conclusions should be based only on your results and should not be influenced by what you think should have happened. For example, if the salt did not make the rubber stickier, then a conclusion might be:

> **Conclusion:** *Based on my data, the salt did not make the rubber more sticky.*

Based on this one experiment, you cannot say why the salt helps the cars drive more easily. You would have to conduct more experiments. But you have been able to eliminate at least one hypothesis using the scientific method. Showing which hypotheses are NOT true is often just as important as showing which one is true.

Using the scientific method is a way for scientists to evaluate whether the answers to their questions are correct. Sometimes, even when scientists use the scientific method, they cannot prove that their answers are right. Furthermore, different scientists will have different ideas about answers to questions.

1.5 Making Scientific Measurements

Aristotle (384-322 BCE) was a Greek philosopher who helped change the way people thought about the natural world. He believed that we should emphasize what we can perceive with our senses. Aristotle conducted his studies in a very hands-on manner by observing the world around him.

Observations allow people to use the technique of inductive reasoning. When employing this type of reasoning, a person draws conclusions from a small number of observations.

For example, if some students observe that three different ice cubes are cold, they are using inductive reasoning when they draw the conclusion that all ice cubes are cold.

Inductive reasoning takes observations of one or a few to draw conclusions about many or all.

Three ice cubes are cold,
therefore all ice cubes are cold.

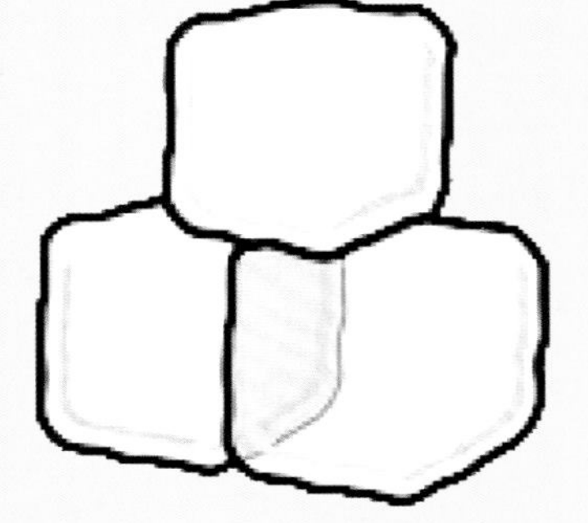

Inductive reasoning has its limitations. We may not look at enough different situations to see all of the possibilities. For example, if black cats are the only type of cat a person has ever seen, they might believe that all cats are black. But we know there are other kinds of cats that are not black. You can see that inductive reasoning might sometimes lead to false conclusions. However, inductive reasoning is very useful in science because it is impossible to measure everything.

When scientists study the natural world, they ask questions and use inductive reasoning to draw conclusions about the measurements they make. Scientists use the term data to refer to the results of their measurements. Data are the "facts" in science. How heavy is a boulder? How tall is a tree? How many legs does a starfish have? Sometimes the "facts" change as scientists learn more about the world and refine their experiments and measurements.

One way scientists refine their measurements is to use scientific tools. Using tools helps scientists with both accuracy and precision. Accuracy is how closely a measurement matches reality, and precision is how closely different measurements match each other.

In chemistry, a beaker or graduated cylinder can be used to accurately measure the volume of a liquid, and a balance or scale is used to accurately measure the weight of chemical compounds. A digital thermometer might be used to get an accurate temperature, and the temperature might be recorded three or more times to get a precise measurement.

1.6 Interpreting Scientific Data

Once the measurements have been made, the next step is to find out what they mean. It is a misunderstanding about science to believe that scientific data yields obvious and straightforward interpretations. Because people, including scientists, don't see things in the same way, there are disagreements about what scientific data mean. There are many theories and ideas that create arguments in science. The disagreements scientists have about how to interpret data are very important for science. Without arguments to stimulate new discoveries, science can't move forward.

Everybody has certain ideas about the world until there is a good reason to change their ideas. Sometimes new information is discovered that presents just a small change to existing ideas. Other times, as a result of new information, there is a major change in the way we understand the world around us. That major change is often called a paradigm shift.

A paradigm is the entire set of beliefs, values, techniques, and ideas that a group of people share. In science, a paradigm is developed over time, and it is based upon scientific information that has been gathered, theories that have been developed, and conclusions that have been reached. Some people change their understanding of scientific information more easily than others. When people who adopt new understandings discuss science with those who are resistant to new ideas, the disagreement can get very heated.

Paradigm shifts have been happening for as long as there have been people. The idea of the paradigm shift was developed in 1962 by Thomas Kuhn (1922–1996), an American science philosopher and historian. He said that scientific understanding is not a slow and steady stream. Rather, it occurs by major shifts in paradigms.

Before a paradigm shift in science can occur, new ideas must give rise to new scientific discoveries. New ideas challenge old, established ideas in science. However, in order for new scientific discoveries to happen, new ideas need to be discussed and debated, and the new ideas need to be given the opportunity to challenge the old ideas. When new ideas that challenge old ideas cannot be discussed and debated, new scientific discoveries don't happen. Scientific discoveries are made when scientists incorporate new data and allow prevailing theories to be modified or changed.

1.7 Summary

- Science is a systematic way to study the world in which we live.
- Science as ideas is called philosophy. Science as observation includes the various scientific disciplines, such as chemistry and biology. And science as invention is called technology.
- Science has a history.
- The scientific method is used to test theories and has 5 steps:
  1. Making observations.
  2. Forming a hypothesis.
  3. Designing an experiment.
  4. Collecting data.
  5. Drawing conclusions.
- Interpreting scientific data is an important part of scientific investigation, and can be the source of many scientific arguments.

Chapter 2 What Is Chemistry?

2.1 Introduction 15

2.2 History of Matter 16

2.3 The Alchemists 20

2.4 Alchemy Meets Experiment 21

2.5 Summary 24

2.1 Introduction

Have you ever wondered what all the objects in the world are made of and why they behave the way they do?

What is soap and why is it slippery? What is air? Why do ice cubes float? Why are dates sweet? What are hair and skin made of? Why is a marble hard and a jellyfish soft?

All of these questions and others like them begin the inquiry into the branch of science we call chemistry.

Chemistry is the study of the "stuff" that makes up the things in the physical world. Scientists call this "stuff" matter.

Everything we see with our eyes and can touch with our fingers is made of matter.

Bananas are made of matter. Cars are made of matter. Even our bodies are made of matter. In Chapter 3 we will learn more about matter and what makes up matter.

2.2 History of Matter

The first person we know of who asked questions about matter was Thales, a Greek philosopher who was born in Miletus, a small trading town on the Aegean coast. Thales studied astronomy and mathematics and is believed to have traveled to Egypt where he learned geometry and astronomy. Thales is credited with bringing this knowledge back to Greece. He used what he knew about the stars to his advantage. One story has it that he bought olive presses for making olive oil because he predicted a large olive harvest. He was right! He made lots of money selling olive oil to everyone.

Thales believed that water was the fundamental unit of matter. He thought that everything in the universe came from water. Thales also felt that water could turn into earth and other types of matter.

Another Greek philosopher from Miletus who asked about what things are made of was Anaximander. Many of the philosophers who lived during the time that Anaximander was alive were looking for the essence (the true nature of a thing) of all things. These philosophers were curious about what everything is composed of. Anaximander came up with the idea of "the boundless," or "the ultimate." Unfortunately, he never explained what that was, and this was not a lot of help to people.

Anaximenes was another Greek philosopher who lived in Miletus and wondered what things are made of. In contrast to Thales, Anaximenes believed that air was the basic substance of matter. According to Anaximenes, when air was thinned, it could become fire. In addition, if air was condensed, it would become wind and clouds. And even more condensing would compress air into water, earth, and even stone. Anaximenes tried to explain many natural processes. For example, he believed that thunder and lightning came from wind breaking out of clouds, that rainbows occurred when the Sun's rays hit the clouds, and that earthquakes took place when the ground dried out after a rainstorm.

Empedocles was all things to all people. Some people believed he was a great healer. Others thought he was a magician. He had some convinced he was a living god. Still others believed he was a total fake. The periodic table of earth, air, fire, and water came from Empedocles. He believed that these four "roots" made up all matter. He believed that even living creatures were composed of these materials.

Another Greek philosopher was Leucippus. We don't know much about Leucippus, but from what we do know, it appears that he was the first person to suggest the idea of empty space. (Today, we would call this a vacuum.) He also developed the idea of atoms. Leucippus believed that different atoms had different sizes and weights. We now know this to be true.

Democritus was another Greek philosopher, and he probably was one of the first weather forecasters. Democritus had people convinced that he could predict the future. He was a student of Leucippus, and he is an example of a pupil who is better known than his teacher. He studied many natural objects, and he gave public lectures.

The Greek philosophers debated about a lot of things. One of their debates had to do with sand on the beach. They asked the following questions: Can you divide a grain of sand indefinitely? —and— Is there a point at which you can no longer break the grain in half?

Most of the philosophers believed that you could divide the grain of sand continuously, without ever stopping. Democritus, however, believed that there was a point at which the grain of sand could no longer be broken into smaller pieces. He called this smallest piece of matter the atom. Today we know that atoms make all matter.

The early Greek philosophers had many arguments over the course of many centuries. They argued about how the world works, how it is made, and how it came into being.

As we saw earlier, Thales thought that everything was made of water. He believed that water was the "primary substance" of all things. He thought that water could not be divided any further. Today we know that water is made of two hydrogen atoms and one oxygen atom.

Anaximander rejected water as the primary substance. As we saw earlier, he thought that everything was made of something that he called "the boundless." Nobody was really sure what Anaximander meant by "the boundless," and this made it difficult for him in arguments.

Anaximenes didn't agree with either Thales or Anaximander. He rejected both water and "the boundless" as the primary substance. He believed that air was the primary substance.

Empedocles disagreed with everyone. He said that all of the things in the world are made up of not just one substance but of four—earth, air, fire, and water.

Democritus and Leucippus didn't agree with any of the other philosophers either. Democritus and Leucippus thought that the world was made up of atoms. They had trouble explaining exactly what atoms were because they didn't have the technology to find out about them. However, they thought that all matter is made of one type of thing which they called an atom. They thought that atoms could be combined to make larger things.

It turns out that Democritus's and Leucippus's ideas were closer to reality than the other philosophers' ideas were. But Democritus and Leucippus didn't get very many people to agree with them. Atoms were not seriously considered as a possibility until the 17th century, almost 2000 years later!

2.3 The Alchemists

Many scholars agree that the word chemistry comes from the word alchemy. The word alchemy comes either from the Egyptian word *khemia* which means "transmutation of earth" or from the Greek word *khymeia*, which means the "art of alloying metals." Both word origins point to the alchemists as the first to experiment with chemistry.

Some early experimenters of chemistry were the alchemists. Alchemists were not considered to be true chemists because they did not approach their work with a scientific method. But they did play with the properties of matter. They believed that they could turn some matter, like lead, into different matter, like gold. A lot of what they tried was based on magic and didn't work. In fact, they never got any lead to turn into gold. Often they would go to a king and ask for money to use to make lead turn into gold. Of course, this never happened. Very often, the king would get angry and put the alchemists in prison (or worse). Sometimes the alchemists would just leave town with the king's money.

Although the alchemists were never successful at turning lead into gold, they did learn quite a lot about the properties of matter. They found out which substances would burn, which substances had a particular taste or smell, and which substances would cause bubbles if mixed with other substances. Through this process, they collected lots of information about the properties of various elements.

2.4 Alchemy Meets Experiment

The alchemists didn't think that everything was made of air, water, fire, and earth. They thought that everything was made of mercury, sulfur, and salt! But the alchemists weren't right either. By the late 16th and early 17th centuries, modern scientific thinking began to take shape. Philosophy and invention started coming together, and many philosophers began thinking about how to do quality scientific experiments.

One such thinker was Sir Robert Boyle (1627-1691), an Irish chemist and philosopher. Boyle believed in running experiments to see what would actually happen and to prove or disprove his ideas. He used elaborate glassware to test the properties of air and fire, and by doing these experiments, he figured out fundamental gas laws that describe how gases behave under different conditions. Boyle's experiments also helped show that different kinds of atoms could combine to form molecules.

While doing experiments with air, Boyle produced oxygen, but he didn't know it! However, his experiments led to the later discovery of oxygen as an element. By doing quality experiments, Boyle made many contributions to chemistry.

Joseph Priestley (1733-1804) was an English philosopher and chemist who never took a science course. However, he enjoyed playing around with different materials. After he met Benjamin Franklin, Priestley became very interested in science. He discovered carbon dioxide gas and invented the first soda water by adding carbon dioxide to water, a process called carbonation. Carbon dioxide gas makes the fizz in soft drinks. Another of his many discoveries was nitrous oxide, also called laughing gas, which is used for anesthesia. Priestley is also well known for his experiments with oxygen.

Antoine Lavoisier (1743-1794) was a French scientist who believed in performing experiments. He called laboratory work "the torch of observation and experiment." This "torch" shed light on scientific facts. Lavoisier was one of the many scientists who earned the title *The Father of Chemistry*.

Lavoisier knew Priestley, and Priestley told him about his experiments with oxygen (which Priestley called dephlogisticated air). Lavoisier did his own experiments with oxygen and is the one who gave oxygen its name. Lavoisier tried to take credit for the discovery of oxygen, but it was known that others had discovered it before he did.

Lavoisier showed that water is not a basic substance but is made of oxygen and hydrogen. This was a very important discovery for the advancement of chemistry. Lavoisier wrote his ideas and findings in the well known book *Elements of Chemistry,* which contained useful information for chemists of his time and is still available today.

Although Lavoisier's research and discoveries were important to science, he became unpopular during the French Revolution, which was a time of great turmoil. He was taken prisoner and executed.

By the early 1800s, it was well established that air, fire, water, and earth were not the basic substances. This paved the way for the work of John Dalton (1766–1844). Dalton was a British schoolteacher for most of his life, and he first became interested in science by studying the weather.

Dalton revived the hypothesis for the atomic theory of elements that had been proposed by Democritus some 2000 years earlier. In his published work, *A New System of Chemical Philosophy,* consisting of several volumes written between 1808 and 1827, Dalton proposed that all elements are made of atoms. He also proposed that each element has its own atomic weight. The atomic weight, he said, is proportional to the size of the atom that makes up the element. This agrees with what we know today.

Dalton drew the first table of elements. In the table, he described the arrangement of the atoms in several elements, and he provided their atomic weights. Dalton did not know all of the elements that we know today, but he laid the foundation for future study. His contributions to the field of chemistry were significant. John Dalton is known as the *Father of Modern Chemistry.*

Dalton's atomic theory tried to explain some basic properties of atoms. He had the right idea, but several points in his theory were later proven incomplete. Today, we know that atoms make up matter and that the model of the atom is a good explanation for how matter works. Like the alchemists, modern chemists continue to experiment with finding ways to change matter from one type to another. Because they understand about atoms, they've even figured out how to change lead into gold!

2.5 Summary

- Chemistry is the study of the matter that makes up the physical world.
- Early Greek philosophers had different ideas about what matter is made of and had many arguments about how the world works.
- The alchemists experimented with matter and tried to turn lead into gold.
- By doing quality experiments, early scientists were able to show that the basic unit of matter is the atom.

Chapter 3 Matter

3.1 The Atom Today 26

3.2 The Periodic Table of Elements 27

3.3 Using the Periodic Table 28

3.4 Summary 33

Chemistry

3.1 The Atom Today

Today we know that the fundamental building blocks of matter are atoms. The word atom comes from the Greek word *atomos*, which means "uncuttable."

Today we know that atoms are not really uncuttable but are made of even smaller particles called protons, neutrons, and electrons. However, during chemical reactions atoms act as whole units, so the model of the atom as an uncuttable unit of matter works well for understanding chemical reactions.

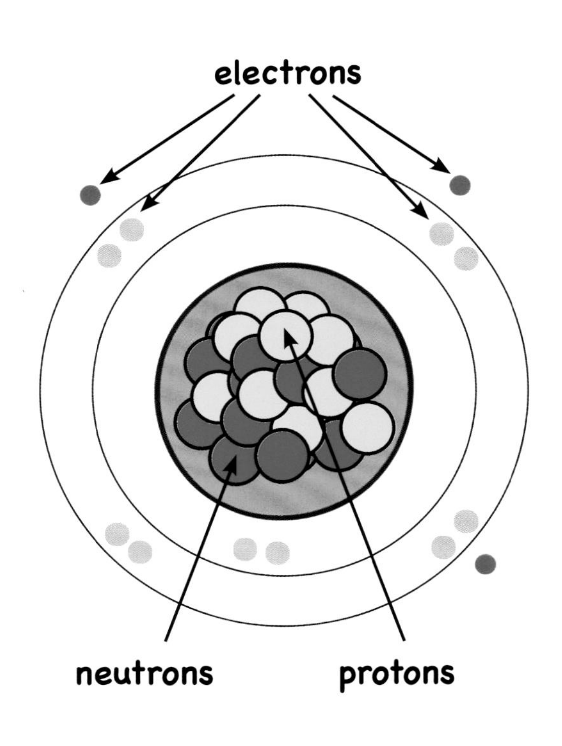

Protons and neutrons are roughly equal in size, but electrons are much smaller than either protons or neutrons. Together, protons, neutrons, and electrons make up an atom. Protons and neutrons combine to form the central core (the nucleus) of an atom, and the electrons occupy the space surrounding the central core.

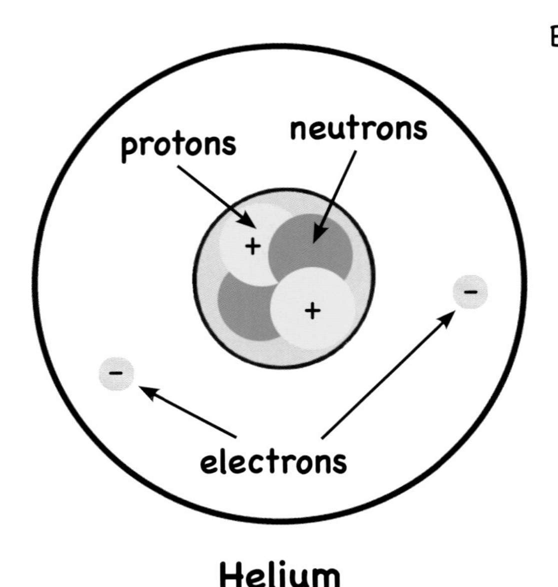

Helium

Electrons have a negative electric charge, protons have a positive charge, and neutrons have no charge. For neutral elements (those that do not have an electric charge) the number of electrons in an atom always equals the number of protons.

Notice that in the helium atom there are two protons and two electrons. Sometimes the number of protons also equals the number of neutrons, as in helium, but this is not always true.

Most of the size of an atom is actually made of the space between the electrons and the core. The protons and neutrons make up only a very small part of the total size.

On the other hand, almost all of the weight of an atom comes from the protons and neutrons. The electrons weigh almost nothing compared to the nucleus.

3.2 The Periodic Table of Elements

The periodic table of elements is a chart used by chemists that categorizes the elements (atoms) and shows their characteristics. Recall from Chapter 2 that the first periodic table of elements was put together by John Dalton (1766-1844) who proposed that all matter is made of atoms.

In 1869 Dmitri Mendeleev, who was a chemist born in Tobolsk, Siberia (Russia), expanded Dalton's table. While scribbling in his notebook, Mendeleev developed the first version of our modern periodic table of elements.

Mendeleev carried with him cards that had the names and weights of the 63 known elements written on them. He thought about the elements and their weights a great deal. After much thinking, he decided to arrange the elements into a chart that was based on their atomic masses.

In 1869 Mendeleev published his chart in a book called *Principles of Chemistry*. He left spaces in his chart because he thought that some elements were missing, and he was right! With his table, he was able to predict a few of the elements that were missing, and while he was still living, the next three elements were indeed discovered. His table gave other scientists the information they needed to find the missing elements. Those missing elements were exactly what Mendeleev predicted! He was famous for the success of his predictions.

Today, the periodic table of elements is much larger than Mendeleev's table and contains 118 elements. Some of the newer elements have been created in the laboratory. The International Union of Pure and Applied Chemistry (IUPAC) is an organization that reviews and verifies the discovery of new elements. As of this writing, the elements ununtrium, ununpentium ununseptium, and ununoctium have been given temporary names until they have been verified and given their official names.

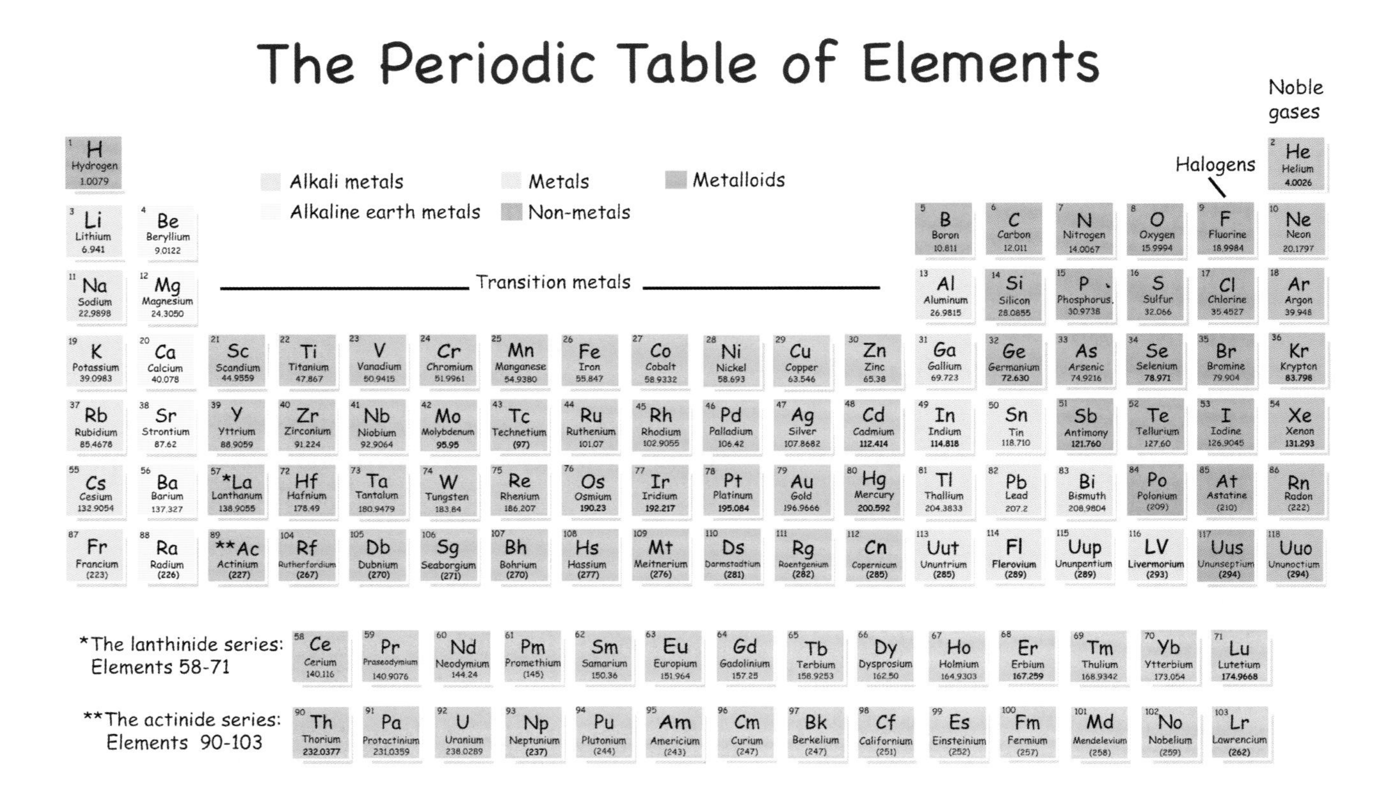

3.3 Using the Periodic Table

In the standard periodic table used by most scientists, the elements are arranged horizontally from left to right in order of increasing atomic number. The atomic number is the number of protons in the nucleus of each atom. For example, carbon has an atomic number of 6. This means carbon has 6 protons in its nucleus. Oxygen has an atomic number of 8, which means it has 8 protons in its nucleus.

Each of the elements has its own symbol. For example, hydrogen has the symbol "H," carbon has the symbol "C," and oxygen has the symbol "O." Notice that for these elements the symbol is the same as the first letter of the name. Other elements have the first two letters of their name as their symbol—for example, "He" for helium and "Ne" for neon.

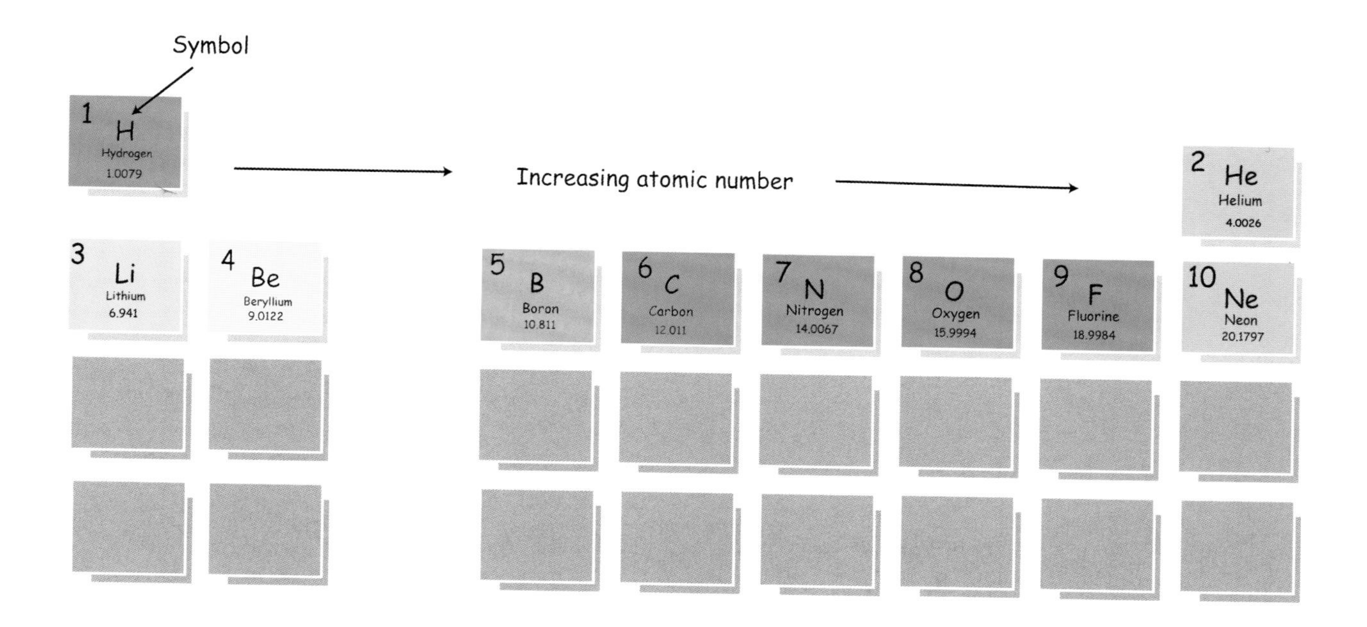

Some elements have a symbol that is different from the first letter or letters of their name. For example, the symbol for gold is "Au" from the word *aurum* which means gold in Latin. The name for sodium comes from the Latin word *natrium*, so sodium has the symbol "Na." Other examples include lead, which has the symbol "Pb" from the Latin word *plumbum*, and tungsten which has the symbol "W" from the German word *wolfram*.

In an atom, the number of protons equals the number of electrons. The atomic number is also the number of electrons in an atom. For example, the smallest element is hydrogen. It has an atomic number of 1, which means it has only one proton. It also has only one electron, since the number of protons equals the number of electrons.

Though atoms are very small, each one has a weight called the atomic weight. For most atoms the atomic weight is very close to the sum of the protons and neutrons in the nucleus. Protons and neutrons each have an atomic weight of 1. Electrons are so small that they are considered to have almost no weight at all. The number of neutrons for an atom can be calculated by subtracting the number of protons from the atomic weight.

For example, the atomic weight of hydrogen is 1.0079, which on this periodic table is the number found below the name. To find the number of neutrons, the number of protons (1) is subtracted from the atomic weight (1.0079 or 1); 1 - 1 = 0. This means that hydrogen has no neutrons and only one proton in its nucleus, or core.

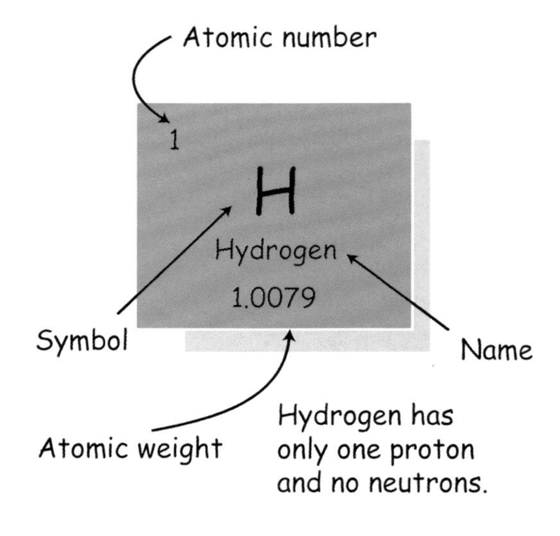

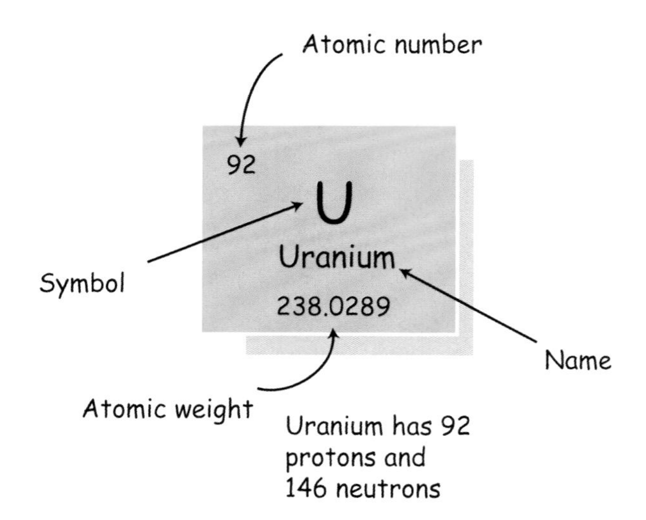

The largest naturally occurring element is uranium. It has an atomic number of 92, which means it has 92 protons and 92 electrons. It has an atomic weight of 238.0289. To calculate the number of neutrons, the number of protons is subtracted from the atomic weight (238 - 92 = 146), so uranium has 146 neutrons.

The elements in the periodic table are arranged vertically according to their chemical properties. All of the elements in a single column undergo similar chemical reactions and have similar chemical properties. All of the elements in the far right-hand column are called the noble gases. They are similar to each other because they don't react with other atoms or molecules. The elements in the far left-hand column are called the alkali metals. They are similar to each other because they react with lots of different atoms and molecules.

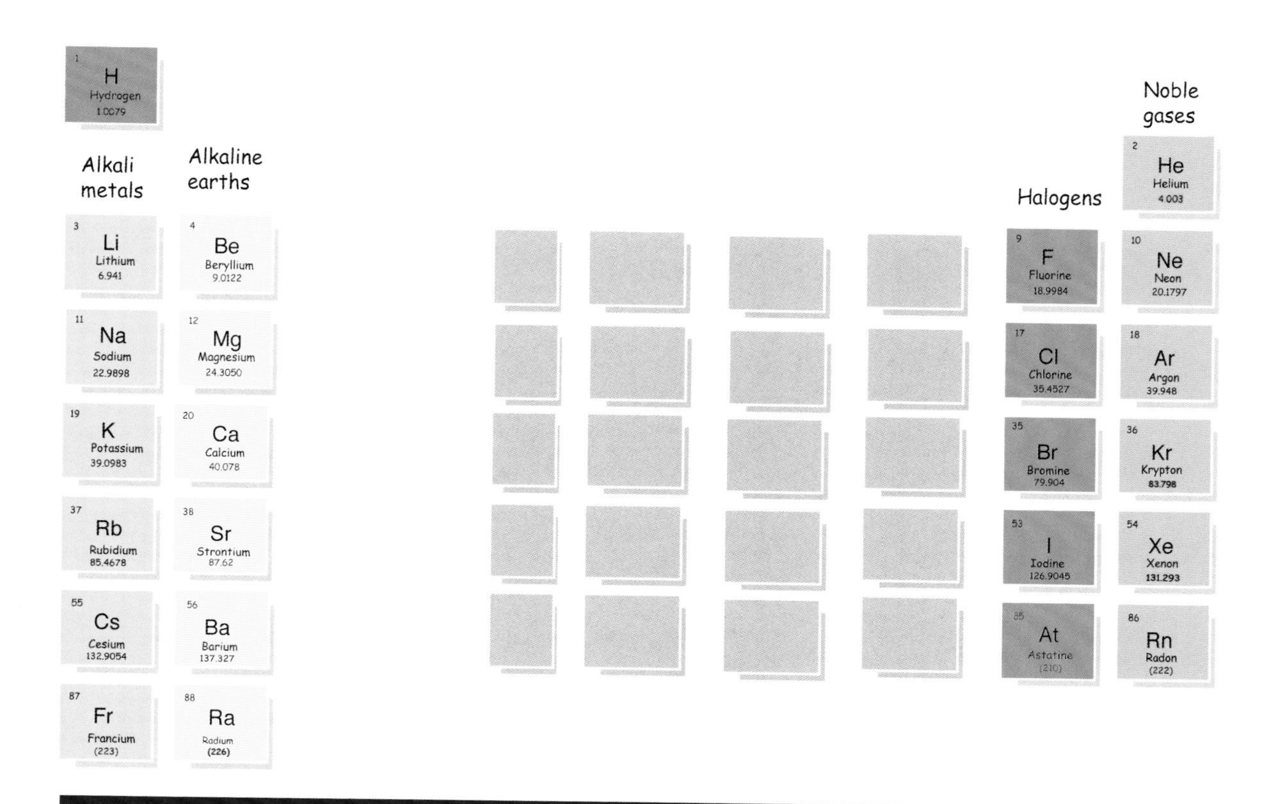

All of the elements in a single column have similar properties.

The periodic table of elements organizes a lot of information about the elements and their chemical properties. This table helps chemists predict the behavior of the elements and how they might interact with each other.

The Periodic Table of Elements

Alkali metals — Alkaline earth metals — Metals — Non-metals — Metalloids

Transition metals — Halogens — Noble gases

1	2	3	4	5	6	7	8	9	10	11	12	13	14	15	16	17	18
1 H Hydrogen 1.0079																	2 He Helium 4.0026
3 Li Lithium 6.941	4 Be Beryllium 9.0122											5 B Boron 10.811	6 C Carbon 12.011	7 N Nitrogen 14.0067	8 O Oxygen 15.9994	9 F Fluorine 18.9984	10 Ne Neon 20.1797
11 Na Sodium 22.9898	12 Mg Magnesium 24.3050											13 Al Aluminum 26.9815	14 Si Silicon 28.0855	15 P Phosphorus 30.9738	16 S Sulfur 32.066	17 Cl Chlorine 35.4527	18 Ar Argon 39.948
19 K Potassium 39.0983	20 Ca Calcium 40.078	21 Sc Scandium 44.9559	22 Ti Titanium 47.867	23 V Vanadium 50.9415	24 Cr Chromium 51.9961	25 Mn Manganese 54.9380	26 Fe Iron 55.847	27 Co Cobalt 58.9332	28 Ni Nickel 58.693	29 Cu Copper 63.546	30 Zn Zinc 65.38	31 Ga Gallium 69.723	32 Ge Germanium 72.630	33 As Arsenic 74.9216	34 Se Selenium 78.971	35 Br Bromine 79.904	36 Kr Krypton 83.798
37 Rb Rubidium 85.4678	38 Sr Strontium 87.62	39 Y Yttrium 88.9059	40 Zr Zirconium 91.224	41 Nb Niobium 92.9064	42 Mo Molybdenum 95.95	43 Tc Technetium (97)	44 Ru Ruthenium 101.07	45 Rh Rhodium 102.9055	46 Pd Palladium 106.42	47 Ag Silver 107.8682	48 Cd Cadmium 112.414	49 In Indium 114.818	50 Sn Tin 118.710	51 Sb Antimony 121.760	52 Te Tellurium 127.60	53 I Iodine 126.9045	54 Xe Xenon 131.293
55 Cs Cesium 132.9054	56 Ba Barium 137.327	57 *La Lanthanum 138.9055	72 Hf Hafnium 178.49	73 Ta Tantalum 180.9479	74 W Tungsten 183.84	75 Re Rhenium 186.207	76 Os Osmium 190.23	77 Ir Iridium 192.217	78 Pt Platinum 195.084	79 Au Gold 196.9666	80 Hg Mercury 200.592	81 Tl Thallium 204.3833	82 Pb Lead 207.2	83 Bi Bismuth 208.9804	84 Po Polonium (209)	85 At Astatine (210)	86 Rn Radon (222)
87 Fr Francium (223)	88 Ra Radium (226)	89 **Ac Actinium (227)	104 Rf Rutherfordium (267)	105 Db Dubnium (270)	106 Sg Seaborgium (271)	107 Bh Bohrium (270)	108 Hs Hassium (277)	109 Mt Meitnerium (276)	110 Ds Darmstadtium (281)	111 Rg Roentgenium (282)	112 Cn Copernicum (285)	113 Uut Ununtrium (285)	114 Fl Flerovium (289)	115 Uup Ununpentium (289)	116 LV Livermorium (293)	117 Uus Ununseptium (294)	118 Uuo Ununoctium (294)

*The lanthinide series: Elements 58-71

58 Ce Cerium 140.116	59 Pr Praseodymium 140.9076	60 Nd Neodymium 144.24	61 Pm Promethium (145)	62 Sm Samarium 150.36	63 Eu Europium 151.964	64 Gd Gadolinium 157.25	65 Tb Terbium 158.9253	66 Dy Dysprosium 162.50	67 Ho Holmium 164.9303	68 Er Erbium 167.259	69 Tm Thulium 168.9342	70 Yb Ytterbium 173.054	71 Lu Lutetium 174.9668

**The actinide series: Elements 90-103

90 Th Thorium 232.0377	91 Pa Protactinium 231.0359	92 U Uranium 238.0289	93 Np Neptunium (237)	94 Pu Plutonium (244)	95 Am Americium (243)	96 Cm Curium (247)	97 Bk Berkelium (247)	98 Cf Californium (251)	99 Es Einsteinium (252)	100 Fm Fermium (257)	101 Md Mendelevium (258)	102 No Nobelium (259)	103 Lr Lawrencium (262)

3.4 Summary

- All things, both living and nonliving, are made of atoms, which are also called elements.
- Atoms are made of protons, neutrons, and electrons.
- In an atom, the number of protons equals the number of electrons.
- All atoms (elements) are found in the periodic table of elements.
- The elements (atoms) are arranged in the periodic table in groups that have similar properties.

Chapter 4 Chemical Bonding

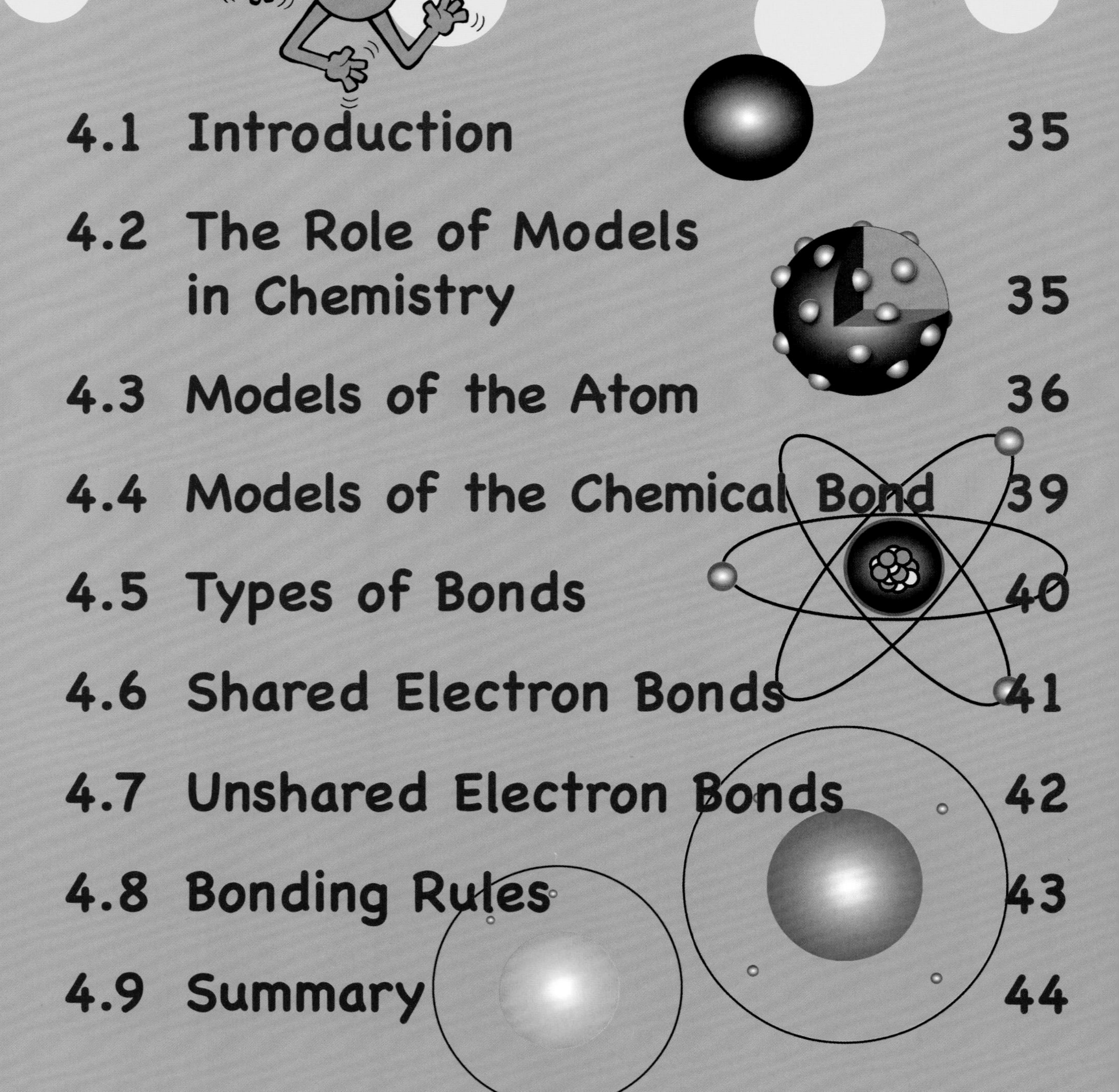

4.1 Introduction 35

4.2 The Role of Models in Chemistry 35

4.3 Models of the Atom 36

4.4 Models of the Chemical Bond 39

4.5 Types of Bonds 40

4.6 Shared Electron Bonds 41

4.7 Unshared Electron Bonds 42

4.8 Bonding Rules 43

4.9 Summary 44

4.1 Introduction

As we saw in the previous chapter, everything is made of atoms. Sometimes substances such as gold and silver are made of a single type of atom. Sometimes substances are made of more than one type of atom. For example, table salt is a combination of sodium and chlorine atoms. When two or more atoms combine with each other, they make a molecule. But how do atoms stick together, or bond, to make a molecule?

4.2 The Role of Models in Chemistry

Before we look at bonds, let's first explore models in chemistry. Our understanding of a chemical bond is based on models of how electrons interact with each other. A model is simply an idea of how something looks or works.

Anything can be represented by a model. Maybe you like to build model airplanes, model ships, or model cars. Even though a model can represent an airplane, ship, or car, we know the model is not the real thing. We understand that models give us an idea of what the real thing looks like, and that idea helps us to understand more about the real thing.

A model in science is the same. We have an idea of what something is, how it is structured, and how it works. We use models to help us think about and further develop our ideas. Models also help us explain our ideas to other people. In science, a model is usually very incomplete and does not have all the details of the real thing. In fact, many times scientists don't know exactly what the real thing looks like!

Even so, building models helps scientists better understand how things work and helps in designing experiments. Running experiments is important in science, and models help scientists decide what experiments to do. We can test the model by doing experiments that will show whether the model fits with the data.

4.3 Models of the Atom

Building models of the atom has been a very important part of chemistry for many years. There have been many different models proposed as new information about atoms has been discovered.

For example, John Dalton was not aware of protons, neutrons, or electrons. He perceived the atom as a small hard sphere, like a billiard ball. This model of the atom is still useful and is used in many illustrations of atoms and molecules. However, because it does not show how electrons are arranged, it is not useful for understanding how atoms form bonds.

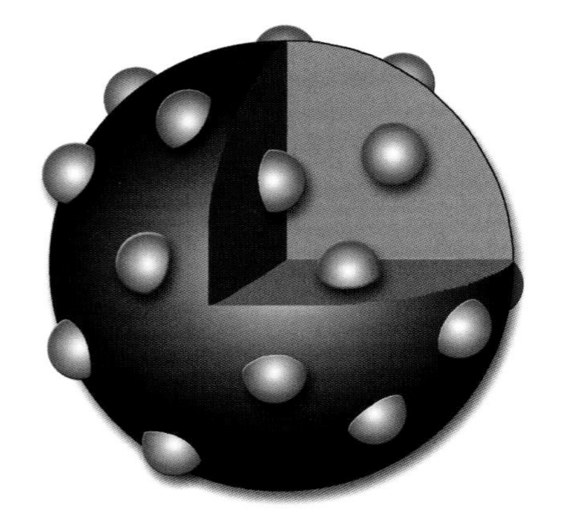

In 1897 Sir Joseph John Thomson (1856-1940) proposed a different model. Thomson was a British physicist who studied electricity and how magnetic fields affect the path of light. Through his research Thomson discovered the electron and its very small size. Thomson proposed a model similar to the billiard ball model but with the electrons randomly embedded. The model looks like plum pudding and is referred to as the plum pudding model.

However, it was later shown that electrons don't sit randomly around the atomic core, so the model needed to be revised again.

In the early 1900s Ernest Rutherford (1871-1937), a British physicist, found that almost all of the mass of an atom is located in the center with the majority of the atom consisting mainly of empty space. Rutherford's finding contributed to a model proposed by Niels Bohr (1885-1962), a Danish physicist, showing that the electrons circle the atomic core in fixed orbits with the low energy electrons orbiting close to the center and the high energy electrons orbiting farther away.

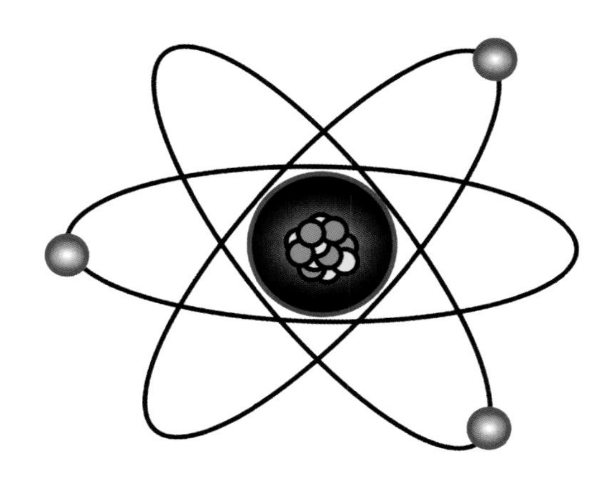

However, as scientists continued to explore atoms, electrons, protons, and neutrons, the model of the atom continued to grow more complex.

Today, scientists use quantum mechanics to understand how electrons move and form bonds. Quantum mechanics uses both physics and math. Sometimes the research done in quantum mechanics results in very strange ideas about how small particles such as electrons behave. Because it's impossible to know both the position of an electron and how fast it is going at exactly the same time, quantum mechanics tells us that electrons exist in orbits as probabilities! In other words, we can only describe how likely (how probable) it is that an electron is located at a specific position around an atom. This means that electrons don't circle the atom in a fixed orbit as Bohr suggested.

Carbon

In the *Real Science-4-Kids* textbooks, we have also used different ways to model the atom. In *Exploring the Building Blocks of Science Books 1, 2,* and *3,* we modeled the atom as a ball with arms and a face. The arms represent the electrons that are available for bonding and show how they link together to form molecules.

In *Book 4* we learned that electrons make the bonds that join atoms together to form molecules. To show this, a new model was needed. The arms in our models were replaced by red dots to represent the electrons that can form bonds, and gray dots were added to represent the electrons that can't form bonds.

Carbon

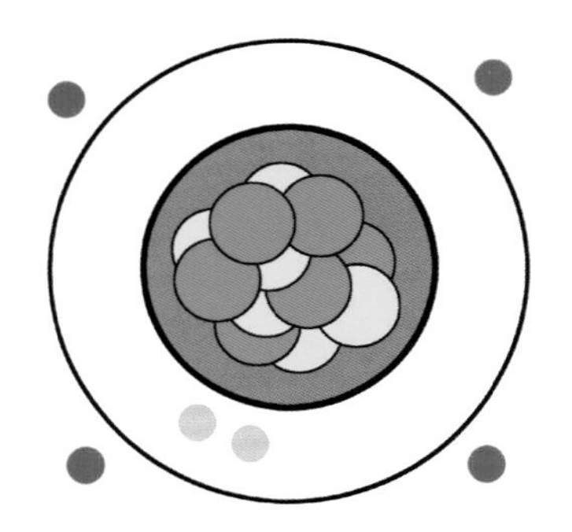

Carbon

Now that we've learned about protons and neutrons, we can add these to our model. We can take away the face and show how protons and neutrons occupy the nucleus, or atomic core.

However, because protons and neutrons don't participate in bonding, we don't need to show them in our model when we are illustrating how atoms make molecules. We can replace the core with a hard sphere or billiard ball, similar to Dalton's model and keep the bonding electrons. We will use this model to illustrate how atoms form bonds, and for larger molecules and chemical reactions, we will use the hard sphere.

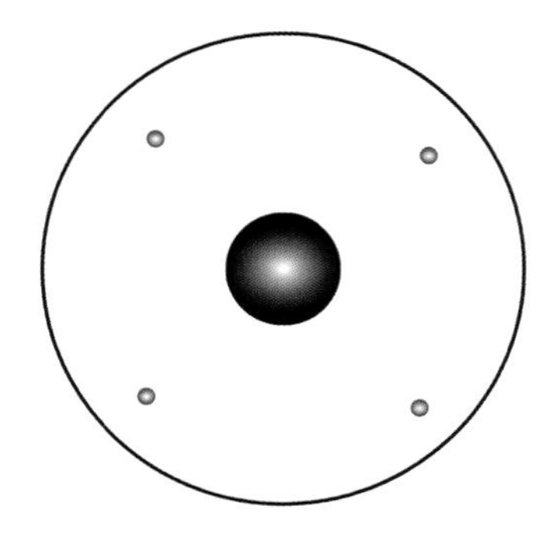

Carbon

All of these different models focus on different features. Some models focus on the number of bonds. Some models focus on the protons and neutrons. Some models focus on both the bonding and non-bonding electrons. None of these models illustrate exactly what an atom looks like, but they can still be used to understand atoms and how atoms form bonds.

4.4 Models of the Chemical Bond

Once scientists knew about electrons in atoms, they could ask how atoms were held together to form molecules. The idea of atoms connecting to form molecules was thought about for centuries. René Descartes (1596-1650), a French philosopher, proposed a model of the chemical bond and believed that molecules were held together by little hooks and eyes. He believed that some atoms had hooks and that others had eyes where the hooks could connect. Today we know that atoms don't have hooks and eyes, but Descartes' model added to our understanding of chemical bonds.

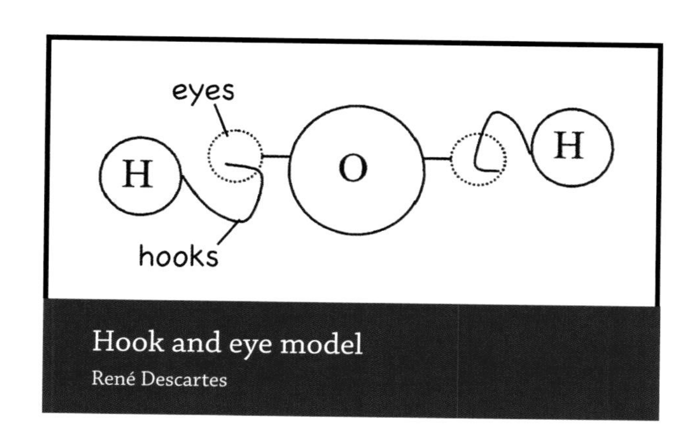

Hook and eye model
René Descartes

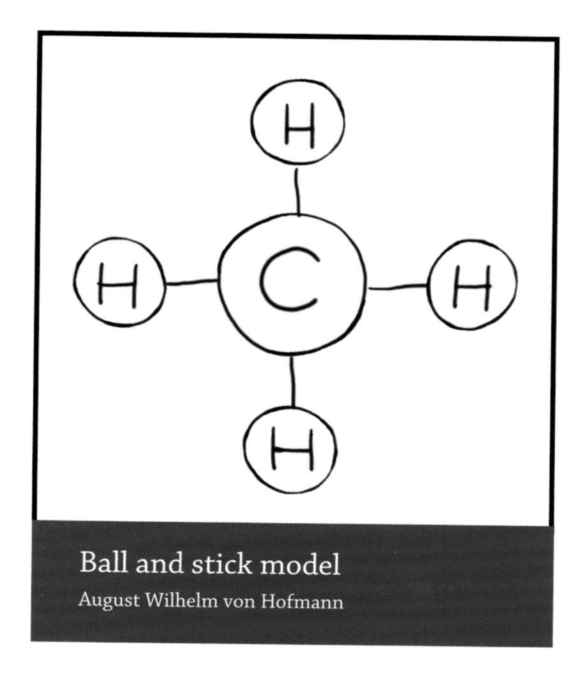

Ball and stick model
August Wilhelm von Hofmann

August Wilhelm von Hofmann (1818-1892), a German chemist, was the first person to build models of molecules instead of just drawing them. He used sticks for chemical bonds and balls for the individual atoms. He did not know the real shapes, but he gave us a start in understanding the science of molecular shape.

The ball and stick model is still in use today, but it does not give a complete idea about a molecule because the model is flat. We need to see a molecule in three dimensions to really understand how it will react with other molecules and atoms.

Hermann Emil Fischer (1852-1919) was a German chemist who proposed some ideas about molecular shape for enzymes (molecules in living things). He also developed a way of drawing on paper a two-dimensional representation of a three-dimensional molecule. In a Fischer projection all of the bonds are drawn as vertical or horizontal lines. For methane, the carbon atom is represented by the intersection of the horizontal and vertical lines. A Fischer projection is a representation of a three-dimensional molecule. The horizontal lines represent bonds that come forward, out of the page.

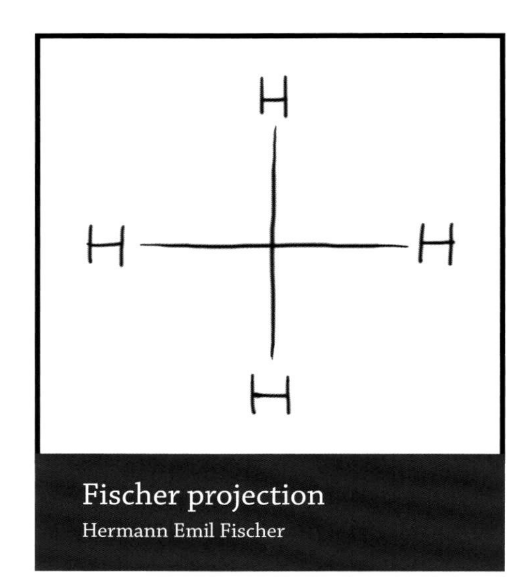

Fischer projection
Hermann Emil Fischer

4.5 Types of Bonds

Today we know that there are two general types of bonds: bonds between atoms where the electrons are shared and bonds between atoms where the electrons are not shared.

Molecules that have shared electron bonds behave very differently from molecules that have unshared electron bonds. This difference is quite important because it determines the way molecules interact with other molecules.

4.6 Shared Electron Bonds

Hydrogen is an example of an atom that has one electron available for bonding. When two hydrogen atoms bond to form a molecule, they form a bond where the electrons are equally shared. Because the atoms are identical (they are both hydrogens), one atom cannot take more electrons for itself than the other atom. This results in a bond with shared electrons, and in this particular case the electrons are equally shared. A bond with shared electrons is a covalent bond.

Bonds that are equally shared are *always* formed between two identical atoms, such as two hydrogens, two oxygens, two nitrogens, or two chlorine atoms.

Two separate hydrogen atoms

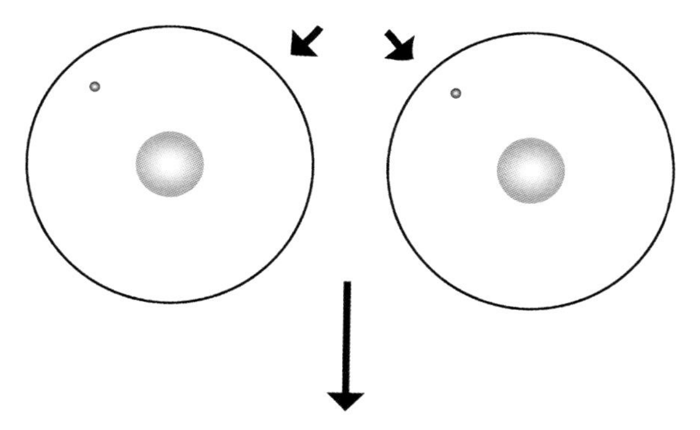

One single hydrogen molecule

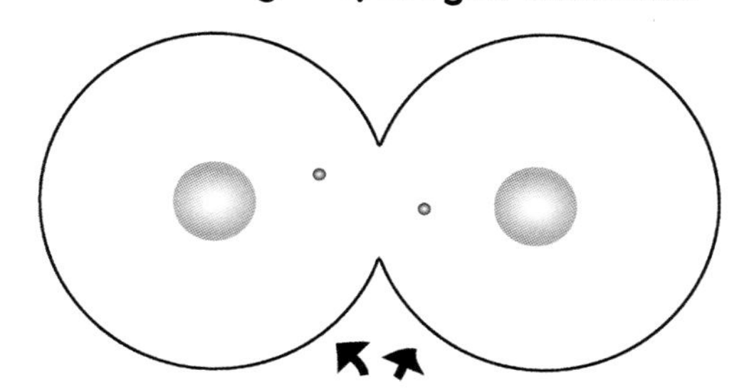

Space shared by both electrons

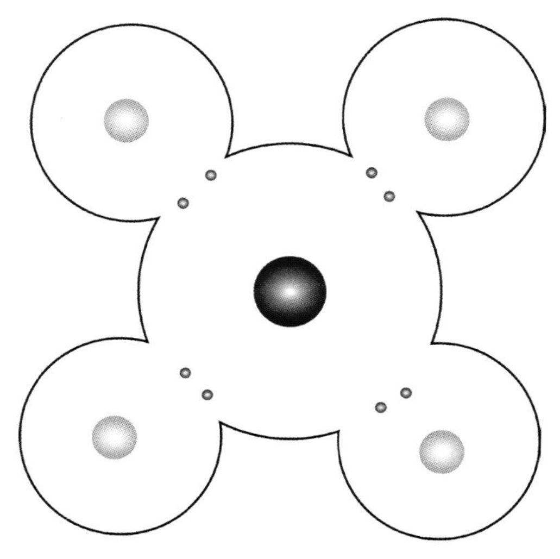

A carbon atom with four hydrogens sharing their electrons (methane)

However, covalent bonds also form between atoms that are not identical but still want to share electrons—such as carbon and oxygen, carbon and hydrogen, and hydrogen and oxygen. The molecule (methane) formed by one carbon atom and four hydrogen atoms also has bonds with shared electrons that are covalent bonds.

4.7 Unshared Electron Bonds

Sometimes the electrons are not shared between two atoms. This happens when there is one atom that wants to get more electrons for itself and is not willing to share its electrons, and the second atom wants to give electrons away. This results in a bond with *unshared* electrons. This type of bond is called an ionic bond. The word *ionic* in this case means that the atoms form ions. An ion is an atom that is positively or negatively charged.

The electrons in the bond between a sodium atom and a chlorine atom are *not* shared. The sodium atom gives away one of its electrons to the chlorine atom. As a result, the sodium atom has fewer electrons than it would normally have if it were alone, and the chlorine atom has more electrons than it would normally have if it were alone.

The molecule formed by sodium and chlorine is called sodium chloride.

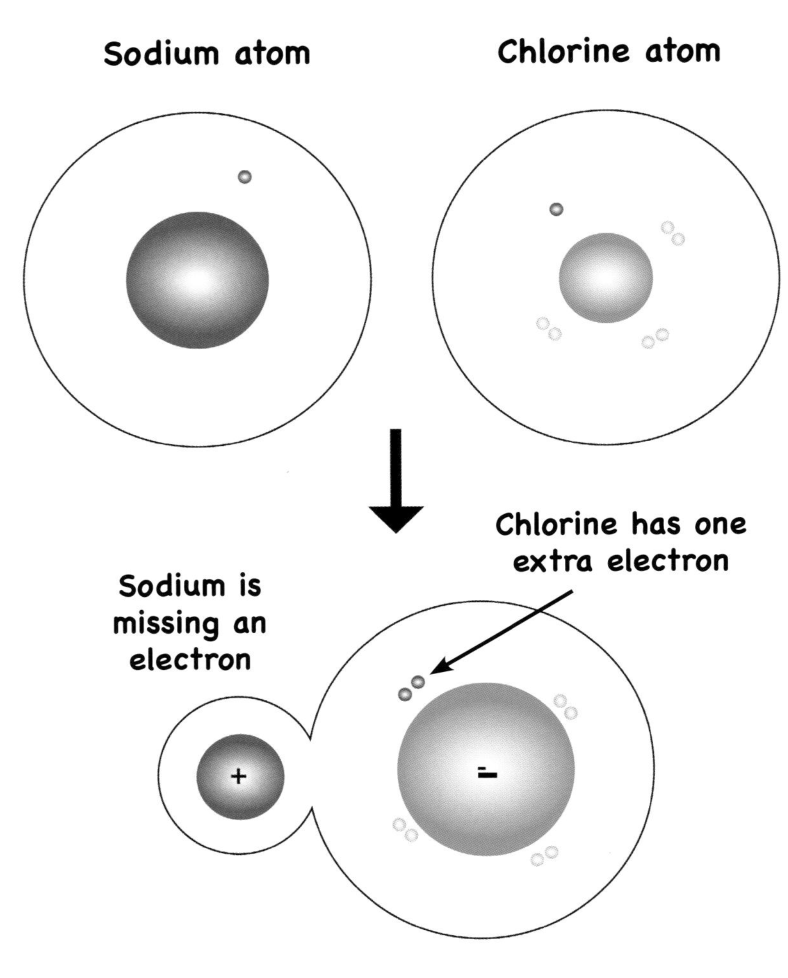

4.8 Bonding Rules

The number of electrons an atom has available for bonding also determines how many bonds an atom can form. An atom cannot form just any number of bonds with another atom. For example, a hydrogen atom has only one electron, so it usually forms only one bond. Carbon, on the other hand, has a total of 6 electrons. However, only 4 of those electrons are available to make bonds, so carbon atoms usually form a total of 4 bonds. Nitrogen has only three available electrons and usually forms three bonds. Oxygen, with two available electrons, typically forms only two bonds.

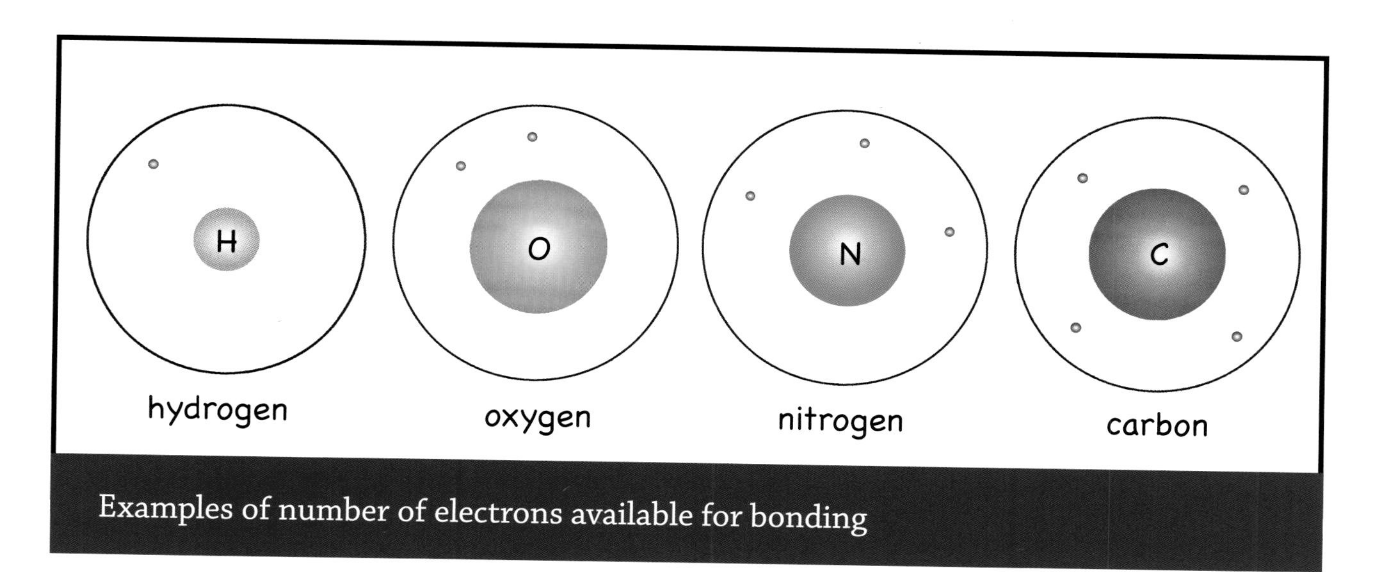

Examples of number of electrons available for bonding

4.9 Summary

- Electrons join together to form chemical bonds between atoms.
- Building models helps scientists understand how things work and how they are made.
- As scientists learn more about electrons and bonding, models change.
- A covalent bond occurs when atoms share electrons.
- An ionic bond occurs when atoms do *not* share electrons.
- Different atoms have different numbers of electrons available for bonding.

Chapter 5 Chemical Reactions

5.1 Introduction 46
5.2 Chemical Reactions and the Atomic Theory 47
5.3 Types of Chemical Reactions 49
5.4 Combination Reaction 49
5.5 Decomposition Reaction 50
5.6 Displacement Reaction 50
5.7 Exchange Reaction 51
5.8 Spontaneous or Not? 51
5.9 Evidences of Chemical Reactions 52
5.10 Summary 53

5.1 Introduction

What happens inside a battery? How does a car use gasoline to run? What happens to an egg when it's fried in a pan? All of these situations are examples of chemical reactions.

Chemical reactions happen everywhere! When we look at the world around us, we see thousands of chemical reactions happening all the time. We see plants using water and sunlight to grow. We see cars using fuel to move. We see foods being cooked, and factories making fabrics. All of these activities require chemical reactions.

People were using chemical reactions even before history was recorded. For example, ancient people used animal skins to make clothes. These people treated animal skins in order to make them soft. During the treatment of the skins, chemical reactions occurred. They didn't know what the reactions were, but they knew that by treating the skins they could change them.

Ancient farmers who grew crops for food discovered other chemical reactions. They knew that there were materials that they could put in the ground, and they knew that those materials would help the plants grow. Today, farmers use chemical reactions to help plants grow and keep pests away!

5.2 Chemical Reactions and the Atomic Theory

By the time John Dalton came up with his atomic theory, there were already some facts known about chemical reactions. People knew that materials could be changed into other materials, but it looked like substances were lost during those changes. For example, when wood is burned, ashes are left. However, the ashes weigh a lot less than the wood did before it was burned. It looks as if a lot of matter is lost during this chemical reaction.

Early chemists didn't know that matter isn't lost when wood turns to ash. Dalton and others realized that burning wood gives off gases. We can't see these gases, but we can show that they exist. When wood burns, part of the chemical reaction involves making gases, and the gases have some of the atoms that were in the original wood.

Recall that part of Dalton's atomic theory involved the idea of molecules. Dalton said that atoms are neither created nor destroyed in a chemical reaction—the atoms are just rearranged into different combinations.

The understanding that atoms are neither created nor destroyed during the process of a chemical reaction is called the law of conservation of matter. The law of conservation of matter was originally proposed by Antoine Lavoisier, the French chemist. By trapping the oxygen that is released when mercuric oxide (a compound of mercury and oxygen) is heated, Lavoisier proved that matter is not lost during a chemical reaction.

The law of conservation of matter is very important in chemistry. Because we know how many and what type of atoms a chemical reaction starts with, we also know how many and what type of atoms are present when the chemical reaction is complete.

The starting materials in a chemical reaction are called reactants and the ending materials are called products.

Because atoms are neither created nor destroyed, all the atoms we have in the universe today are the same atoms that existed thousands of years ago! It's strange to imagine that the oxygen atoms we are breathing could be the same oxygen atoms breathed by George Washington, Mendeleev, Cleopatra, or Ibn al-Haytham. They could even be the oxygen atoms that Democritus breathed long ago!

It's even more strange to think about where the atoms in our bodies came from. In your body, you could have carbon atoms that were once in the body of Julius Caesar, the great Roman emperor. Or maybe you have atoms in you that were once in an eagle that flew over the mountains thousands of years ago.

5.3 Types of Chemical Reactions

A chemical reaction occurs:

whenever bonds between atoms and molecules are created or destroyed.

Whenever two atoms, two molecules, or an atom and a molecule interact with each other and cause bonds to be created or destroyed, a chemical reaction has occurred.

Because there are many different kinds of chemical reactions, it is useful to categorize them. There are different ways to categorize chemical reactions, but to make it simple we will look at the following four general types:

1. Combination reactions occur when two or more molecules combine with each other to make a new molecule.
2. Decomposition reactions occur when a molecule decomposes, or breaks apart, into two or more molecules.
3. Displacement reactions occur when one atom kicks another atom out of a molecule.
4. Exchange reactions occur when one atom trades places with another atom.

5.4 Combination Reaction

In a combination reaction, two or more molecules combine to form a single product.

The reaction of sodium and chlorine to make sodium chloride (table salt) is an example of a combination reaction. In this reaction two sodium atoms combine with one molecule of chlorine gas to make two molecules of sodium chloride. The sodium and chlorine atoms are the reactants and the sodium chloride is the product.

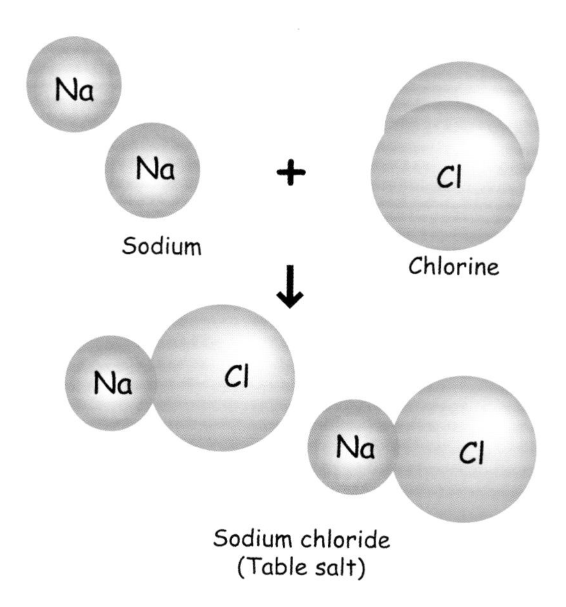

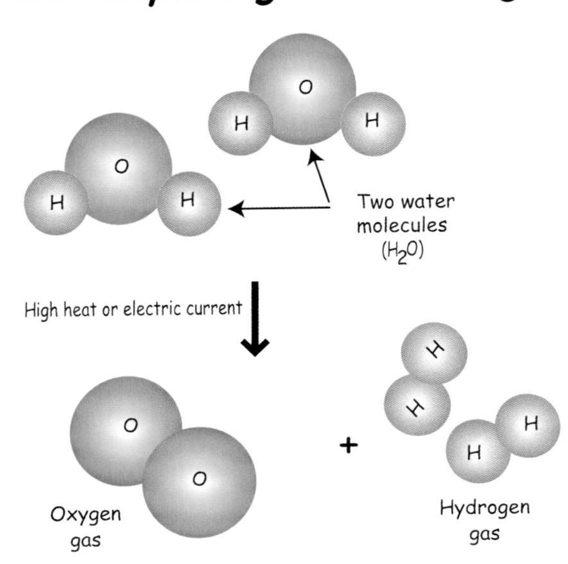

5.5 Decomposition Reaction

In a decomposition reaction, molecules of one type break apart, or *decompose,* to make two or more products. The breakup of water into hydrogen and oxygen gases is an example of a decomposition reaction.

5.6 Displacement Reaction

A third general type of chemical reaction is the displacement reaction.

In this reaction, one atom will remove another atom from a compound to form a new product.

The formation of sodium hydroxide from two water molecules and two metallic sodium atoms is an example of a displacement reaction. The sodium atoms (labeled "Na" and shown as blue balls) kick out hydrogen atoms (labeled "H" and shown as gray balls) from the water molecules. The sodium atoms combine with the remaining oxygen atom and hydrogen atom from the water molecule (called a hydroxide ion) to make a new molecule called sodium hydroxide. The two hydrogen atoms that were kicked out by the sodium atoms form a hydrogen gas molecule.

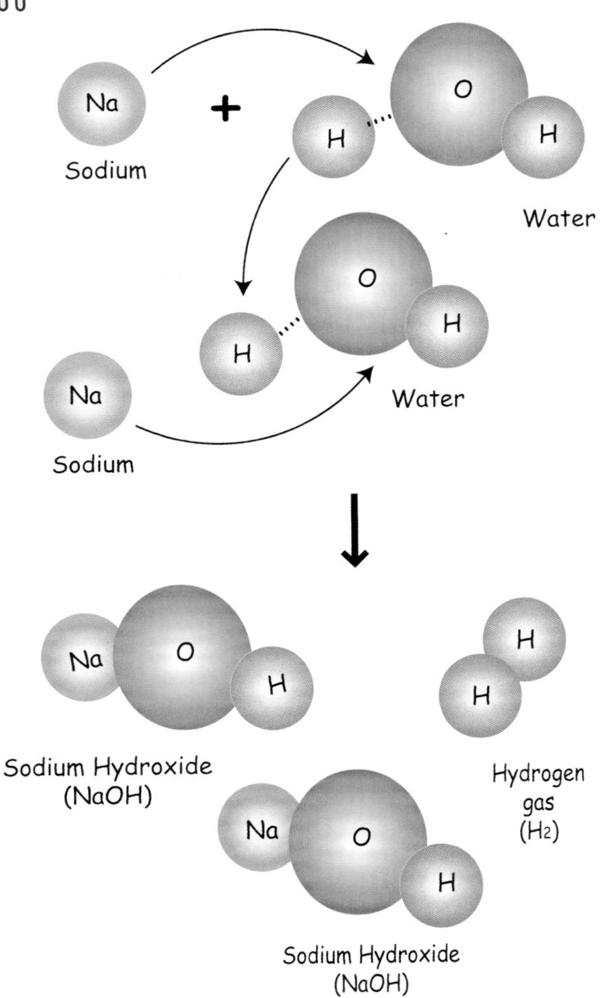

5.7 Exchange Reaction

The fourth type of general chemical reaction is the exchange reaction. In this reaction, the atoms of one molecule trade places with the atoms of another molecule to form two new molecules.

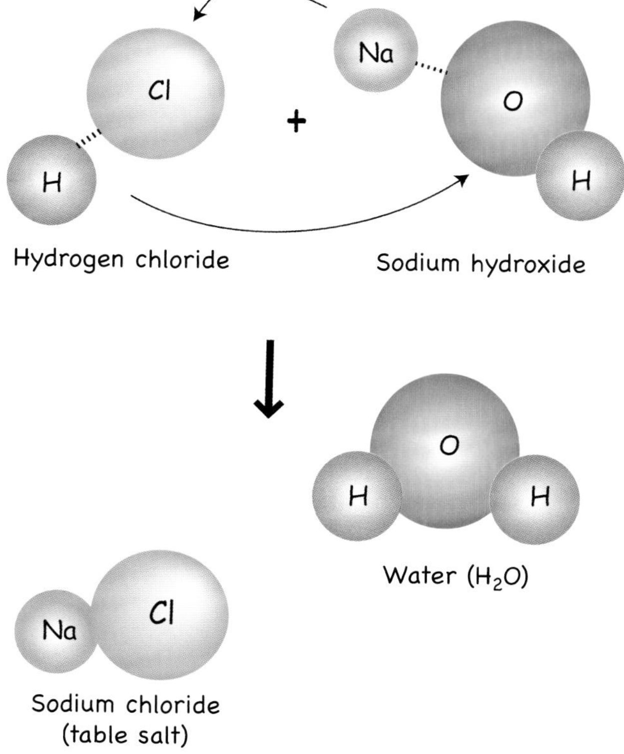

The reaction of hydrochloric acid (HCl) and sodium hydroxide (NaOH) is an example of an exchange reaction. The hydrogen atom in the HCl molecule trades places with the sodium atom in the NaOH molecule to make two new molecules, sodium chloride (NaCl, or table salt) and water (H_2O).

These are the basic types of simple chemical reactions. Some reactions that have many components are much more complicated than those outlined in this chapter, but most chemical reactions fall into one of these four categories.

5.8 Spontaneous or Not?

Not all chemical reactions are spontaneous. Spontaneous means the reaction happens all by itself by just mixing the chemicals. The reaction of hydrochloric acid (HCl) and sodium hydroxide (NaOH) (an exchange reaction) is a spontaneous reaction. However, not all chemical reactions are spontaneous. The decomposition reaction of water into hydrogen gas and oxygen gas is *not* a spontaneous reaction. It requires either high heat or an electric current. It's a good thing that not all reactions occur spontaneously. Imagine how difficult it would be to swim or sail a boat, or even get a drink, if water spontaneously decomposed into hydrogen gas and oxygen gas!

5.9 Evidences of Chemical Reactions

To determine whether or not a chemical reaction has occurred, chemists look for certain signs, or evidences, of a change. There are several signs that tell scientists when a chemical reaction has occurred.

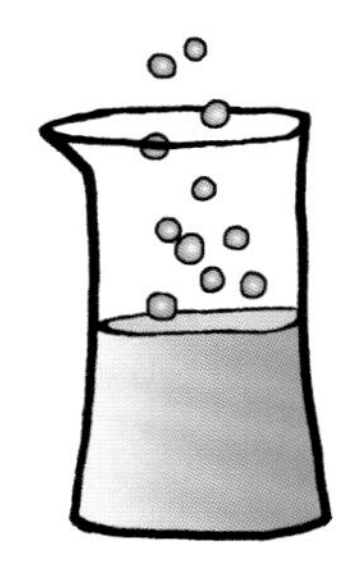

Bubbles

A chemist may look for bubbles being released when something gets added to something else. Bubbles indicate that a gas formed during the reaction.

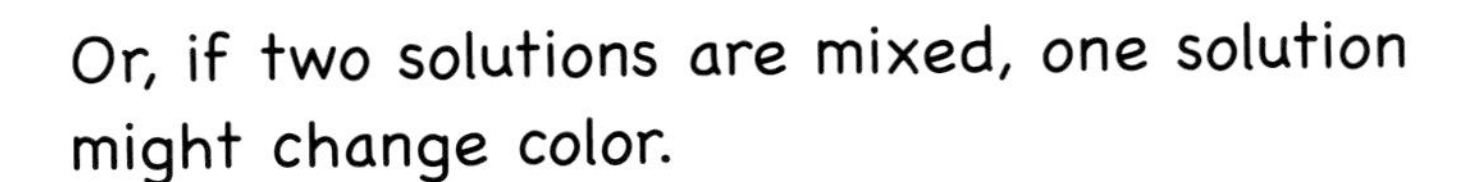

Or, if two solutions are mixed, one solution might change color.

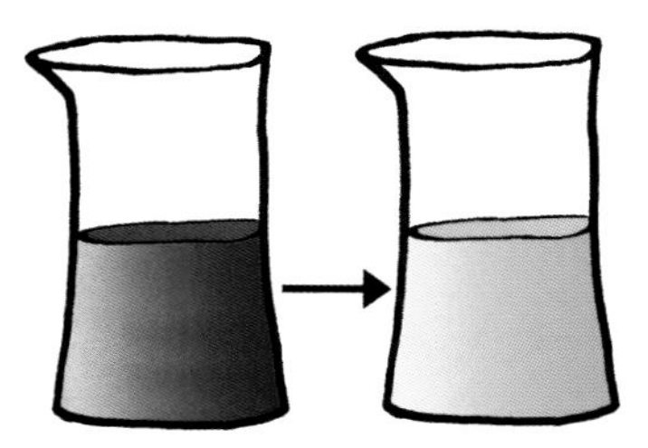

Color change

Sometimes when two solutions are mixed, a temperature change occurs, and the solution gets either hotter or colder.

Finally, another indication that a chemical reaction has taken place is the formation of a precipitate, which can look like colored sand, mud, dust, or snow forming in a solution. A precipitate forms when new molecules being made from the chemical reaction do not dissolve in the solution.

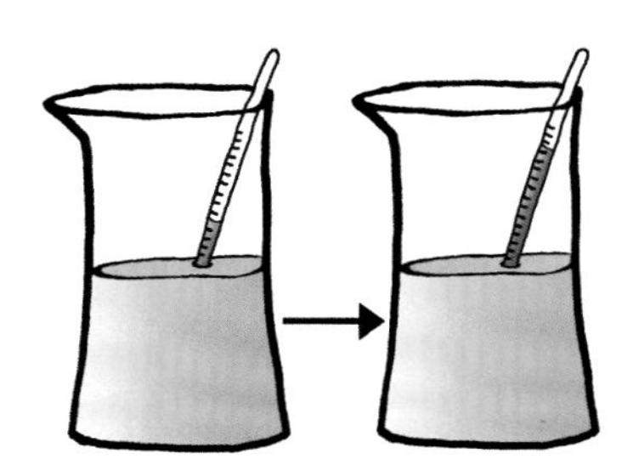

Temperature change

These are some of the ways that chemists can tell when a chemical reaction has taken place.

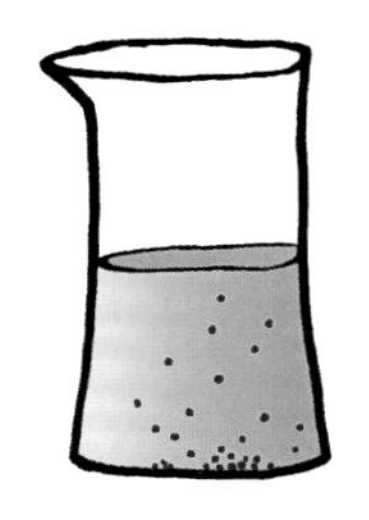

Precipitation

5.10 Summary

- The law of conservation of matter states that matter is neither created nor destroyed during a chemical reaction.
- A chemical reaction occurs whenever bonds between atoms and molecules are created or destroyed.
- There are different kinds of chemical reactions. Four of these are as follows:

  Combination reactions occur when molecules join.

  Decomposition reactions occur when molecules break apart.

  Displacement reactions occur when molecules are removed.

  Exchange reactions occur when molecules trade places.
- Not all chemical reactions occur spontaneously.
- Sometimes changes occur that indicate a chemical reaction has taken place. These changes include bubble formation, color changes, temperature changes, and precipitates.

Chapter 6 What Is Biology?

6.1 Introduction 55

6.2 What Is Life? 56

6.3 Philosophical Maps Help Us Inerpret Science 60

6.4 Organizing Life 61

6.5 Summary 68

6.1 Introduction

Biology is the study of life. The word biology comes from the Greek words *bios*, which means "life," and *logos*, which means "description." Biology is the field of science that "describes life." Biology is concerned with all living things and how they interact with one another.

Living creatures come in many different sizes, shapes, and colors. Some are big and some are very small. Some are green, some are red, some are black, and some are white. Some see with two eyes, some see with eight eyes, and some have no eyes at all! Some fly, some walk, some swim, and some crawl.

There are many different kinds of living things, but they all have one thing in common. They all are alive. But what does it mean for something to be alive?

Both living things and nonliving things are made of the same material—atoms! But if living things and nonliving things are all made of atoms, why are they so different? Why can a butterfly land on a rock, but a rock cannot fly away to find food?

6.2 What Is Life?

It seems that defining life should be easy. Even a young child knows the difference between living things and nonliving things. But finding a definition for life is actually very difficult!

One way to define life is to list the properties that are unique to living things. For example, living things have the ability to grow, the ability to reproduce, and the ability to adapt to the environment. However, a computer program can be designed to grow, reproduce, and adapt to the environment, yet we wouldn't say a computer program is alive. What else is needed to define life?

The struggle to define life goes back many centuries. The Greek philosophers thought a lot about life and how to define life. Aristotle believed that living things have a moving principle. Aristotle defined the moving principle as the mover, force, or creator that causes an object to become itself. For example, all life needs the Sun to grow, so the Sun could be considered a moving principle. But something caused the Sun to become the Sun, and that would also be a moving principle.

Aristotle felt that plants, animals, and humans have moving principles. Aristotle believed that, for plants, the functions of the moving principle are nutrition and reproduction. For animals, the functions of the moving principle are nutrition and sensation (or the ability to feel). In addition to nutrition and sensation, Artistotle believed that human moving principles also have the function of reasoning. Aristotle saw this idea of the moving principle as the ladder of creation. He placed plants at the low end and animals next. Humans were placed at the top because he believed humans have the most moving principle.

GALEN
circa 129–circa 199 CE

Galen (circa 129–circa 199 CE) was a Greek physician who studied anatomy. He agreed with Aristotle and further developed the idea of life having a moving principle. He referred to the moving principle as the vital spirit. Galen studied anatomy and the organs of the body, and he believed that the vital spirit moves in the bloodstream. The idea of a vital spirit led to the idea of vitalism—the idea that an unknown force is responsible for making creatures be alive.

Not all of the Greek philosophers agreed with the idea of a moving principle, or vital spirit. Hippocrates (circa 460–circa 377 BCE) was an early Greek physician who disagreed with Aristotle. He said that life is not caused by a moving principle, but by the ether. This ether is a type of fire that always existed and is present in air and in other matter.

HIPPOCRATES
circa 460–circa 377 BCE

Other Greek philosophers called atomists believed that life is simply the result of movements and combinations of small invisible, indestructible particles. Probably the most famous atomist was Democritus. Recall that Democritus proposed that all matter is composed of indivisible particles called atoms.

According to Democritus, the objects formed by atoms are not permanent. Democritus and others taught that all of life comes from collisions of these atoms and that life would disintegrate in time. However, the atomists' views were not very popular. Vitalism was the most popular philosophy of Democritus's day because it fit with the religious ideas of the times. It would take more than 2000 years for the atomists' view to be revisited.

Many new ideas about life developed in the sixteenth and seventeenth centuries. These ideas usually combined some sort of mechanical theory (the idea that living things function like machines) with some explanation of purpose (why the living things exist).

Recall that Descartes thought about how atoms form molecules. He also developed a "mechanical philosophy" or the idea of mechanism. He believed that all living creatures are like machines. Their behaviors are controlled solely by forces pushing the organs of the body.

Descartes was an atomist, but not a strict atomist. He thought that humans have a moving principle but believed even humans are basically just machines.

During the 1800s as we learned much more about the cell, it became much easier to explain life in terms of chemical reactions. By the end of the twentieth century, a completely non-vitalist philosophy had emerged. This idea is called materialism. According to materialism, everything is made of matter only, so all life can be explained solely by the laws of chemistry and physics.

A particular facet of materialism is called reductionism. Reductionism is the belief that because life can be explained by the laws of chemistry and physics (materialism) you can completely understand something by studying the parts. For example, if you don't know what a bicycle is, then you can take it apart, and by understanding the tires, the spokes, and the gears, you can understand a bicycle.

Reductionism and materialism have played a very important role in shaping scientific understanding, particularly in biology. For example, we can understand a great deal about cells by looking at their individual parts. But modern science appears to be moving away from strict reductionism and materialism.

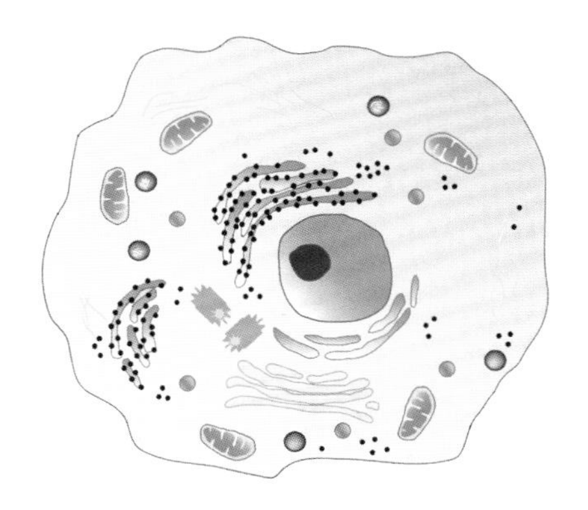

Cells are the basic building blocks from which all living things are made. Biologists have found out that a single cell is much more complex than they had originally thought. The cell was once believed to be a simple bag full of molecules. But today we know the cell is a very complicated structure with thousands of parts that all work together. Because the cell is so complex, scientists don't yet understand everything a cell does.

Some scientists who work with the brain also think there is more to how we process information than just the laws of chemistry and physics. They see a mind that can work in ways that we cannot understand with chemistry and physics alone. As a result of these observations, we are seeing a recognition of the complexity of life, and vitalism is once again playing a role in some new scientific discussions.

6.3 Philosophical Maps Help Us Interpret Science

All of these "-isms" are particular ways to interpret the world. Vitalism, materialism, mechanism, and reductionism are philosophical maps that help us get a clearer picture of the world around us. Just like physical maps help us navigate directions in cities, philosophical maps help us interpret and understand scientific data.

However, it's important that we don't confuse the map with reality. A map is just a map, and although it is useful, it does not always give the most accurate picture of reality. Also, the best way to navigate any territory is to use more than one map.

Often scientists disagree about which map is the "right" map for understanding science. However, there is not one "right" map for all questions. Materialism and reductionism can be useful in answering some questions, and vitalism and mechanism can be useful for answering other questions. The scientist who understands and can use multiple maps has a better chance of seeing the world more clearly than the scientist who only uses one map. Also, the scientist who uses many maps will find more opportunities to make new discoveries.

6.4 Organizing Life

Taxonomy

One way to understand living things is to organize or classify them. By organizing the different types of living things into groups, scientists can better study both their similarities and their differences.

The branch of biology concerned with naming and classifying the many different types of living things is called taxonomy. Carolus Linnaeus (1707-1778), a Swedish physician, was the founder of taxonomy. Linnaeus viewed science as a way to understand how the world is organized. He began to carefully study all the living things he could find. Whenever he found animals that were similar, like dogs and wolves or bees and wasps, he grouped them together. Grouping things together is what is meant by classifying. A new creature is classified in a group depending on which creatures it has the most in common with. Sometimes it is very hard to decide which group a creature fits into.

LINNAEUS
1707-1778 CE

Domains and Kingdoms

Because there are so many different kinds of living creatures, it has been hard for scientists to figure out exactly how to organize them. Several different approaches are currently in use. Until recently, the most commonly used approach divided all living things into five kingdoms.

However, modern taxonomy is beginning to use a system introduced in 1990 by Carl Woese. In this system living things are divided into three domains which are then further divided into six kingdoms. The three domains are called Eukarya, Bacteria, and Archaea. The kingdoms in those domains are Protista,

Plantae, Fungi, Animalia, Bacteria (also called Eubacteria), and Archaea (also called Archaebacteria).

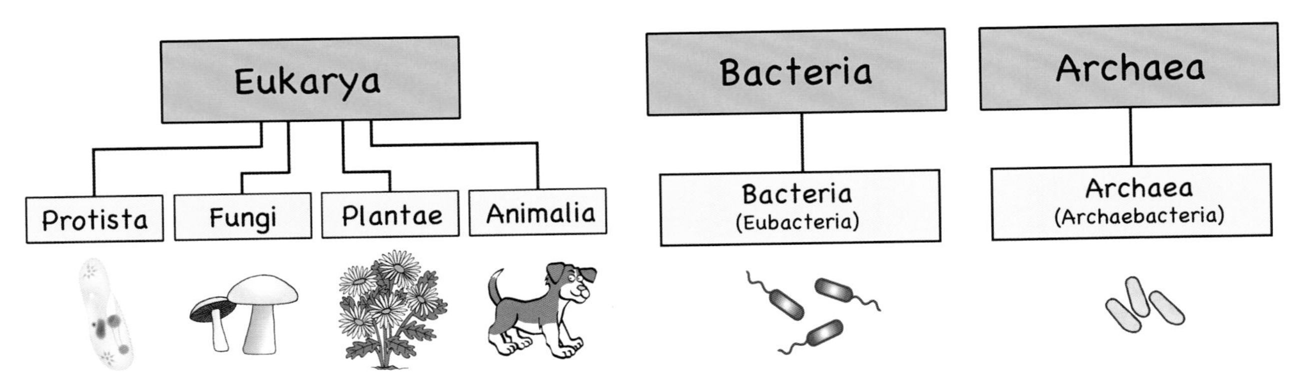

Taxonomy is continuing to change as scientists make new discoveries about living things, and scientists may use different taxonomic systems according to what they are trying to find out about living things.

How do we decide in which domain and which kingdom a living thing should be placed?

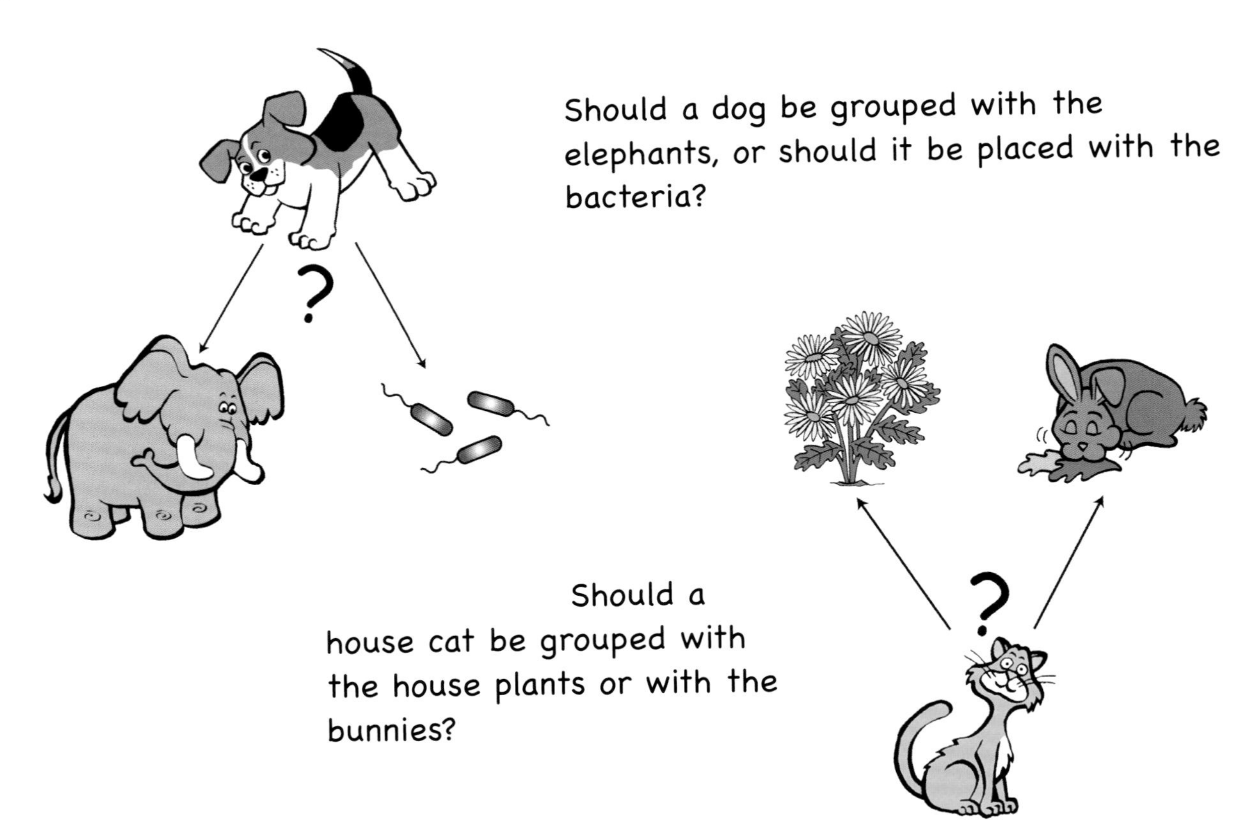

Should a dog be grouped with the elephants, or should it be placed with the bacteria?

Should a house cat be grouped with the house plants or with the bunnies?

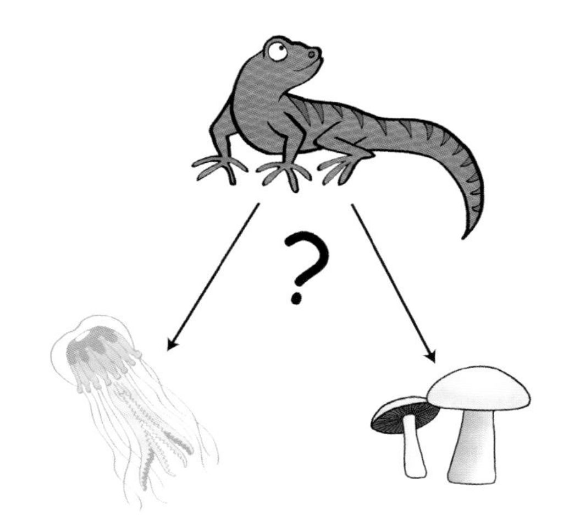

What about a lizard?
Is it like a mushroom or
like a jellyfish?

Before placing a living thing into a particular kingdom, it must first be placed in a domain. It is primarily the difference in the structure of the cells that ultimately determines the domain in which an organism is placed.

Dog cells are more like elephant cells than they are like bacteria, so dogs are grouped with elephants in the domain Eukarya. Cat cells are more like bunny cells than archaeal cells, so cats are grouped with bunnies in the domain Eukarya. Lizards and jellyfish, although very different from each other, have similar cells, so lizards are grouped with jellyfish in the domain Eukarya and not grouped with bacteria or archaea.

Once an organism is placed into a domain, it is further categorized and placed in a kingdom. The animal kingdom, Animalia, includes ALL of the animals: dogs, cats, frogs, sea urchins, bees, birds, snakes, jellyfish, bunnies, and even us! The animal kingdom has a wide variety of living creatures in it. Some are similar to each other, like dogs and wolves, and some are not so similar, like bees and snails, but ALL animals in the kingdom Animalia have animal cells. (See Chapter 8.) This distinguishes them from other living things.

The plant kingdom, Plantae, includes all plants: trees, grass, flowers, ferns, dandelions, seaweed, and even asparagus! Again, some plants are similar to each other and some plants are very, very different, but ALL plants have plant cells. (See Chapter 8.)

The fungus kingdom, Fungi, includes mushrooms, toadstools, truffles, and even athlete's foot! The fungi were once grouped with plants, but they have many unique features and are now placed in a kingdom of their own.

The last three kingdoms, Protista, Bacteria (Eubacteria), and Archaea (Archaebacteria), include most of the microscopic organisms, such as paramecia and amoebas. These organisms cannot be seen with the unaided eye and were unknown before microscopes were invented.

The kingdom Protista is in the domain Eukarya because protists have cells similar to other Eukarya. In the kingdom Protista, there are creatures that have both plant-like and animal-like features. Some, like euglena, are green and can use the Sun's energy to make food, like plants do. Others, like amoebas, catch and eat prey like animals do.

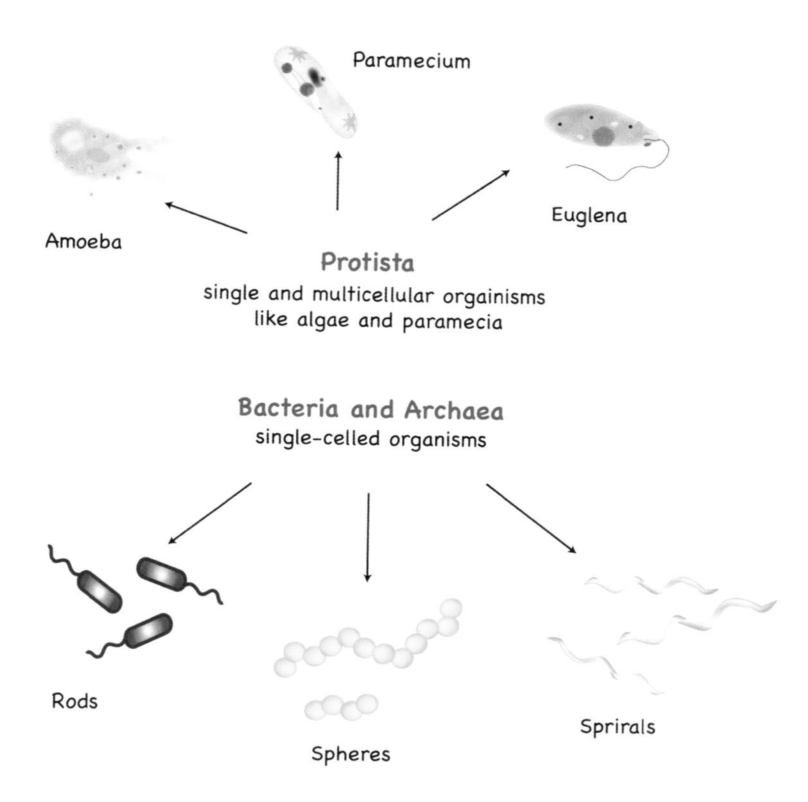

Bacteria and Archaea have cells different from each other and from Eukarya, and they therefore have their own domains. Most of the organisms in the kingdoms Bacteria (Eubacteria) and Archaea (Archaebacteria) are unicellular. That is, they have only one cell. These organisms have a variety of shapes. The three most common shapes are spheres, rods, and spirals.

Further Classification

Once a living thing has been placed in a kingdom, the classification continues. Living things are further organized by being placed in additional categories that depend on a variety of criteria, like whether or not they have a backbone or whether or not they lay eggs. For example, although all animals are in the kingdom Animalia, it seems obvious that dogs and bees and snakes should be in different groups.

Kingdoms are divided into smaller groups called phyla. Dogs, frogs, and cats are members of the phylum Chordata because they all have backbones, and bees are in the phylum Arthropoda because they have "jointed feet (legs)."

In the same way, the phyla are divided into smaller groups called classes. Dogs and cats are all in the class Mammalia because they nurse their young, and frogs are in the class Amphibia because they live both in water and on land.

Classes are further divided into orders. Both cats and dogs are in the order Carnivora because they eat meat. Orders are further divided into families. Cats are in the family Felidae, and dogs are in the family Canidae.

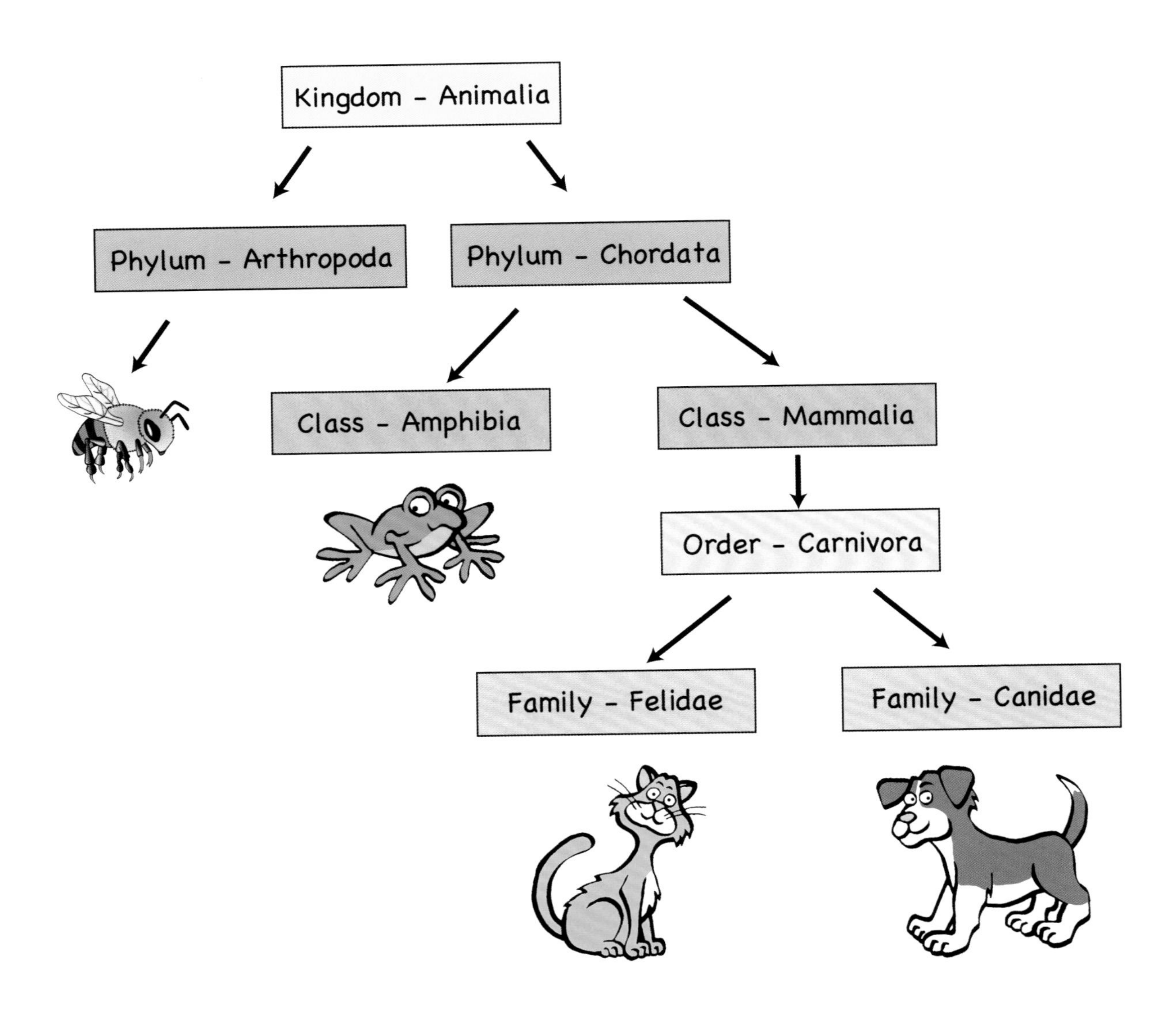

Naming Living Things

Finally, families are further divided into the genus, and the genus is divided into the species. The genus is the last group in which a living creature is placed, and the species identifies each creature placed in the genus, so each different living thing has a unique genus and species name. For example both a bobcat and a house cat are in the genus Felis. A bobcat has the species name rufa and a house cat has the species name catus. So a house cat is a Felis catus and a bobcat is a Felis rufa.

A tiger is a kind of cat, but it is different from both bobcats and house cats. It is in the genus Panthera and has a species name tigris. So, a tiger is called a Panthera tigris. A lion is like a tiger and is also in the genus Panthera, but it has a species name leo, so a lion is a Panthera leo.

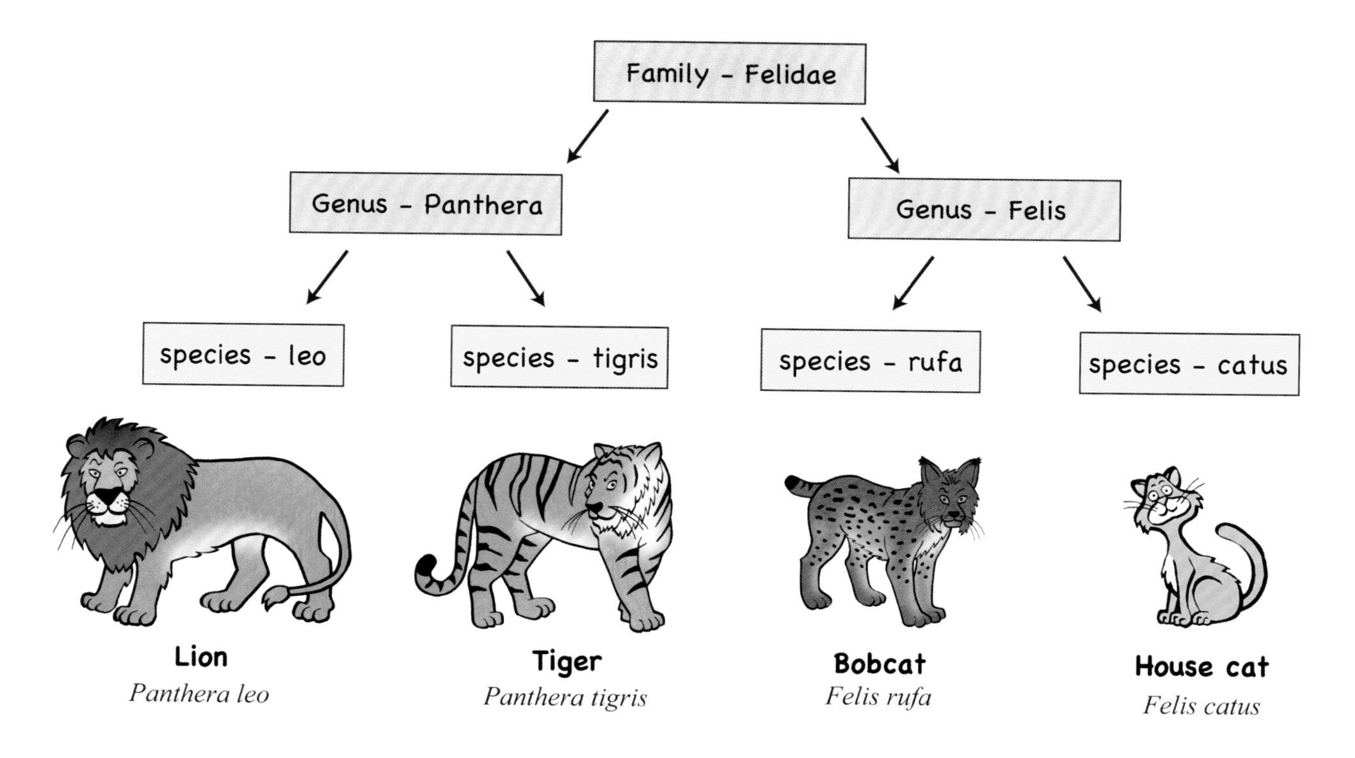

All living things have a particular genus and species name. The name for household dogs is Canis familiaris, and for humans it is Homo sapiens from the Latin words meaning "man wise."

6.5 Summary

- Providing an exact definition of life is difficult, and both scientists and philosophers have contributed.
- Greek philosophers such as Aristotle, Galen, Hippocrates, and Democritus had different ideas about what causes living things to be alive.
- Vitalism, materialism, mechanism, and reductionism are philosophical maps that help us explore the world around us.
- Taxonomy is the branch of biology that classifies living things.
- Living things are grouped into categories so scientists can learn more about how they are the same and how they are different. Also, if a new creature is discovered, for instance, on the deep ocean floor, placing it into a group of known creatures will help scientists better understand how it lives.
- Living things are placed in a group depending on many characteristics, including what kind of cells they have, whether they have hair or scales, and whether or not they lay eggs.
- Several different systems of taxonomy are in use today, and taxonomy continues to change as new discoveries are made.
- All living things are classified into different groups. The largest group is the domain. There are three domains that are divided into six kingdoms, followed by phylum, class, order, family, genus, and species.

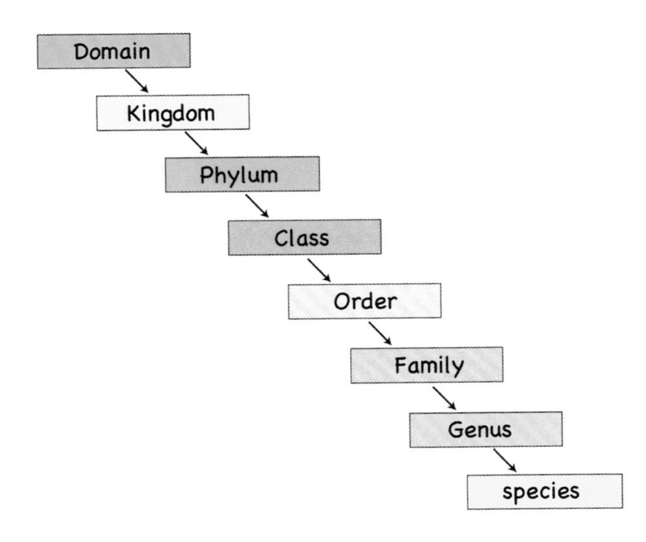

Chapter 7 The Chemistry of Life

7.1 Introduction 70

7.2 Types of Atoms Inside Cells 71

7.3 Types of Biological Molecules 71

7.4 Energy Molecules 72

7.5 Structural Molecules 73

7.6 Molecular Machines 75

7.7 Information Storage and Transfer 76

7.8 Chemical Reactions in Cells: Metabolism 77

7.9 Summary 78

7.1 Introduction

In Chapters 2-5 we saw that all things, including living things, are made of small units of matter called atoms and molecules. Atoms and molecules join to form cells, which are the basic building blocks of life. What makes a cell special is the high organization of atoms and molecules that work together through chemical reactions to keep the cell alive.

For example, in order for a cell to be alive, it must convert food into energy. To convert food into energy, food molecules are broken down into smaller pieces during a series of chemical reactions within the cell. When this happens, chemical bonds are created and destroyed and energy is released. These processes keep cells alive.

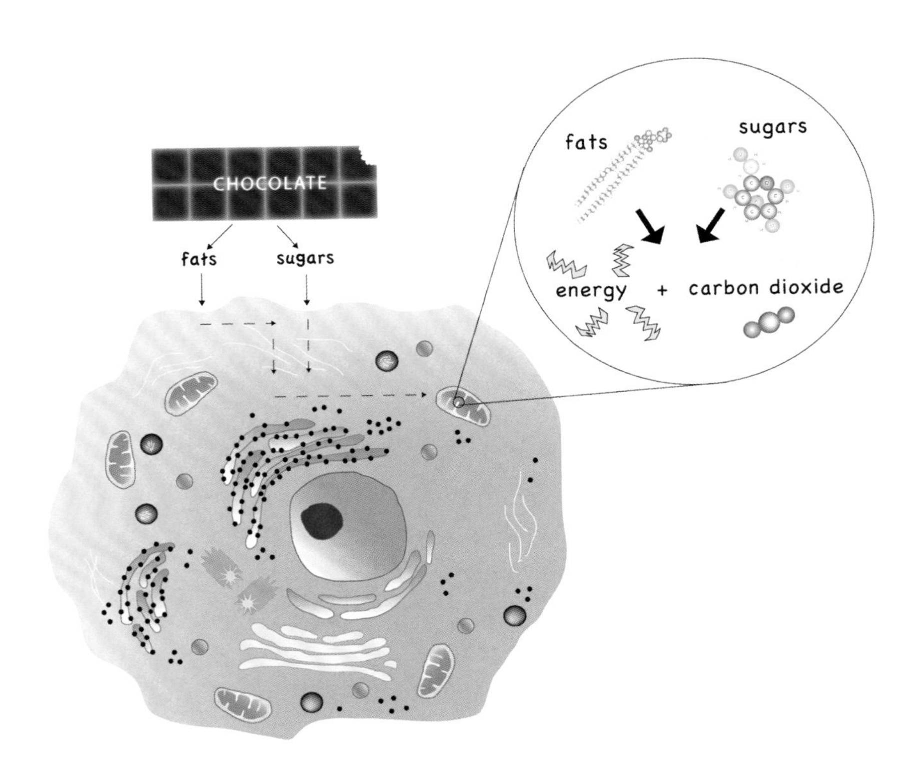

There are literally millions of chemical reactions going on in each cell at every moment. All of these chemical reactions are performed by millions of little molecules reacting with each other. When these chemical reactions stop, the cell dies.

7.2 Types of Atoms Inside Cells

As we saw in Chapter 3 there are over 100 different atoms, but the majority of biological molecules are made up of just six different atoms. This set of atoms is called the HCNOPS group and includes hydrogen, carbon, nitrogen, oxygen, phosphorus, and sulfur.

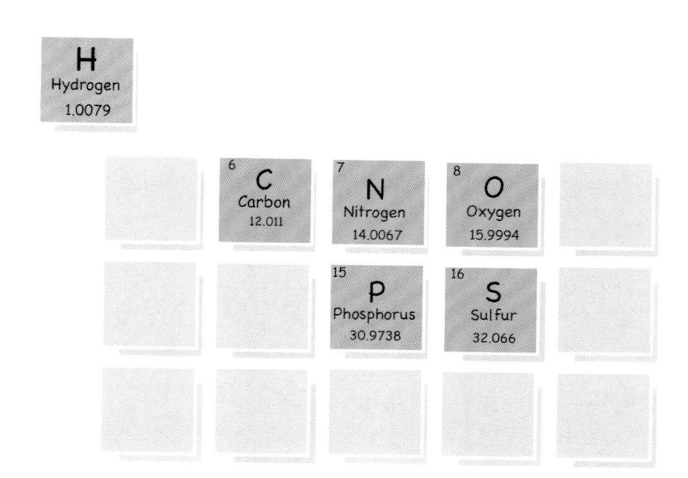

One of the special features that distinguishes living things from nonliving things is that living things have biological molecules. Most biological molecules are made of the five atoms in the HCNOPS group.

7.3 Types of Biological Molecules

There are many different types of biological molecules, including large biological molecules made up of millions of atoms and small biological molecules made up of only a few atoms. Some biological molecules are made up of smaller molecules that are hooked together to form long chains, and these molecular chains are grouped together in particular shapes.

Biological molecules perform different jobs inside cells. Some biological molecules provide energy for chemical reactions. These are called energy molecules. Other biological molecules are used to hold different parts of the cell together. These are called structural molecules. Some molecules move other molecules, break down unwanted molecules, and make molecules. These molecules are all molecular machines. And some molecules give the cell instructions for how to grow and when to die. These molecules are called information molecules.

All of these different types of biological molecules work together to keep cells alive, make them grow, process energy, and eventually tell the cell when to die.

7.4 Energy Molecules

Energy molecules play an important role in many different biological processes. One of the most important jobs that molecules perform inside cells is storing and transferring energy. In order for a cell to use glucose, the cell must have a way to store and transfer the energy it gets from the glucose molecules. To store and transfer energy, cells use special energy molecules.

The most important energy molecule inside cells is called adenosine triphosphate, or ATP. The ATP molecule gets its name because it has an adenosine group attached to three phosphate groups. A phosphate group is a cluster of phosphorus, oxygen, and hydrogen molecules. In an ATP molecule, the energy is stored in the phosphate bonds. A phosphate bond is the bond between two phosphate groups.

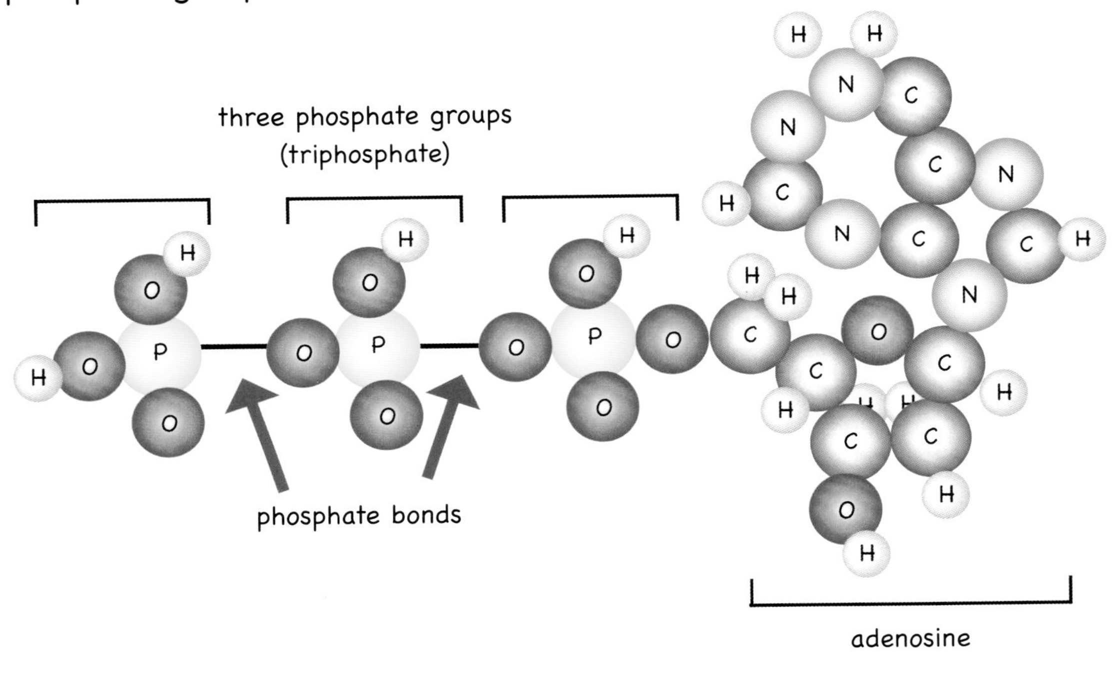

When the phosphate bonds are broken during a chemical reaction, energy is released. Energy can be put back into the molecule when the phosphate bonds form again. The phosphate bonds can be broken and created over and over again, so the cell can store and release energy as often as needed. It is useful to think of ATP as being like a little rechargeable battery that stores and releases energy as the cell needs it.

7.5 Structural Molecules

Cells also have molecules that hold the cell together. These molecules are called structural molecules.

Plant cells, for example, have a stiff outer wall that helps the plant stand upright. This stiff outer wall is made of cellulose. Cellulose is a structural molecule composed of millions of glucose molecules.

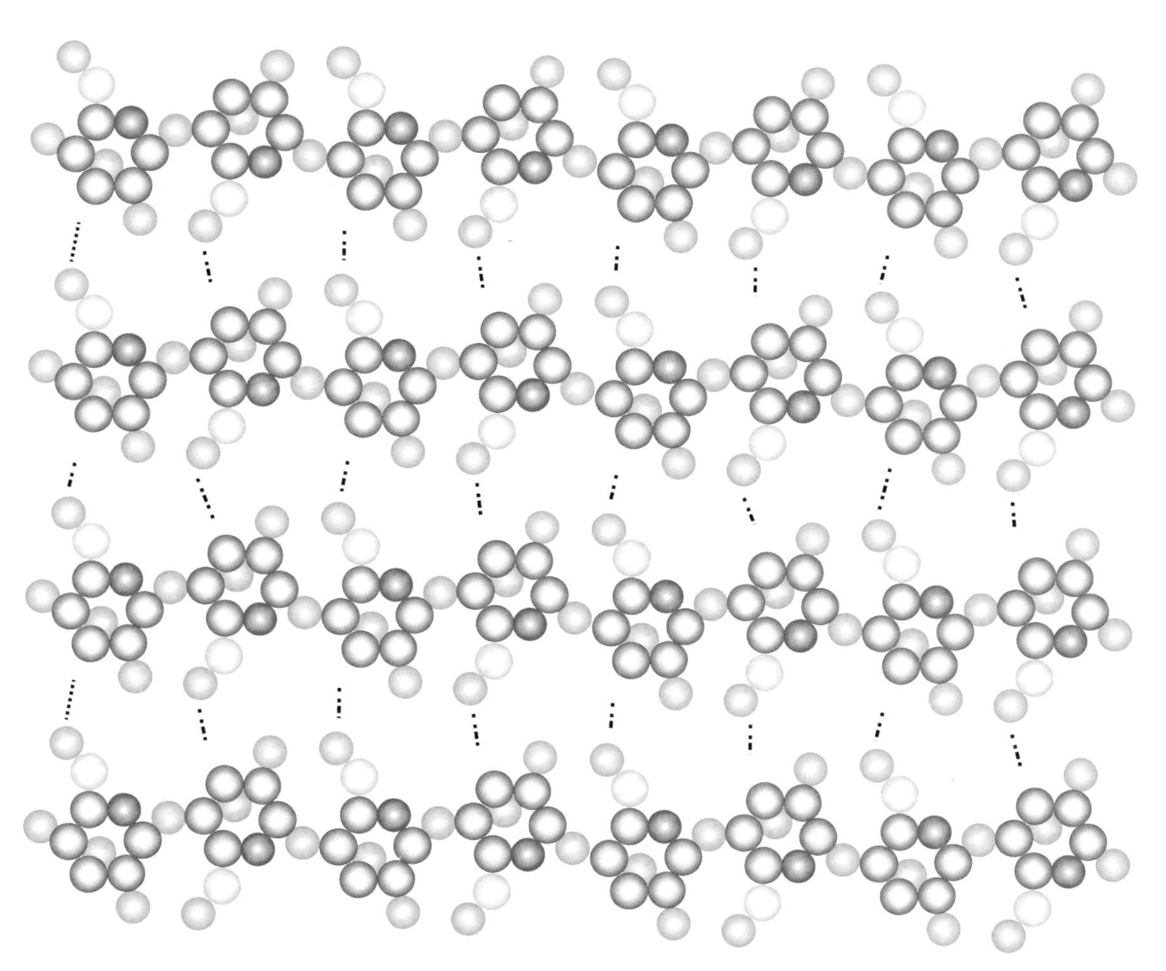

Cellulose

An animal cell is surrounded by a cell membrane. The cell membrane is made of a type of fat molecule called a lipid. The lipid molecules in a cell membrane form two layers that together are called a lipid bilayer. The lipid bilayer is a structural molecule made of lipids, and it holds a cell together.

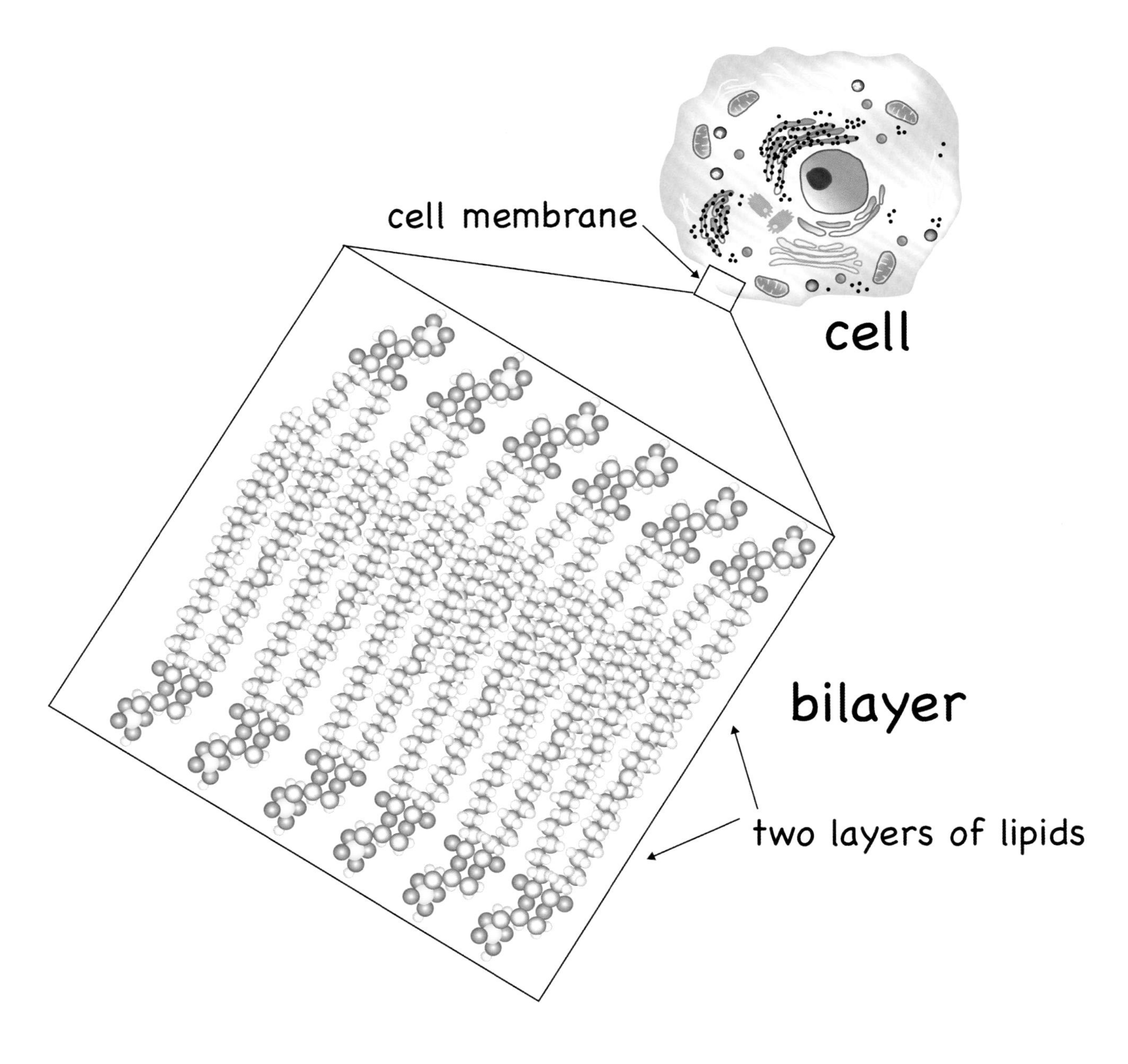

Structure is provided to cells by the molecules in both cellulose and lipid bilayers. Both types of molecules are structural molecules.

7.6 Molecular Machines

Cells perform a variety of different jobs, and to do those jobs cells use molecular machines. Molecular machines are specialized molecules that can cut other molecules apart and glue them back together. Molecular machines can also move other molecules around inside the cell or transport them outside the cell. Some molecular machines read molecules, others transcribe molecules from one molecular language to another, and others move molecules from one end of the cell to the other end.

Kinesin is a molecular machine that moves cargo around within the cell on a molecular "road."

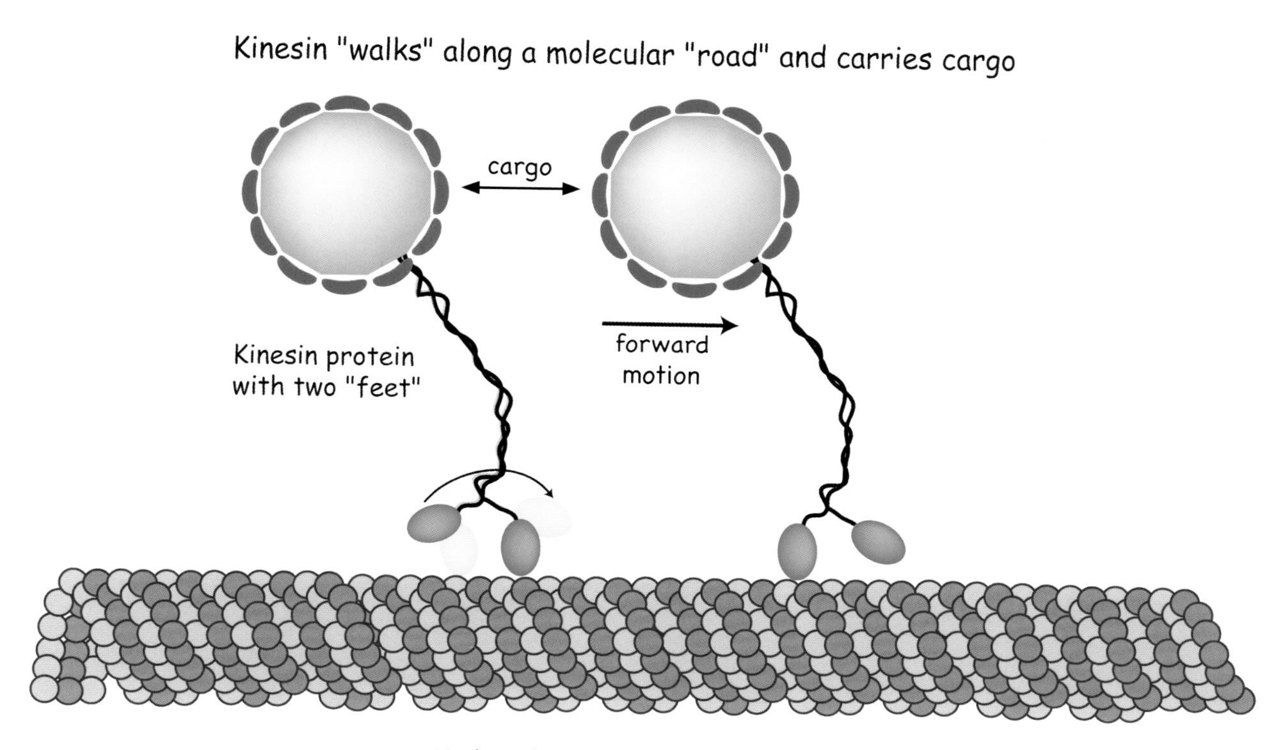

Molecular machines are made mostly of proteins. Proteins are a special type of biological molecule made of long chains of molecules (polymers) that can fold into a variety of structures. The structure of the folded protein is important. If a protein does not fold properly, it won't function. Proteins can perform a wide array of important jobs for the cell because they can fold into so many different shapes.

7.7 Information Storage and Transfer

Deoxyribonucleic acid (DNA) and ribonucleic acid (RNA) are special types of biological molecules that are used by the cell to store and transfer information. DNA and RNA store and transfer all the information a cell needs to grow, divide, make proteins, and eventually die. The information in DNA and RNA molecules is like the code in a computer. This code tells the cell when to grow, how to convert food into energy, when to stop growing, and when to die. The cell uses molecular machines to read the DNA code and make sense of it so the cell can know what functions to perform.

Deoxyribonucleic acid (DNA) is a polymer that is made of nucleotides which are made of two parts: nucleic acid bases and ribose sugars. The bases are connected to the sugars, and the sugars are connected to each other. RNA is similar to DNA but lacks an oxygen group on the sugar. RNA also folds differently than DNA.

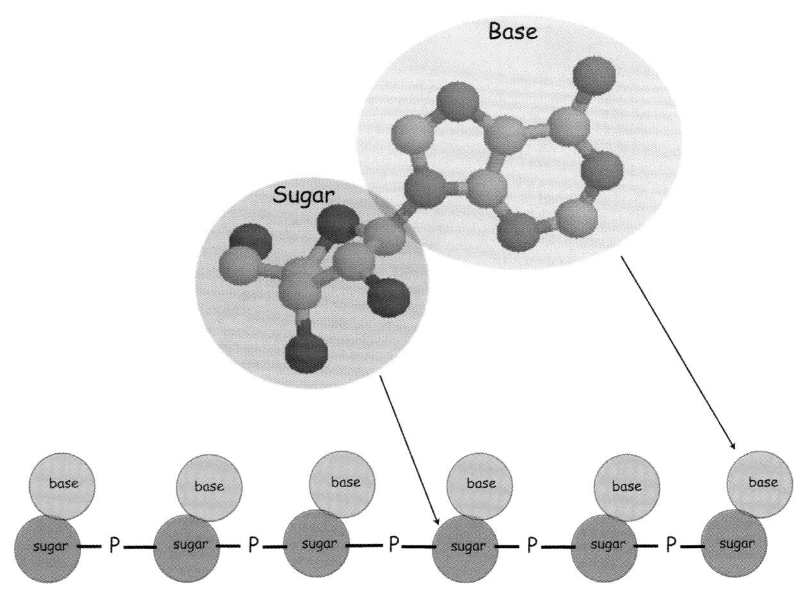

7.8 Chemical Reactions in Cells: Metabolism

Metabolism is the term used to refer to all of the chemical processes your body uses to stay alive. The word metabolism comes from the Greek word *metabole* which means "to change or overthrow." In biology, the word metabolism describes all of the chemical reactions living things use to change food into energy and other materials in order to live and grow.

There are literally millions of chemical reactions happening in your body every minute. Your cells are constantly making and destroying molecules, which converts them from one form to another, and cells are constantly creating and using energy.

Today we know a great deal about the chemical reactions cells use for metabolism. Chemical reactions in a cell follow a certain order, with one chemical reaction leading to another. This order is called a metabolic pathway. There is a different metabolic pathway for each function the cell is performing.

Two of the most important metabolic processes cells perform are the conversion of food into energy and the conversion of energy into food. The conversion of food into energy is called glycolysis. The conversion of energy into food is called photosynthesis.

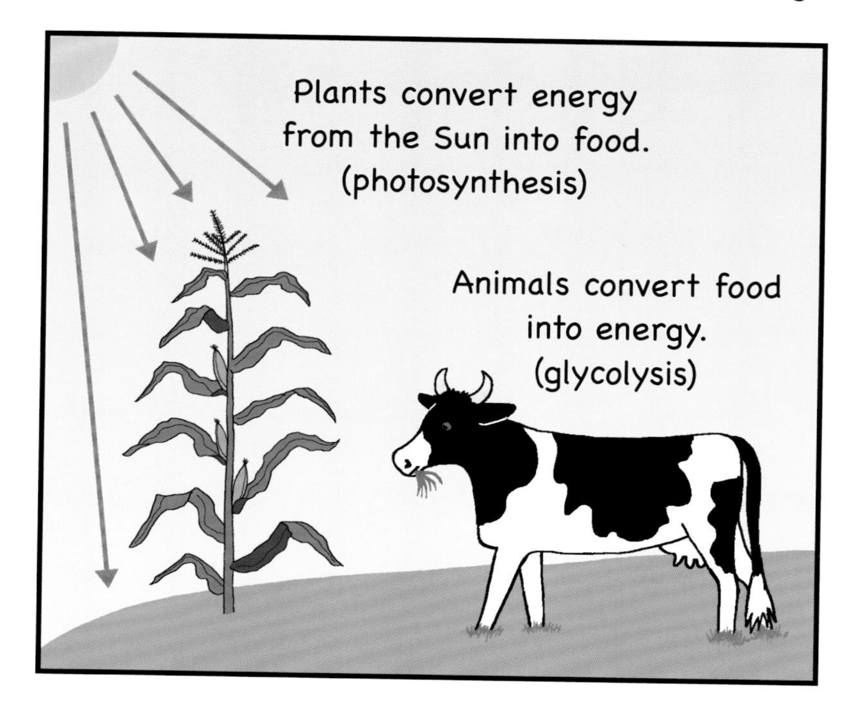

Animals use glycolysis to convert the food they eat into energy, and plants use photosynthesis to convert energy from the Sun into food. Both glycolysis and photosynthesis are metabolic pathways with many chemical reactions linked together. And photosynthesis and glycolysis depend on each other. Without photosynthesis, glycolysis cannot happen and without glycolysis, photosynthesis cannot happen. Because these processes depend on each other, the organisms that perform them depend on each other. Plants depend on animals and animals depend on plants!

7.9 Summary

- Living things are made of atoms and molecules that are highly organized and perform millions of chemical reactions every moment.
- Most biological molecules are made of five different atoms called the HCNOPS group which includes hydrogen, carbon, nitrogen, oxygen, phosphorus, and sulfur.
- There are different types of biological molecules that perform different functions inside cells.
- Energy molecules, such as ATP, are like little batteries that store and release energy.
- Structural molecules, such as cellulose and lipid bilayers, give cells the structure they need to function properly.
- Molecular machines are mostly proteins that can read, cut, transcribe, and move molecules inside a cell.
- Molecules such as DNA share and transfer information.
- All of the chemical processes in a cell together are called metabolism.

Chapter 8 Cells—The Building Blocks of Life

8.1 Introduction 80

8.2 Types of Cells 81

8.3 Bacterial Prokaryotic Cells 82

8.4 Archaeal Prokaryotic Cells 84

8.5 Eukaryotic Cells 84

8.6 Cell Division 88

8.7 Bacterial and Archaeal Cell Division 88

8.8 The Eukaryotic Cell Cycle: Mitosis 89

8.9 Summary 90

8.1 Introduction

Recall that all living things are made of a complex and highly ordered arrangement of atoms and molecules that fit together to form cells. Cells are the building blocks of all living things.

Each cell is like a little factory. All of the molecules in the cell have special jobs to do. There are many different kinds of molecules inside cells. Most of the big molecules are proteins, but there are also sugars and nucleic acids. Small molecules such as water and salt are also in cells.

The cell "knows" where all of the molecules are and how many molecules are doing work. This way the cell always has just the right number of molecules working in a particular area, and there are not too many or too few molecules.

The molecules in a cell never rest. They are always working. If they stop working, the cell can no longer live. When cells get old or are damaged, the molecules cannot work, and the cell dies. When a cell dies, all of the parts of the cell break down into smaller molecules. The molecules from dead cells are used again to make new molecules for different cells. Eventually, all cells in all living things die.

8.2 Types of Cells

There are three major types of cells that correspond to the three main taxonomic domain divisions. Organisms in the domain Bacteria have bacterial prokaryotic cells, organisms in the domain Archaea have archaeal prokaryotic cells, and organisms in the domain Eukaryra have eukaryotic cells. All three cell types have some similarities and some differences.

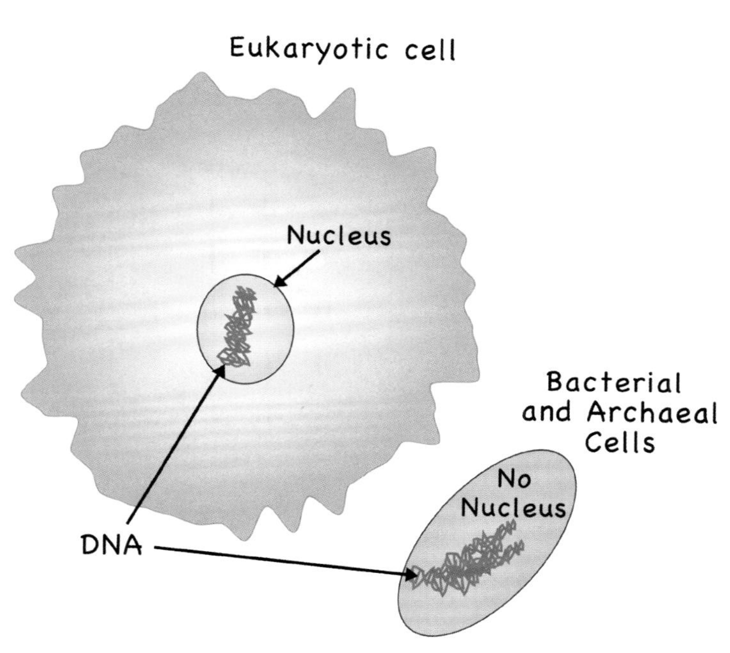

All three cell types are similar because they all are made of atoms and molecules. Also, all three types of cells act as little chemical factories, making the molecules and structures needed by the cells and breaking down the molecules that the cells don't need.

However, these three cells types are different from each other in significant ways. For example, eukaryotic cells have a nucleus. A nucleus is a small "sack" that is inside the cell and holds the DNA. Neither bacterial nor archaeal cells have a nucleus to hold their DNA.

Both eukaryotic cells and bacterial cells have plasma membranes that are different from the plasma membrane of archaeal cells. A plasma membrane is a thin, soft, greasy film that surrounds the cell and controls what goes into and out of the cell. Bacterial and eukaryotic cells have a glycerol ester plasma membrane, and the archaea have a slightly different plasma membrane called a glycerol ether plasma membrane. Glycerol ester and glycerol ether plasma membranes get their names from the kind of molecules they are made of.

Bacterial and archaeal cells do not have organelles, but eukaryotic cells do. (An organelle is like a little organ because it is a structure that performs specific functions inside a cell.) Both archaea and eukarya have eukaryotic ribosomal proteins, and bacteria have prokaryotic ribosomal proteins. (A ribosomal protein is the molecular machine that makes proteins.) Although there are similarities between these three cell types, there are enough differences that three different domains are needed.

	Comparison of Cell Types		
	Bacteria Prokaryotic Cells	**Archaea** Archaeal Cells	**Eukarya** Eukaryotic Cells
Nucleus	No	No	Yes
Organelles	No	No	Yes
Plasma Membrane	Glycerol ester	Glycerol ether	Glycerol ester
Ribosomal Proteins	Prokaryotic	Eukaryotic	Both eukaryotic and prokaryotic

8.3 Bacterial Prokaryotic Cells

Bacteria are single-celled organisms. The word bacterium comes the Greek word *bakterion* which means "small staff or rod" and was used because the first bacteria observed were rod-shaped.

The word prokaryote comes from the Greek word *pro*, which means "before" and *karyon* which means "kernel." So prokaryote means "before kernel." This term refers to the fact that prokaryotes do not have a nucleus, the small "sack" inside the cell that holds the DNA in eukaryotes. Instead, the DNA is kept in a region called the nucleoid. A nucleoid is a central region in the cell that is not physically separated from the rest of the cell by a membrane.

Bacterial prokaryotic cells are surrounded by a cell wall and a glycerol ester plasma membrane. The cell wall is rigid, like a coat of armor, and protects the cell from being broken.

Many prokaryotic cells have flagella. These are long or short "whips" that help the cell move around. A flagellum is connected to a complicated molecular motor that twirls around with great speed and propels the cell in all directions. Some prokaryotes also have pili. Pili are long "threads" that help the cell stick to surfaces and to other cells.

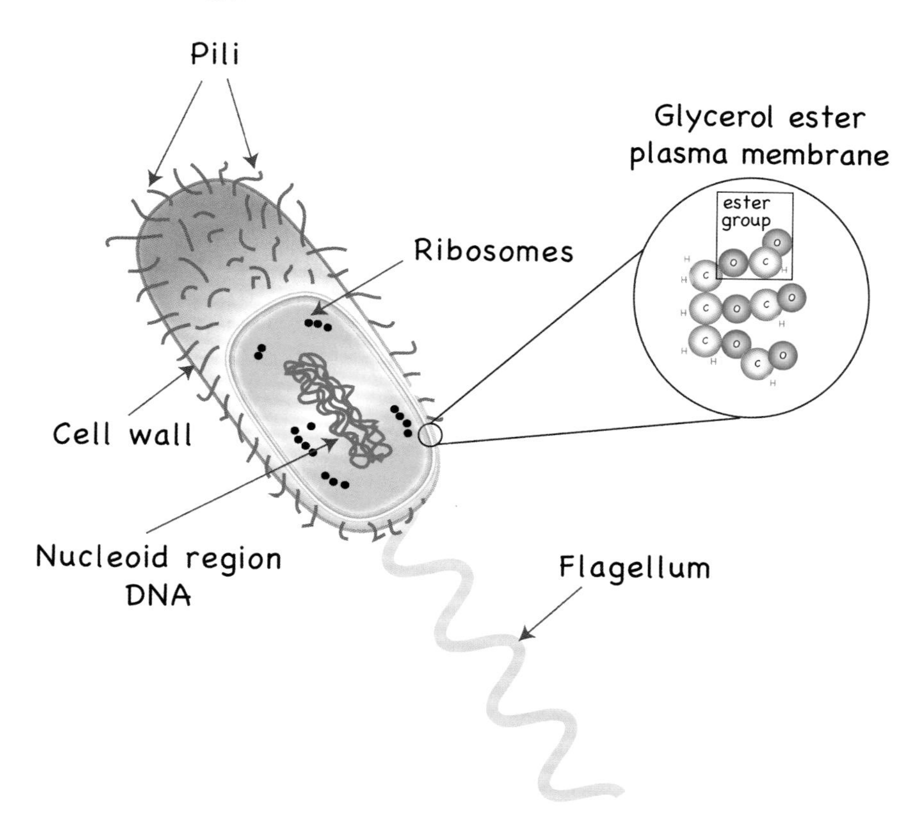

Bacterial prokaryotic cell

8.4 Archaeal Prokaryotic Cells

Archaea are single-celled organisms. The word archaea comes from the Greek word *archein* which means "the first" or "to rule." Some scientists believe that archaeal cells were the first type of cells to exist. However, since archaeal cells have some similarities with eukaryotic cells, it isn't perfectly understood what the first cells may or may not have been.

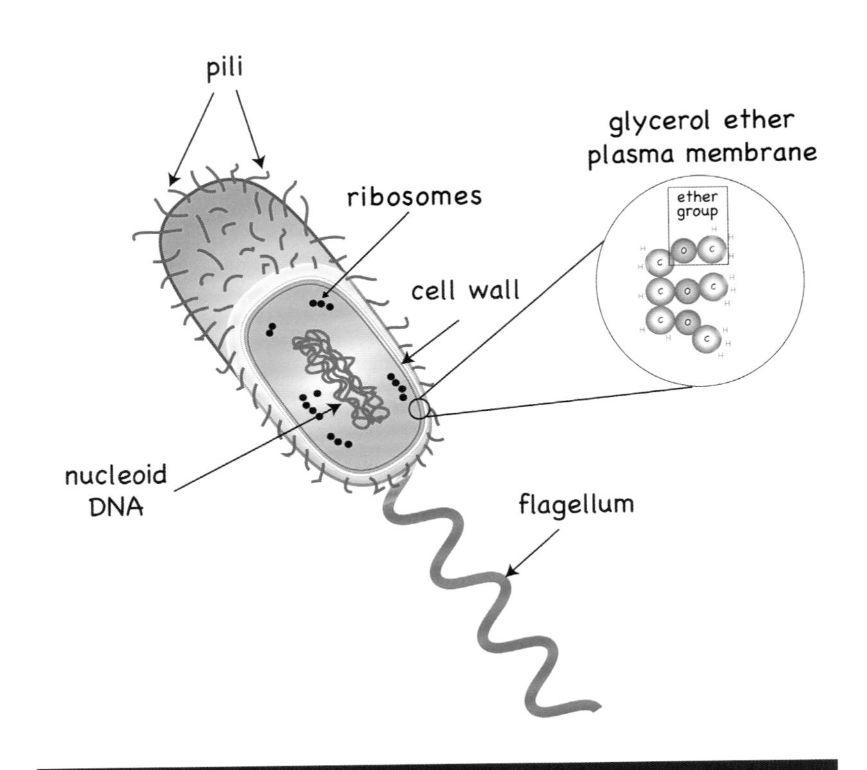

Archaeal prokaryotic cell

Like bacterial prokaryotic cells, archaeal cells don't have a true nucleus or organelles. Archaeal cells have a glycerol ether plasma membrane, and some have flagella and pili. Most have a cell wall.

8.5 Eukaryotic Cells

The word eukaryote comes from the Greek word *eu* meaning "true" and *karyon*, meaning "kernel." Eukaryotic cells have a nucleus in the central part of the cell. Eukaryotic cells are usually much bigger and more complicated than either bacterial prokaryotic cells or archaeal prokaryotic cells. All living things in the domain Eukarya and the kingdoms Plantae, Animalia, Fungi, and Protista have eukaryotic cells.

There are two main types of eukaryotic cells—plant cells and animal cells. Because plant cells are eukaryotic cells, they have a nucleus, a glycerol ester plasma membrane, and organelles. Organelles function like little organs inside a cell. They are not true organs because true organs, such as the heart, are made up of many cells and an organelle is contained within an individual cell. But because each type of organelle performs specific functions, organelles can be thought of as little organs inside cells.

Many plants make their food from the Sun and have a type of organelle called a chloroplast. By using chloroplasts, many plants can convert the Sun's energy into food through photosynthesis. Plant cells have other organelles, including mitochondria (small factories that make ATP energy molecules), microtubules to move things from place to place, and a golgi apparatus where proteins are modified, shipped, and stored.

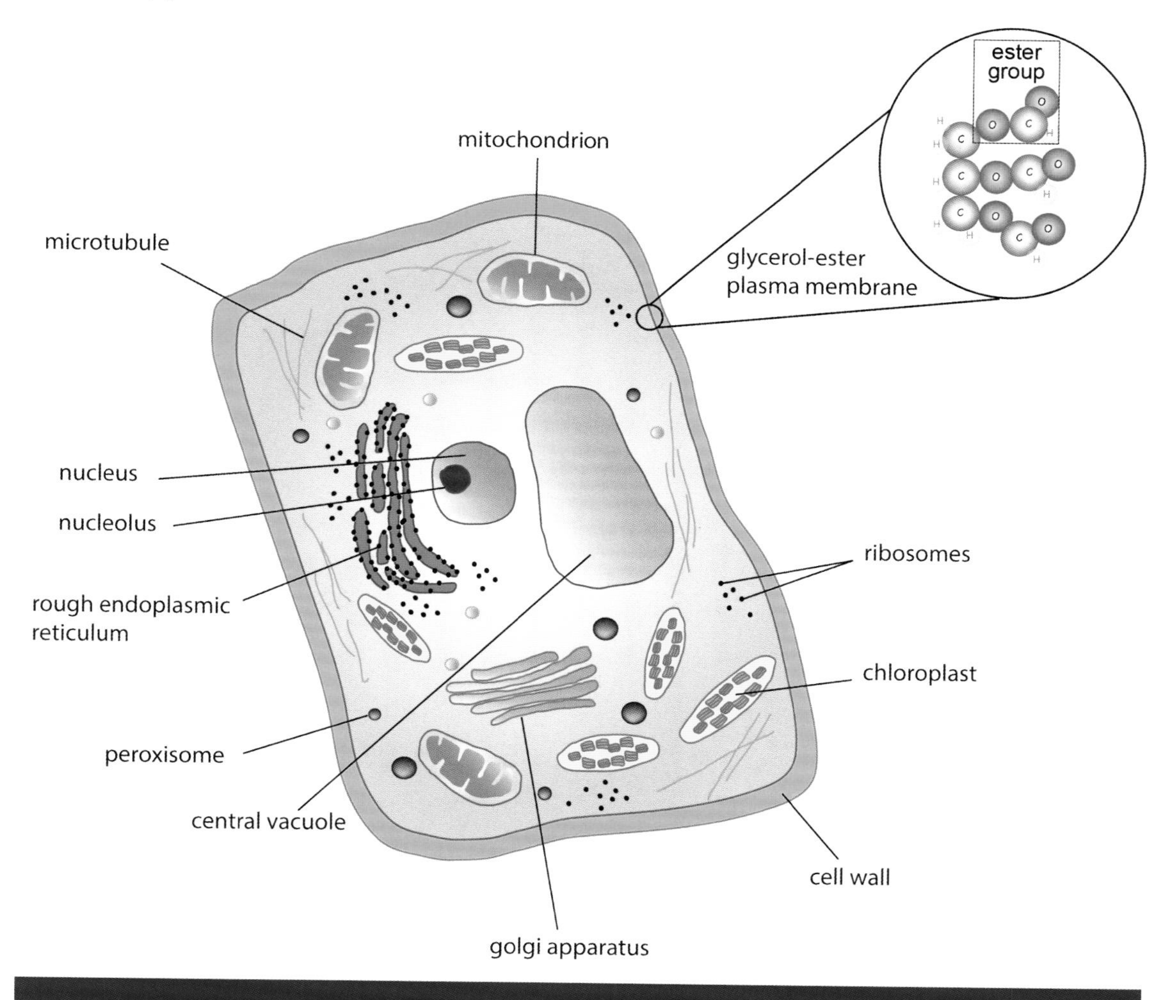

Plant cell

Animal cells have many features similar to plant cells, and they also have important differences. Animal cells do *not* have a cell wall. Instead they are surrounded only by the plasma membrane. Also, animal cells don't have chloroplasts and cannot make their own food with sunlight.

Animal cells do have many other organelles that are the same as those found in plant cells. Animal cells have a nucleus, mitochondria, a rough endoplasmic reticulum, and microtubules that move things from place to place in the cell. Both also have a golgi apparatus that behaves like a shipping and receiving area for the cell.

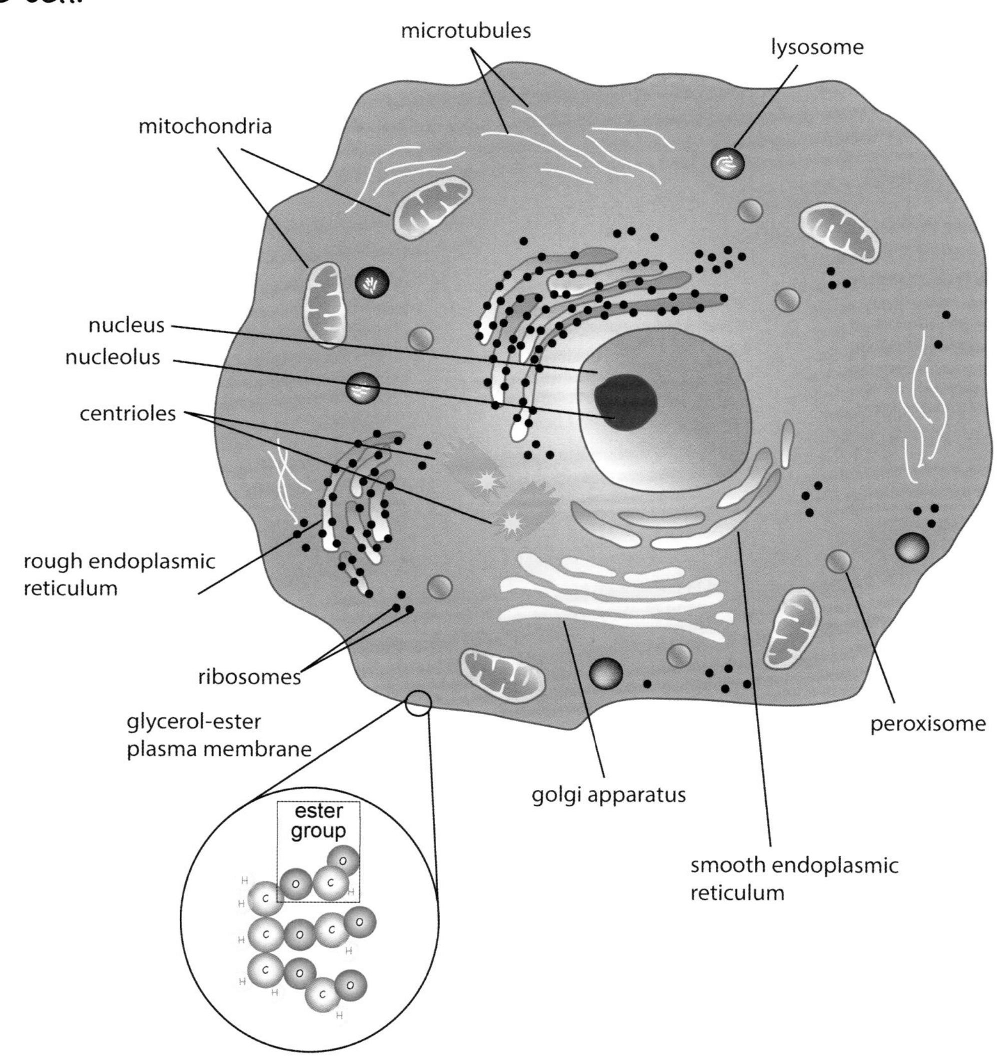

Animal cell

Some Organelles and Cell Machinery		
Nucleus		Organelle - The nucleus is the central part of the cell. It holds all of the information the cell needs to live and reproduce.
Mitochondrion		Organelle - The cell's energy molecules are made in the mitochondria.
Ribosome		Molecular machine - The ribosomes make proteins.
Lysosome		Organelle - The lysosomes are the places in the cell where some big molecules are digested for other uses by the cell.
Chloroplast		Organelle - The chloroplast uses light energy from the Sun to make energy molecules for plant cells.
Nucleolus		Organelle - Pieces of ribosomes are made in the nucleolus.
Rough Endoplasmic Reticulum		Organelle - Proteins and new membranes are made in the rough endoplasmic reticulum.
Peroxisome		Organelle - Peroxisomes rid the cell of dangerous and poisonous substances.
Golgi Apparatus		Organelle - The golgi apparatus receives, modifies, ships, and stores proteins.
Cell Wall		Organelle - The rigid cell wall gives shape to plants, bacteria, and most archaea.

8.6 Cell Division

How does your body grow? As you grow, do your cells just get bigger or do they make more cells? Can you think of some advantages of being able to make more cells instead of just making bigger cells?

For you to grow and live a long life, your cells need to divide to make new cells. There are different reasons why our cells need to make new cells. The body needs to make different kinds of cells in order to have all the different organs it needs to function properly, and new cells are needed to grow and form these organs. New cells are needed to

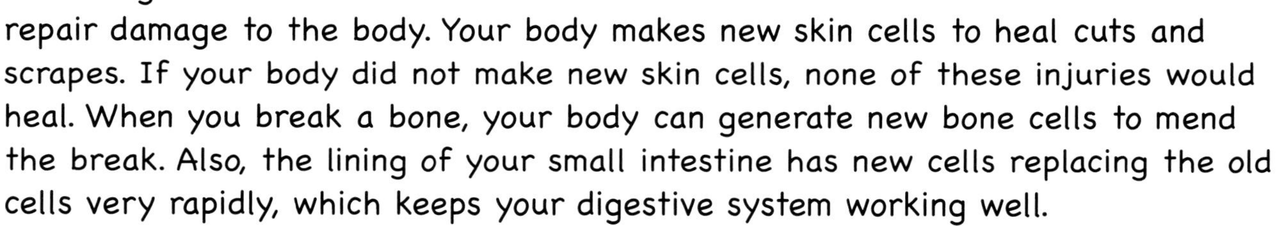

repair damage to the body. Your body makes new skin cells to heal cuts and scrapes. If your body did not make new skin cells, none of these injuries would heal. When you break a bone, your body can generate new bone cells to mend the break. Also, the lining of your small intestine has new cells replacing the old cells very rapidly, which keeps your digestive system working well.

The cells in your body are constantly replacing themselves. Old cells die and new ones are formed. When cells divide and make new cells, the DNA is copied so the new cells will have the correct instructions to function properly.

8.7 Bacterial and Archaeal Cell Division

Both bacterial prokaryotic cells and archaeal prokaryotic cells divide by binary fission. Binary means two parts, and fission means splitting. Binary fission literally means splitting into two parts.

When it is time for a prokaryotic cell to divide, the cell begins to elongate and to duplicate its DNA. As the DNA is duplicated and separated, the cell is also growing bigger. When it is almost twice its normal size, the middle of the cell begins to pinch together, dividing the cell in two. The cell wall and plasma membrane grow down the middle of the cell, and when a new wall has formed, the cell divides into two new cells.

Under good growth conditions, bacteria will often grow, duplicate DNA, and divide almost constantly. If you start with one bacterium in ideal conditions, after a few hours you can have many millions of bacteria!

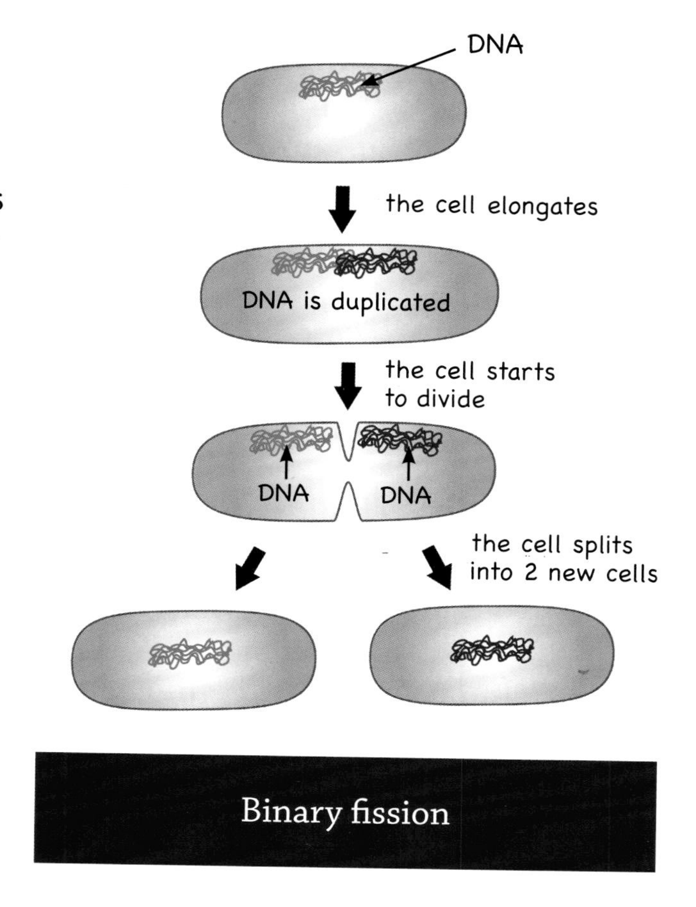

Binary fission

8.8 The Eukaryotic Cell Cycle: Mitosis

A eukaryotic cell goes through a much more complicated process with a series of stages that together make up its cell cycle. When eukaryotic cells divide to repair or grow, they divide by a process called mitosis.

The cell cycle of mitosis has four main steps. The first step is called the G1 phase. G stands for gap, and this is the first gap, or space, between cell divisions. During this phase the cell has finished dividing, and the cell is resting, possibly getting bigger but not actively doing anything to prepare for the next division. Cells can stay in this phase for a short time or for a very long time.

S phase: S stands for synthesis, which means "making." In S phase the cell is beginning to prepare to divide by copying all of its DNA. At the end of S phase, there will be two copies of all the DNA.

G2 phase: During the second gap phase, the cell is finishing preparations to divide. It organizes some of the machinery that it will need to divide.

During mitosis (M phase) the two copies of DNA are pulled to opposite sides of the cell and the cell divides. After mitosis the cell goes back to the G1 phase and the process starts again.

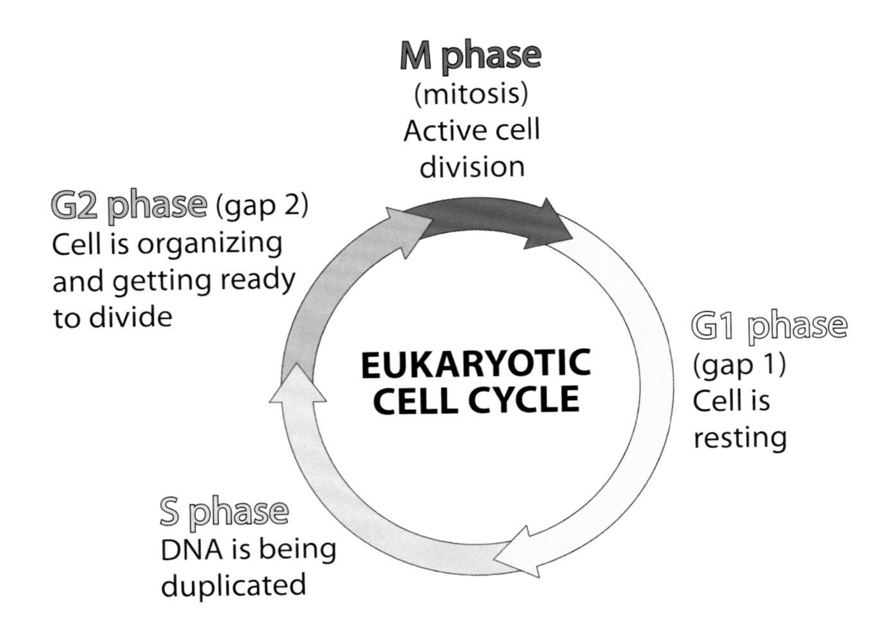

8.9 Summary

- All living things are made of cells.
- There are three main types of cells: bacterial prokaryotic cells, archaeal prokaryotic cells, and eukaryotic cells.
- Prokaryotic cells do not have a nucleus or organelles and eukaryotic cells do.
- To live and grow, cells need to divide to make new cells.
- Bacterial prokaryotic cells and archaeal prokaryotic cells divide by binary fission.
- When they need to divide to repair or grow, eukaryotic cells divide by a process called mitosis.

Chapter 9 Viruses, Bacteria, and Archaea

9.1 Introduction 92

9.2 Viruses 92

9.3 Bacteria 94

9.4 Shapes of Bacteria 95

9.5 Archaea 97

9.6 Summary 99

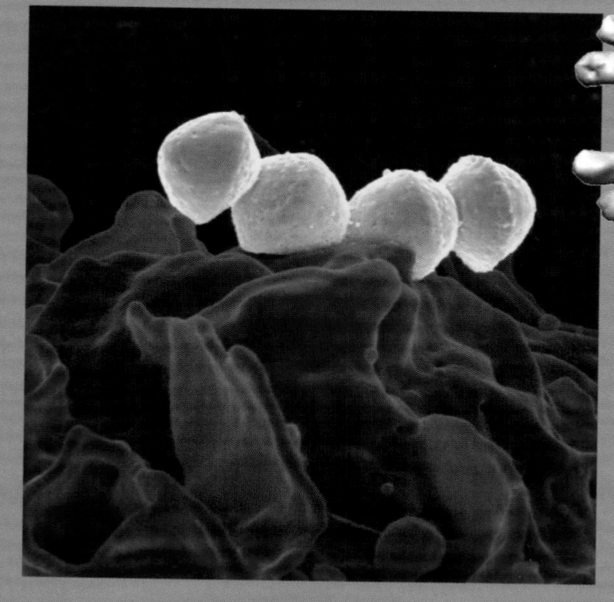

9.1 Introduction

As we saw in the last several chapters, all living things are made of atoms and molecules, and all living things assemble these atoms and molecules into small units called cells. Cells are the basic units of life. In the last chapter we took a close look at cells, the different types of cells, and how cells divide. In this chapter we will take a look at some of the smallest living things: viruses, bacteria, and archaea.

9.2 Viruses

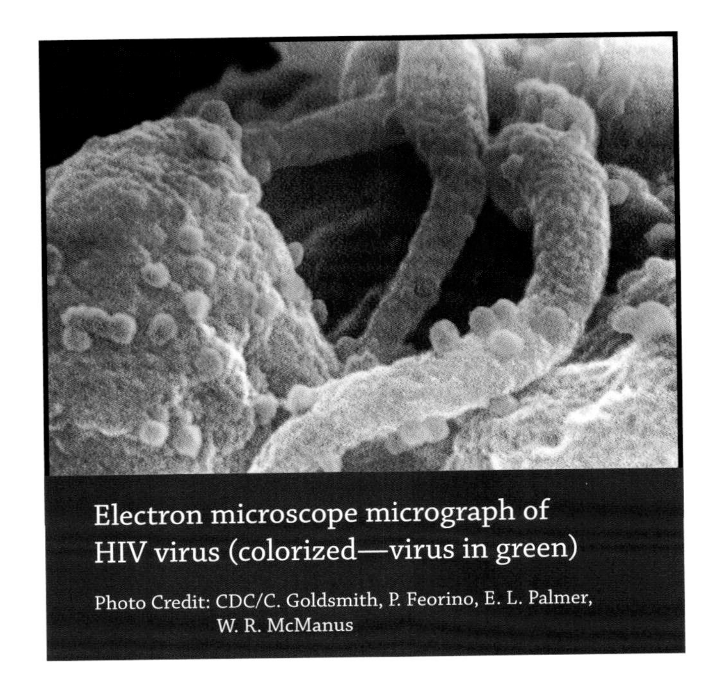

Electron microscope micrograph of HIV virus (colorized—virus in green)

Photo Credit: CDC/C. Goldsmith, P. Feorino, E. L. Palmer, W. R. McManus

If you start sneezing and two days later you feel achy and tired with a sore throat and a stuffy nose, you've probably been hit with a virus.

Viruses are odd, and many scientists still don't know how to classify them. Are viruses really alive or are they just some proteins and DNA codes that infect living things? Because it isn't clear how to catalog viruses, they are not in a domain and don't have their own kingdom.

Viruses are often classified according to the type of organism they infect. For example, Bunyaviruses are grouped together because they infect plants and animals, and Totiviruses are in a different group because they infect protists and fungi.

Viruses don't have all the features that bacterial, archaeal, or eukaryotic cells have. Viruses don't have a nucleus, a cell wall, or a cell membrane. Viruses are technically not cells but small sacks containing DNA or RNA that are surrounded by a tough outer coat made of protein. Most viruses are much smaller than either bacteria or archaea and are too small to be visualized with

Electron microscope

Photo Credit: CDC by James Gathany

a regular light microscope. A special type of microscope called an electron microscope is needed to see viruses. An electron microscope uses electrons instead of light to visualize very small particles.

Viruses can be spiral in shape and look like a tightly coiled garden hose, or they can be icosahedral and shaped like a soccer ball.

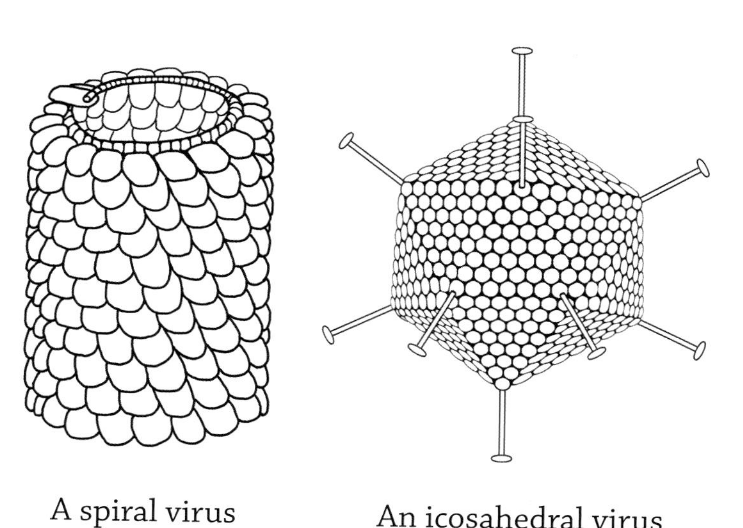

A spiral virus

An icosahedral virus

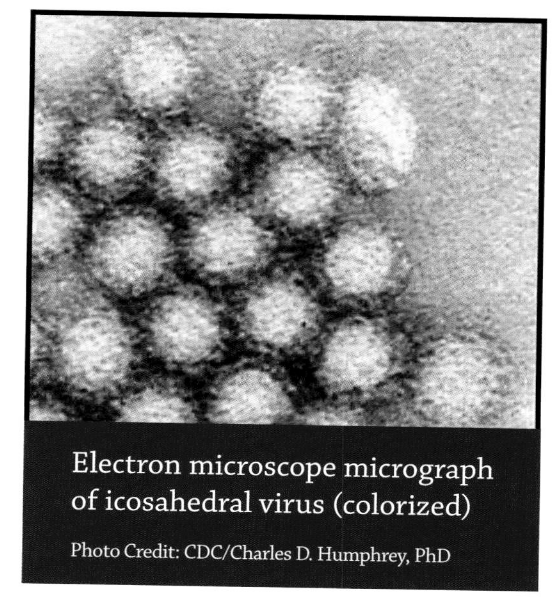

Electron microscope micrograph of icosahedral virus (colorized)

Photo Credit: CDC/Charles D. Humphrey, PhD

The group of viruses that causes most common colds is the rhinovirus group. There are actually three different categories of rhinoviruses: Rhinovirus-A, Rhinovirus-B, and Rhinovirus-C. Rhinoviruses-A and B cause most of the less severe common cold symptoms in humans, and Rhinovirus-C is believed to cause more severe cold symptoms.

When a rhinovirus is interacting with human proteins and cells, it looks like a soccer ball with spikes. Most rhinoviruses cause mild to severe infections in the lungs with occasional headaches and sometimes fever.

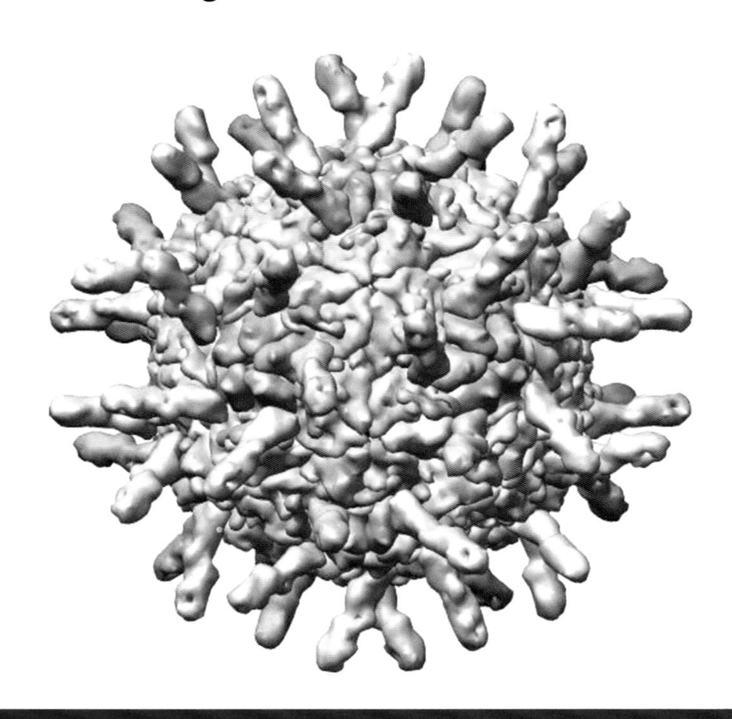

Illustration of Human Rhinovirus 16

Reference Protein Data Bank structural studies of two rhinovirus serotypes complexed with fragments of their cellular receptor
Kolatkar, P. R., Bella, J., Olson, N. H., Bator, C. M., Baker, T. S., Rossmann, M. G.
Journal: (1999) EMBO J. 18: 6249-6259]

9.3 Bacteria

Bacteria have gotten a bad name because many bacteria make humans, plants, and animals sick. But not all bacteria are harmful. It may (or may not) make you feel better to know that there are lots of bacteria that don't hurt us, and some bacteria even help us. Scientists guess that there may be something like 100,000,000,000,000,000 (100 quadrillion) bacteria that live on and in each one of us!

In fact, bacteria live everywhere. People have found bacteria almost everywhere they have looked. As scientists have learned more about these tiny organisms, we have been able to use this knowledge to cure disease, grow food, and clean up our world.

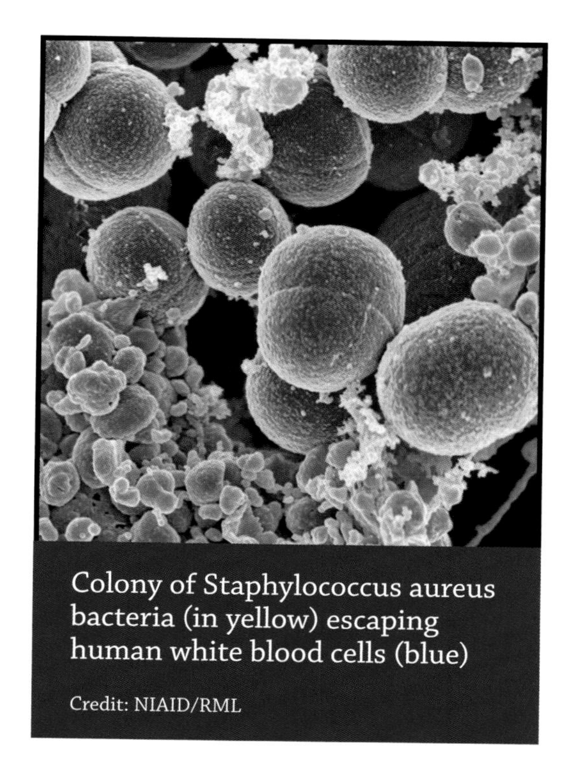
Colony of Staphylococcus aureus bacteria (in yellow) escaping human white blood cells (blue)

Credit: NIAID/RML

Bacteria are single-celled organisms with a prokaryotic cell type. Recall that bacteria have no nucleus and their DNA is "loose" in the cell, located in a centralized place called the nucleoid. Single bacteria are too small to see without a microscope, but a huge group of bacteria, called a colony, can be easily seen with the unaided eye.

Bacteria reproduce fast. Some take only ten minutes to grow and divide. If you started with one, after ten minutes you would have two; after twenty minutes, four; after thirty minutes, 8; after forty minutes, 16; after fifty minutes, 32; and after an hour, 64. If they have the right growing conditions, after a few hours or days there are so many bacteria that you can see the colony without using a microscope or magnifying glass. It's a good thing bacteria can't reproduce that quickly forever. They need the right conditions to grow so fast. If a colony gets too big, it can run out of food. Also, bacteria need moisture and don't thrive on dry surfaces.

When people boil water to make it safe to use, they destroy the bacteria cells. Bacteria can be killed by very high temperatures, like the temperature of boiling water (100° C, 212° F). Very low temperatures slow the rate at which bacteria divide. This is why refrigeration allows food to last for a longer period of time. However, low temperatures do not generally kill bacteria.

9.4 Shapes of Bacteria

Bacteria come in many different sizes and shapes. The three most common shapes are rods, spheres, and spirals, although some bacteria can be star-shaped or even rectangular.

E. coli is an example of a rod-shaped bacterium. Rod-shaped bacteria are called bacilli. Most bacilli appear as single rods. Some bacilli form pairs after they divide and are called diplobacilli. Others form a chain and are called streptobacilli.

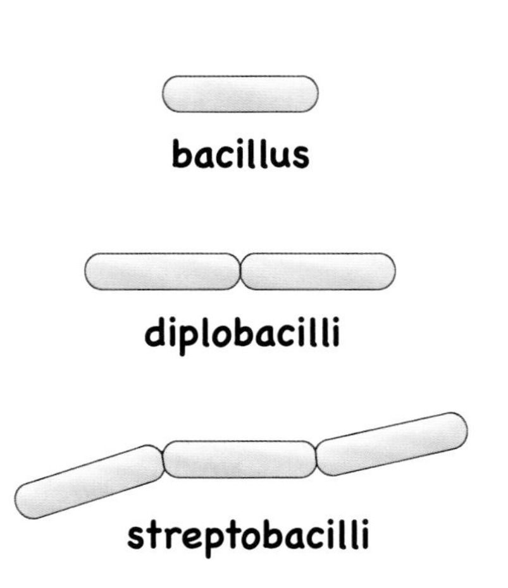

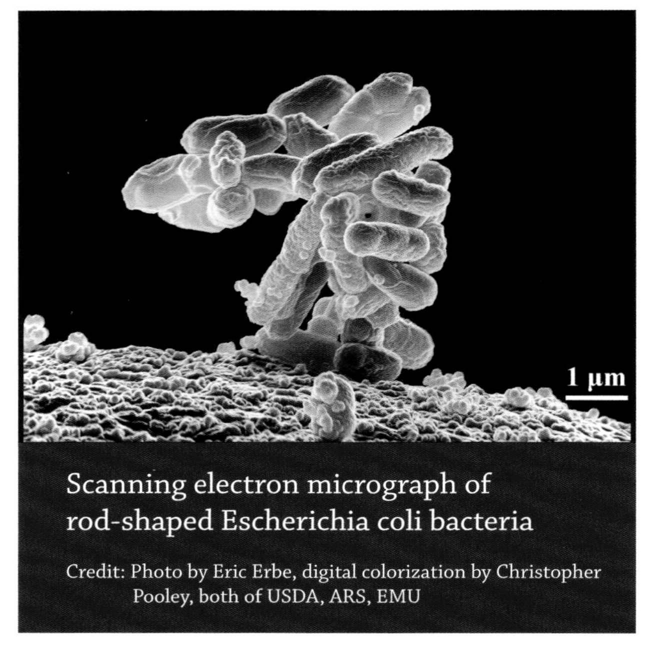

Scanning electron micrograph of rod-shaped Escherichia coli bacteria

Credit: Photo by Eric Erbe, digital colorization by Christopher Pooley, both of USDA, ARS, EMU

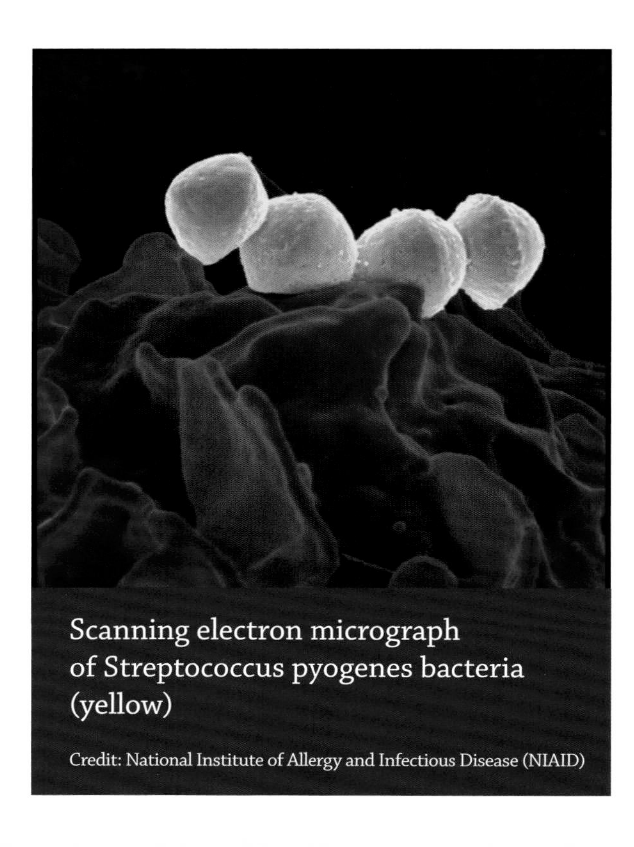

Scanning electron micrograph of Streptococcus pyogenes bacteria (yellow)

Credit: National Institute of Allergy and Infectious Disease (NIAID)

Sphere-shaped bacteria are called cocci, from the Greek word *kokkus* which means "grain, seed, or berry." Most cocci are round, but they can also be elongated or flattened on one side. After cocci divide, they can remain in pairs, form long chains, or form clusters. When you have strep throat, it is an infection of Streptococcus bacteria.

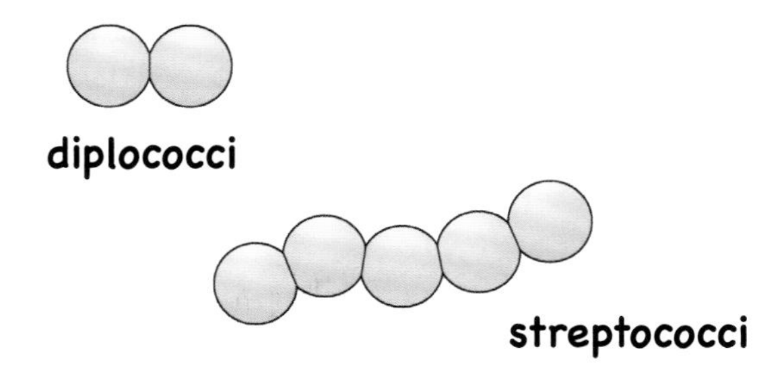

There are three different types of spiral bacteria called vibrio, spirillum, and spirochete. Vibrio bacteria are almost like rods, but are curved. Spririlla are fairly stiff and look like a short corkscrew. Spirochetes are long and thin with flexible bodies, and they look like a long corkscrew.

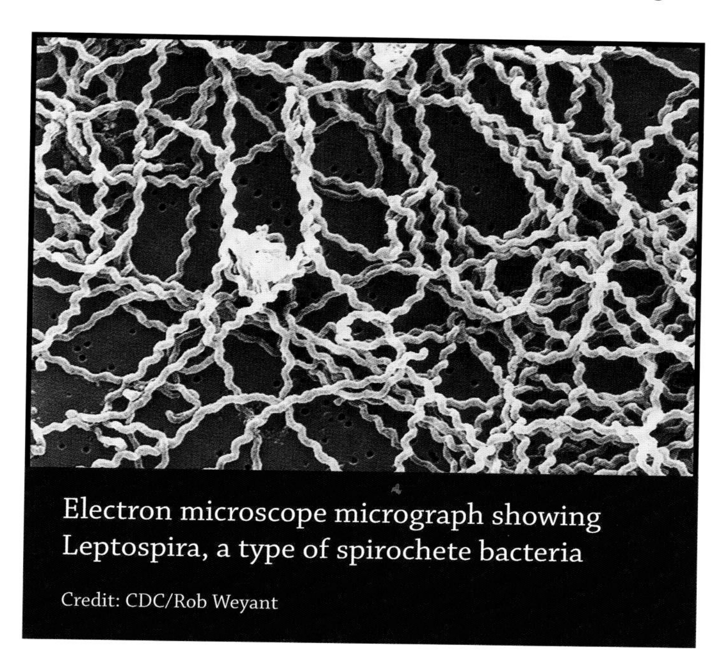

Electron microscope micrograph showing Leptospira, a type of spirochete bacteria

Credit: CDC/Rob Weyant

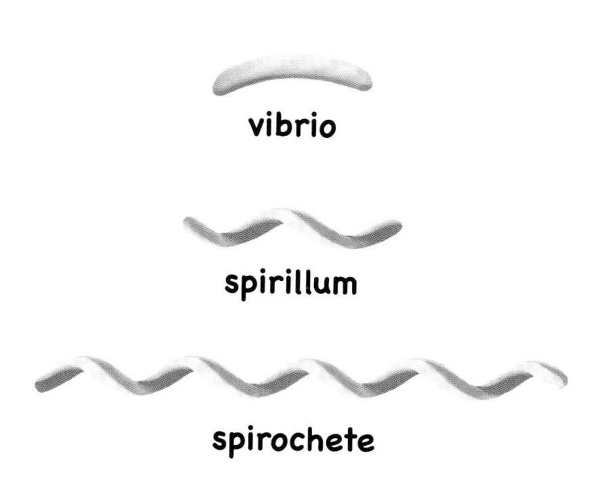

9.5 Archaea

Arahaea are similar to bacteria in size and shape, but as we saw in Chapter 8, they are not identical and therefore have their own domain. Scientists first found archaea in environments where nothing else could survive. Three types of extreme environments where archaea can live are places without oxygen, places with extreme amounts of salt, and places that are very hot.

Methanogens are a type of archaea that cannot survive where there is oxygen. These archaea use carbon dioxide, nitrogen, and hydrogen for energy and give off methane. Methane is a gas that stinks! Many stinky places smell of methane—swamps, marshes, and cows' guts, for example. Cows need archaea to help them digest their food, and methane is made during the digestive process. When plants in a swamp die and the decomposing bacteria use up all the oxygen, it is the perfect environment for the methanogens. For this reason, people can use methanogens to treat sewage (waste water). Because methane can be burned, scientists are experimenting with ways to collect methane and use it for fuel.

Another group of archaea are the halophiles. Their name comes from the Greek words *hals* which means "salt" and *philein* which means "to love," so the halophiles love a salty environment. Halophiles live in bodies of water that have lots of extra salt; for example, the Dead Sea.

San Francisco Bay salt ponds with colorful halophiles

Credit: Grombo Permission: GFDL, cc-by-sa-2.5. 2.0, 1.0

Deep sea vents at the Champagne Vent Site near Japan

Credit: NOAA (oceanexplorer.noaa.gov/gallery)

Thermoacidophiles like it hot! Thermoacidophiles are "hot acid lovers." These archaea live in the hot water right over volcanic areas, like deep sea vents where cracks in the Earth's crust spew out hot seawater full of minerals. The thermoacidophiles use these minerals for food.

9.6 Summary

- Viruses, bacteria, and archaea are some of the smallest living things.
- Viruses can be spiral or icosahedral in shape. They are difficult to classify, and some scientists don't think viruses should be considered to be "alive."
- Bacteria live everywhere and can reproduce rapidly.
- Bacteria have three main shapes: rod, sphere, and spiral.
- Archaea were once grouped with bacteria but are different enough to have their own domain.
- Archaea can live in extreme environments.

Chapter 10 What Is Physics?

10.1 Introduction 101

10.2 The Basic Laws of Physics 101

10.3 How We Get Laws 102

10.4 Summary 104

10.1 Introduction

Have you ever wondered what makes a feather float but a boulder fall, or why a bird can fly but a whale can't fly? Have you ever noticed that when your mom quickly puts on the brakes, the car stops, but your ice cream ends up on the dashboard? Have you ever wondered why, when you slide your stocking feet on the carpet, you can "shock" your dad?

All of these observations, and others like them, begin the inquiry into the field of science called physics. The name physics comes from the Greek word *physika*, which means "physical or natural." Physics investigates the most basic laws that govern the physical or natural world.

10.2 The Basic Laws of Physics

What is a basic law of physics? Are the laws of physics like the laws that tell us not to speed or not to steal? No. In fact, physical laws are statements that tell us about how the physical world works. Using these laws, we can understand why baseballs go up and then come down, why airplanes can fly, why rockets can land on the Moon, and why we see rainbows after it rains.

Physical laws are never broken, unlike laws that tell us not to speed or not to steal. For example, Newton's law of gravity tells us why we stay firmly on the surface of the Earth and do not sometimes just fly off. People have always known that the world behaves in regular and reliable ways. For example, people have observed for centuries that the Sun always rises and sets, that water always flows downhill, or that if it is cold enough, water will turn into ice. The laws of physics are statements about these regular and reliable observations.

We know that objects such as baseballs, airplanes, and people consistently obey the laws of physics and don't suddenly break one or two. It would be hard to play baseball if every once in a while the ball hit by the batter landed on the Moon!

10.3 How We Get Laws

How do we know what these laws are, and how did we discover them? Did the Earth come with a big instruction book that spelled out all of the laws? Not exactly. People had to figure them out on their own. Scientists use scientific investigation to discover how the world works.

One early scientist who used scientific investigation and helped develop the scientific method was Galileo Galilei. Galileo was an Italian astronomer born in Pisa, Italy in 1564. He showed how two lead balls fall at the same rate even if one is larger than the other. He performed a famous experiment where he is said to have dropped two cannon balls off the Leaning Tower of Pisa. He found that, even though the two cannon balls were different weights, they landed on the ground at exactly the same time!

People had trouble believing the results of Galileo's experiments, and it wasn't until Isaac Newton showed mathematically why this was true that it was finally accepted.

Isaac Newton is considered to be one of the greatest scientists of all time. He is also considered to be the founder of physics as we know it today.

SIR ISAAC NEWTON
1643–1727 CE

Sir Isaac Newton was born on January 4, 1643 in Woolsthorpe, Lincolnshire, England. When Newton was 18 years old, he went to the University of Cambridge to study mathematics, physics, and astronomy. By combining his interests in physics, mathematics, and astronomy, Newton was able to calculate how objects move and worked out a proof that showed the effect of gravity on the planets. Through his work, Newton determined the mathematical equations for the laws of motion.

One law that Newton discovered is called the law of universal gravitation. (We will discuss gravity in the next chapter.) Newton was able to confirm Galileo's experiments and showed mathematically why two falling objects will reach the ground at the same time even if one is heavier than the other.

One of the great discoveries of Newton's time is that mathematics can be used to describe events that happen in nature. For example, Newton was able to show that the force acting on an object is proportional to the mass of each object and inversely proportional to the square of the distance between them. The equation is:

$$F=G\frac{m_1 m_2}{r^2}$$

where F is *gravitational force,* G is the *gravitational constant,* m_1 is the *mass of object 1,* m_2 is the *mass of object 2,* and r is the *distance between them.* (F, m_1, m_2, and r are called variables because the amount they stand for can change, or vary. G is called a constant because its amount stays the same in different equations. Inversely proportional means that as one variable increases in value, another decreases.)

How can this equation be used to explain Galileo's experiment? If we fill in the values for each variable and use m_1 for the mass of Earth, we can see that because the mass of Earth (m_1) is huge and the mass of each ball (m_2) is very tiny in comparison, when the mass of Earth is multiplied by the mass of the ball, the value of F won't be affected by the mass of the ball. Therefore, the mass of each ball can be ignored because it doesn't make any difference to the answer to the equation. In other words, the equation shows that the gravitational force on any object is the same regardless of its mass as long as its mass is much smaller than the mass of Earth. This means that any two objects will fall at the same rate even if one object is heavier than the other. The equation that expresses this is:

$$F=Gm \quad (m=\text{mass of Earth}) \quad (\text{for both balls})$$

By using mathematics, Newton was able to prove Galileo's experiment.

10.4 Summary

- Physics is the study of how things move and behave in nature.
- The laws of physics are precise statements about how things behave.
- The laws of physics were determined using scientific investigation.
- Mathematics can be used to describe events that happen in nature.

Chapter 11 Force, Energy, and Work

11.1 Introduction 106

11.2 Force 106

11.3 Balanced Forces 107

11.4 Unbalanced Forces 108

11.5 Work 109

11.6 Energy 110

11.7 Summary 111

11.1 Introduction

What is energy? When your mom says, "I am out of energy," what does she mean?

Energy is actually defined as the *ability to do work*. The term *work*, as used in physics, describes what happens when a force moves an object. Your mom may need to rest to get back the energy she needs in order to have the force to move herself and other objects *(do work)*.

This can seem a little confusing, so let's look at force, work, and energy in more detail.

11.2 Force

What is force? Have you ever dropped an egg on the floor? What happened? Probably you heard a noise and noticed that the egg was no longer available for your cake. In fact, you probably had to clean up a sticky mess. What happened to the egg? Why did it break? It broke because of force. The egg hit the floor with enough *force* to break it open.

Have you ever pushed on a heavy door that just wouldn't open? Did the door feel like it was pushing you back? When we push on a door, we apply a force to the door to open it or to move it. The door pushes back. The same thing happens when we pull on the door; the door pulls back. Both the pushing on the door and the pulling on the door are forces. A *force* is...

> something that changes the *position, shape, or speed* of an object.

There are many different sources of force. You experience one source of force every day, all day long. That is the force of gravity. The Earth is the source of the gravitational force you experience. It pulls on you and makes you, and everything else, stick to the ground.

The force of gravity is actually exerted by every object. You also are a source of gravitational force, and you pull on the Earth at the same time the Earth pulls on you. However, because you are so much smaller than the Earth, your gravitational force is very small compared to the gravitational force of the Earth. So, instead of dragging the Earth with you out into space, the Earth keeps you tightly stuck on its surface. In fact, all of the planets exert gravitational force. They pull and push on each other, and as a result, their distances from the Sun and their orbits around it are balanced and stay the same.

11.3 Balanced Forces

An object that is not moving has balanced forces. For example, a toy sitting motionless on your bookshelf is actually applying a force downward toward the shelf, and the shelf is applying a force upward toward the toy. The forces are *balanced*; they cancel each other out, so the toy does not move.

Another way to look at this is to consider what happens if you and your friend are pulling

a rope in opposite directions. If you both pull with equal strength and neither of you can move the other, then the forces with which you pull are equal. The forces are *balanced*. You both remain motionless.

Balanced forces can also occur with objects that are moving. For example, an air hockey puck slides gracefully, at the same speed, across a hockey table until it is struck with an opponent's paddle. As it is moving and as it is at constant speed, the forces between the puck and the table are balanced. This happens with anything that slides, such as snow skis, ice skates, or even magnetic trains!

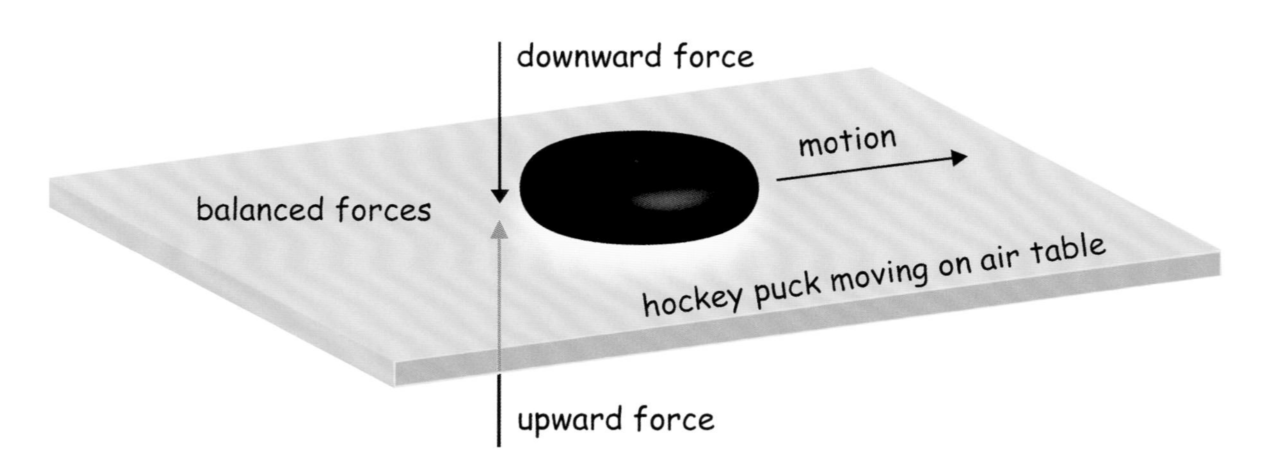

11.4 Unbalanced Forces

If the forces are unbalanced, that is, one force is greater than the other, the object will move. As long as the force keeps acting on the object, the object keeps moving faster. If the object keeps going faster and faster, it is said to accelerate. Unbalanced forces always cause acceleration.

Suppose that when you and your friend are both pulling on the rope, you suddenly pull less hard on your end. What happens? Your friend keeps his force the same, but because you are pulling less hard, BAM! He's in the puddle! Why?

Your force decreased, and your friend's force became greater than your force. These unbalanced forces caused him to fall backward into the puddle. When the forces were equal, you and your friend did not move. As your force decreased (you pulled less hard), your friend began to move. In other words, he went from no speed (standing still), to some greater speed (falling in the puddle).

This change in speed is called acceleration, and this acceleration was caused by a force. In this case, your pulling less strongly on your end of the rope caused your friend to accelerate into the puddle.

11.5 Work

What is work? You probably hear comments like, "I am late for work," by your dad, or "I have too much work," exclaimed by your mom. You might think that work is a very grown-up thing that causes lots of stress, and your parents might agree. But in physics, work is something very simple. *Work* is the result of a force moving an object a certain distance.

When force is used to move an object a given distance, work has been done on that object. The amount of work done is calculated by multiplying the force times the distance the object has traveled. This can be expressed as a mathematical equation:

$$w = d \times f$$

where w stands for *work*, d stands for *distance*, and f stands for *force*.

For example, as the expression on the face of a weight lifter shows, a tremendous amount of work is needed to lift a heavy barbell from its resting position on the ground to its final position above the weight lifter's head. The amount of work the weight lifter does is proportional to the distance he has to lift the barbell. *Proportional* means that work and distance are related; if there is twice as much distance, the weight lifter does twice as much work.

For example, a very short weight lifter would have to do less work to get the bar above his head than a very tall weight lifter. If the short weight lifter were half the height of the tall weight lifter, then he would do exactly half the amount of work.

11.6 Energy

When work has been done, and forces have been used to do that work, energy has been used. It's hard to define energy exactly, but one thing energy *does* is to give objects the ability to do work. Take a look at the weight lifter we studied in the last section. When the barbell is on the ground, it requires the force of pulling up on the barbell to lift it above the weight lifter's head.

When this happens, work has been done. But where did the weight lifter get what he needs to lift the barbell? Wheaties! Yes! The weight lifter had to have energy in his body to be able to use his muscles to do the work of lifting the barbell above his head. By eating food, living things get a type of energy needed to do work.

There are actually different kinds of energy because there are different ways to do work. The different types of energy are given different names. A few of these different types of energy are potential energy, kinetic energy, and heat energy. We will look at some different types of energy in more detail in later chapters.

11.7 Summary

- A force is something that changes the *position, shape, or speed* of an object.
- Forces can be balanced or unbalanced. Objects that are not moving, or objects that are moving at constant speed, have balanced forces. Objects that are accelerating have unbalanced forces.
- Energy is hard to define, but it gives objects the ability to do work.
- Work = distance x force. This means that, for example, twice the distance gives twice the work for the same force.

Chapter 12 Potential and Kinetic Energy

12.1 Potential Energy 113

12.2 A Note About Units 114

12.3 Types of Potential Energy 115

12.4 Energy Is Converted 116

12.5 Kinetic Energy 116

12.6 Kinetic Energy and Work 117

12.7 Summary 119

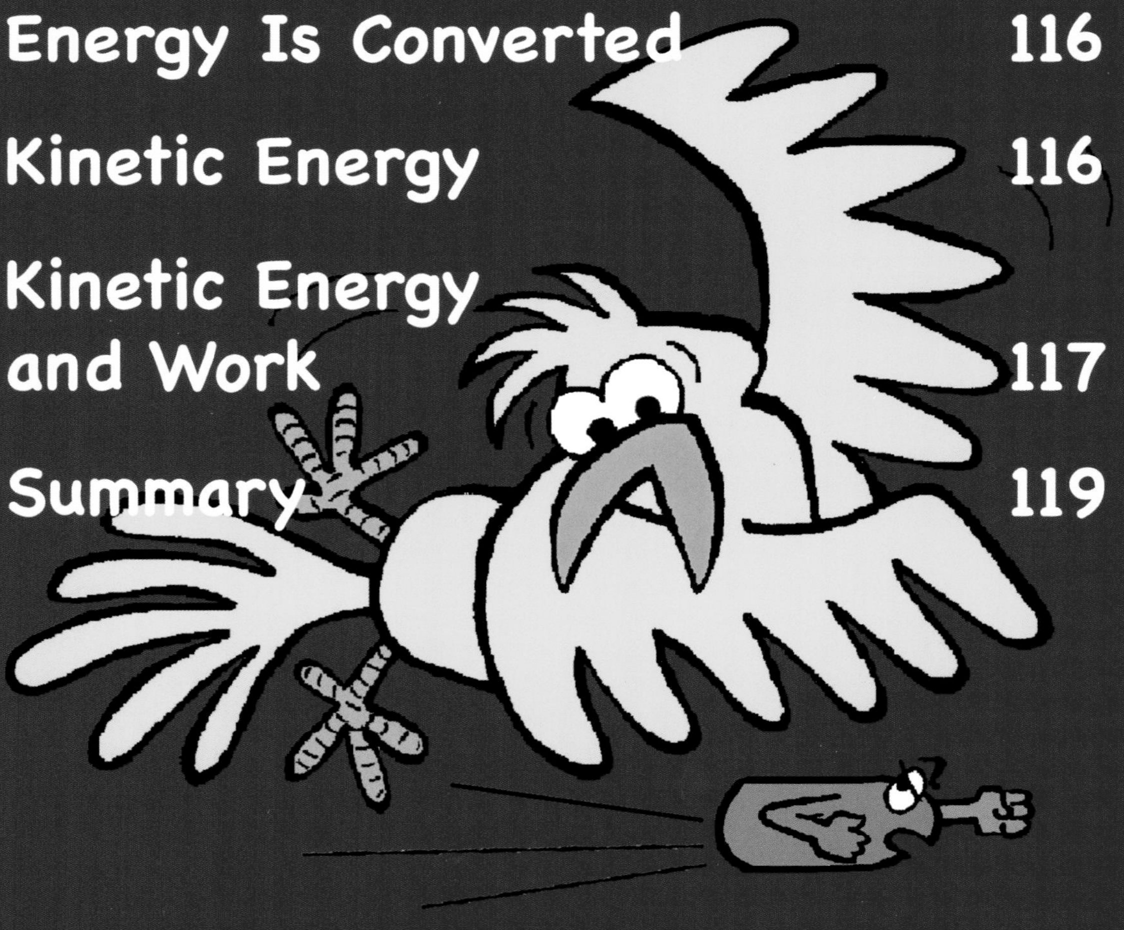

12.1 Potential Energy

What is potential energy? You've probably heard the word *potential* used before. For example, you may have heard someone say, "He's got potential," or "The tropical storm has the potential to become a hurricane." In both of these statements, the word *potential* refers to something that has the capacity to happen or become. "He's got potential" simply means that someone has the possibility of becoming something like a great basketball player or leader in the future but isn't one right now. The tropical storm may become a hurricane, but it isn't right now. It only has the potential to become one. Recall that energy is used to do work. Simply put, *potential energy* is energy that has the potential to do work.

Potential energy is a type of energy often called stored energy. An example of an object with potential energy is a book on a table. It may not seem like the book can do work, but because the book is not on the floor but is raised, it has the potential to fall off the table.

When the book falls off the table, it strikes the floor with a *force*. This force could be used to crack open a peanut, smash a marshmallow, or make a big noise. The book can use the potential energy to do work.

This type of potential energy is called gravitational potential energy because the force of gravity is required to bring the book from its elevated position (on the table) to its final position (on the floor). The amount of gravitational potential energy of an object equals the amount of work that was needed to lift the object in the first place.

The amount of gravitational potential energy can be calculated by multiplying the weight of the object by the height:

gravitational potential energy (GPE) = weight x height

For example, if the book on the table is 1 meter (3.28 feet) above the floor and it weighs 1 kilogram (2.2 pounds), the gravitational potential energy (GPE) is:

GPE = 1 meter x 1 kilogram (3.28 feet x 2.2 pounds)

or

GPE = 1 kilogram-meter (7.2 foot-pounds)

12.2 A Note About Units

What is a unit? In physics, a *unit* is simply the name given to a type of measurement. For example, to measure your height you might stand next to a wall and have your mom mark a place on the wall by the top of your head. Using a ruler, she can then measure how tall you are by putting one end of the ruler on the floor and the other end on the mark on the wall. Your height might be something like 1.25 meters (4 feet, 2 inches). *Meters* and *feet* and *inches* are called *units.*

Meters, feet, and inches measure how long something is, but other units, like kilograms and pounds, may tell us how much something weighs, or like liters and gallons, how much liquid something can hold. Time also has units, like hours, minutes, and seconds. It tells us how long something takes to happen; for instance, how long it might take for an egg to reach the ground if it is dropped from a tall building.

In the United States, we often use what are called British units, for example, feet and inches. But most scientists use metric units. Metric units are usually easier to work with than British units because they can be evenly divided by 10. British units are usually converted to metric units when used in science. The table shows some units in both metric and British.

British Units		Metric Units	
	1 inch	10 millimeters	1 centimeter
12 inches	1 foot	100 centimeters	1 meter
5280 feet	1 mile	1000 meters	1 kilometer

12.3 Types of Potential Energy

There are actually several different types of potential energy. We already saw gravitational potential energy, which is energy associated with the position of an object. Other types of potential energy include nuclear potential energy, elastic or strain potential energy, chemical potential energy, and several others.

Nuclear potential energy is the energy that is stored in an atom. Nuclear reactors use the nuclear potential energy that is stored in uranium atoms to heat water, which can then be used to make electrical energy. Nuclear reactors can provide electricity for very large communities and even whole countries!

Elastic or strain potential energy is the energy stored in an extended rubber band or a compressed spring. Chemical potential energy is the energy that is stored in molecules, such as that found in batteries, fuels, or foods.

12.4 Energy Is Converted

What happens to the potential energy of the book, the battery, or the rubber band once the energy is released? Is it still potential energy? No. The potential energy of the book, the battery, and the rubber band have all been released and converted into another type of energy. It is important to know that:

Potential energy is useful (can do work) only when it has been converted into another form of energy.

Can you think of other uses for batteries? Tree decorations perhaps? Or maybe a nice hood ornament? Not really. In fact, batteries are useless unless their potential energy is converted—for instance, to light a flashlight or power a CD player. When a battery is used to power a CD player or a flashlight, the chemical potential energy inside the battery is released by chemical reactions and converted to electrical energy. The electrical energy can then be converted into light energy in the flashlight or mechanical energy in the CD player.

12.5 Kinetic Energy

We saw in the last section that potential energy must be converted into another form of energy before it can do work. What kind of energy is it converted into? When the book was dropped from the table, the gravitational potential energy had to first be converted into kinetic energy before it could do work on the peanut.

What is kinetic energy? The word kinetic comes from the Greek word *kinetikos*, which means "putting into motion," and kinetic energy is the energy associated with things that are moving.

The potential energy of the book on the table is converted into kinetic energy when the book falls—that is, while it is moving toward the floor. The book has no kinetic energy as it sits on the table, only potential energy. When the book is moved from the table and begins to fall, the potential energy is converted into kinetic energy. The farther it falls, the more kinetic energy it gains and the more potential energy it loses.

By the time it hits the floor, all of the potential energy has been converted into kinetic energy. The total amount of energy has not changed—only the form of energy. Physicists say that the total energy is conserved. That is, all of the potential energy has been converted into another form of energy. Energy is never lost—only converted. We will learn more about the conservation of energy in the following chapter.

How much kinetic energy does the book have? It depends. The kinetic energy of an object depends on two things—one is the *mass* of the object, and the other is the *speed* of the object.

What we need to remember about kinetic energy is the following:

For a certain speed, the more mass an object has,the more kinetic energy it has;

and

For a certain mass, the more speed an object has,the more kinetic energy it has.

Therefore, a heavy book will have more kinetic energy than a lighter book moving at the same speed. Also, a book that is thrown will have more kinetic energy than a book that is dropped.

12.6 Kinetic Energy and Work

We already saw in the last chapter that energy is the ability to do work. When a rubber band is stretched across the prongs of a slingshot, it has *elastic potential energy*. When the rubber band is released, the elastic potential energy is transferred to the pellet in the slingshot as the pellet is propelled toward the target. The pellet now has *kinetic energy*. All, or almost all, of the potential energy that was in the slingshot is now kinetic energy in the pellet.

What happens to the kinetic energy in the pellet when it hits the target? The kinetic energy is converted to other forms of energy, such as heat and sound. As a result, the energy is transferred to the target in the form of work as it pushes on the target.

We say that:

The pellet is doing work on the target.

12.7 Summary

- Potential energy is energy that has the potential to do work.
- A book on a table has gravitational potential energy.
- The energy in a stretched rubber band is called elastic potential energy.
- Kinetic energy is the energy of motion.
- Potential energy can do work only when it is converted into another form of energy, such as kinetic energy.

Chapter 13 Conservation of Energy

13.1 Introduction 121

13.2 Energy Is Conserved 121

13.3 Usable Energy 123

13.4 Energy Sources 123

13.5 Summary 128

13.1 Introduction

Recall the different types of energy we have looked at, such as *potential energy, kinetic energy, chemical energy,* and *electrical energy*. We have seen how one form of energy can be converted into another form of energy. The *gravitational potential energy* of a toy car can be converted into *kinetic energy* as it rolls down a ramp to smash a banana.

We have seen how *chemical potential energy* inside a battery can be converted to *light energy* in a flashlight and how *mechanical energy* can be converted to sound in a CD player. If we recall from biology how plants make food, we can see that chloroplasts convert *light energy* from the Sun into *chemical energy* in leaves. From chemistry, we have seen that when we eat food, like carbohydrates, we get *chemical energy* for our bodies. When we lift a weight or run a race, this *chemical energy* is converted into *mechanical energy*.

13.2 Energy Is Conserved

In all of these processes, energy is neither created nor destroyed. Energy is simply converted from one form to another. In fact, energy cannot be created or destroyed, but only converted. There is a fundamental law of physics, called the law of conservation of energy, which states that energy is conserved. This simply means that the total amount of energy we convert to other forms of energy does not increase or decrease—it stays the same. In fact, the whole universe has the same amount of energy today that it had ten or even twenty years ago. It will have the same amount of energy tomorrow and the next day that it has today! Even a hundred or a thousand years from now, the energy in the universe will stay the same. Energy is conserved.

How is energy conserved? In the experiment for Chapter 12, we saw how gravitational potential energy (GPE) was converted into kinetic energy (KE) when a toy car was used to smash a banana. The energy of this system, called total energy, is equal to GPE plus KE. We saw that as the toy car rolled down the ramp, it lost GPE and gained KE. But what happened to the total energy? Did it change too? No, in fact the total energy stayed the same. We can see how this happens if we look at both the GPE and KE at several places on the ramp.

Imagine that when the car is at the top of the ramp it has 100 joules (joules are a unit of energy) of GPE. Because it is not moving, it has no KE. When the car is halfway down the ramp, it has lost half of its GPE, but it has gained KE because it is moving. In fact, it has gained the same amount of KE that has been lost as GPE. Just before the car hits the bottom of the ramp, it has lost all of the GPE, but has gained more KE. The total energy (GPE + KE) remains the same at each point. The total energy does not change. This is what is meant by conservation of energy.

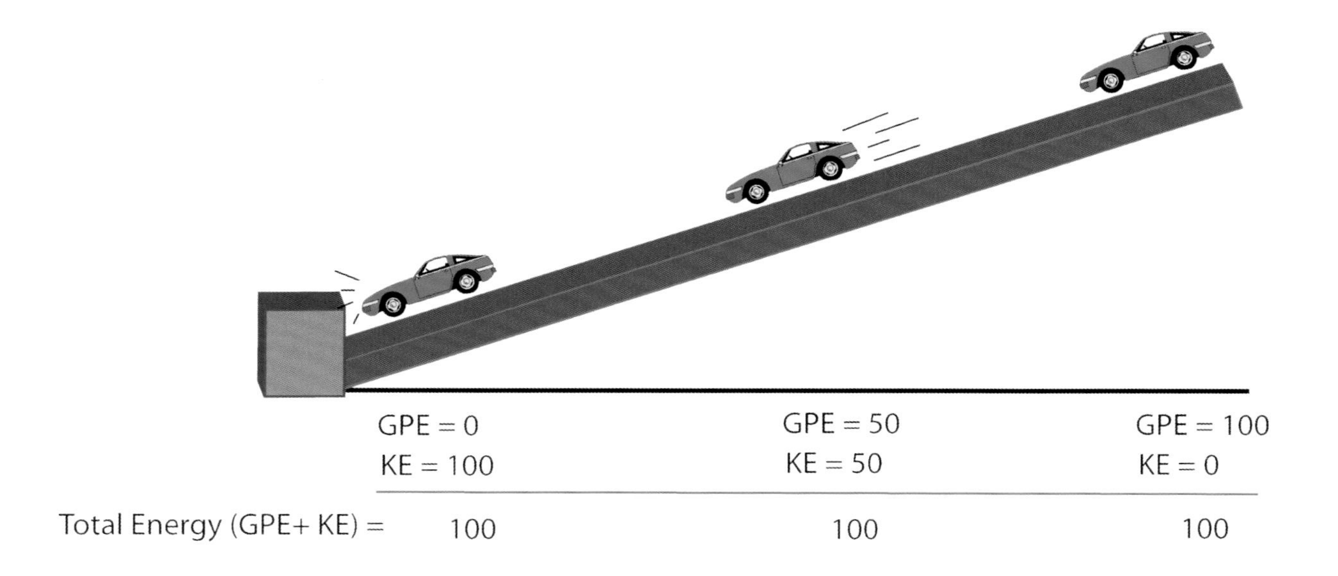

13.3 Usable Energy

Why is it that we often hear of an energy crisis or an energy shortage? Why are we concerned about fossil fuels or ways to save electricity? Why are we told not to waste energy? If we always have the same amount of energy, why do we care if we convert all of the chemical energy in a flashlight into light energy?

We care because not all energy is usable energy. That is, we cannot convert all of the energy into a form that we can use. For example, when a flashlight is left turned on behind the sofa, the stored chemical energy gets converted into light energy and heat energy. The usable energy in the flashlight is "lost" when all of the stored chemical energy has been converted into light and heat energy. We can't use it anymore. In fact, we have to throw the batteries away and get new ones! But the energy isn't gone, it has just been converted into a form that we can't use. So, when someone talks about an energy crisis, they mean that all of the *usable energy* is disappearing because it is being converted into unusable forms of energy, like heat energy.

13.4 Energy Sources

Plant fossil

What are some of the forms of energy we use? We've already seen that batteries store chemical energy, but what about other forms of energy? Where do we get gasoline, electricity, and natural gas?

Some of the energy we use comes from fossil fuels, such as oil, natural gas, and coal. Fossil fuels are formed from plants and animals that died a very long time ago and have been subjected to extreme heat and pressure. When a plant or an animal dies, the tissues and cells that the plant or animal is made of decompose or break down into smaller pieces. One of the smallest pieces that all living things break down into is the carbon atom. Sometimes, if the conditions are just right, the carbon from the dead plants and animals combines with hydrogen and turns into oil, coal, or natural gas. These are called fossil fuels, or hydrocarbons. Hydrocarbons contain chemical potential energy. When hydrocarbons burn, the molecules combine with oxygen in a chemical reaction that converts chemical potential energy to other forms of energy.

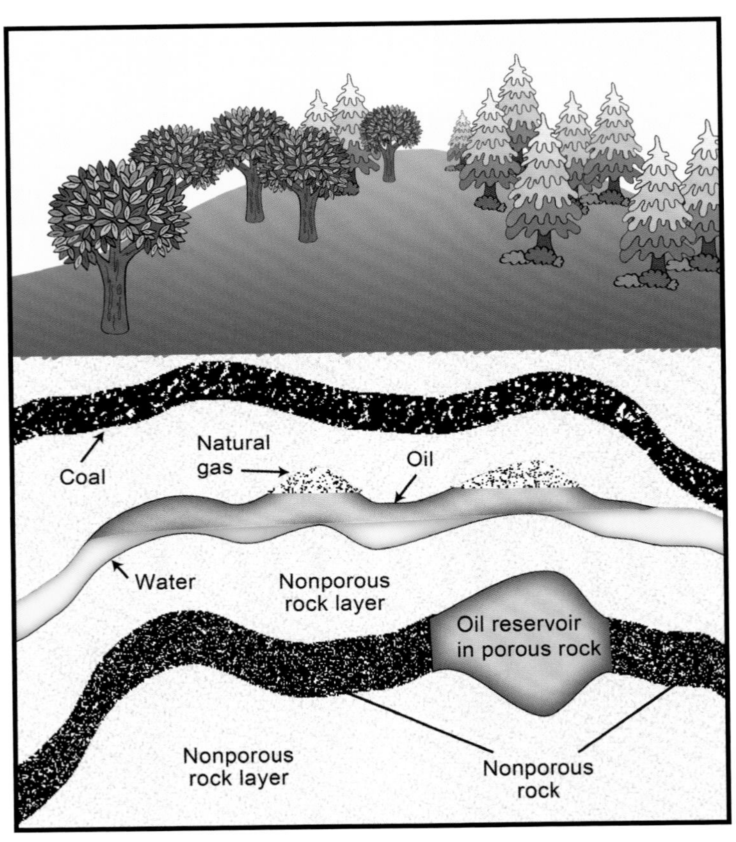

Oil is found in underground rocks and is called crude oil or petroleum. Certain types of rocks, such as sandstone and limestone, are porous and hold oil in reservoirs, which are places where the oil collects and is stored. Porous rocks contain lots of empty spaces, or pores, and when the pores connect to each other, oil can flow through the rock. When these porous rocks are surrounded with nonporous rocks that the oil can't travel through, the oil will accumulate in reservoirs within the porous rock. Oil can be removed from a reservoir by drilling a hole deep into the rock and pumping the oil out.

Crude oil is refined into different products, such as gasoline, kerosene, and jet fuel for cars, trucks, planes, and heating buildings. Petroleum is also used to produce substances such as plastics, waxes, fibers, and dyes. The chemical potential energy in petroleum fuels is converted into heat, light, mechanical, kinetic, and electrical energy.

Like oil, natural gas is formed from tiny plants and animals that have died, decomposed, and fossilized, and natural gas is often found in the same reservoirs as oil. Natural gas is made mostly of methane, which is a carbon atom with four hydrogens attached. Since it is lighter than oil, natural gas is found above the oil in a reservoir. Chemical reactions are used to convert the chemical potential energy in natural gas into heat, light, mechanical, kinetic, and electrical energy.

Coal is another fossil fuel found underground. It is formed from decaying plants that have fossilized and is found in layers, or seams. Coal is hard and cannot be pumped out of the ground like oil but must be removed by digging, or mining. Large holes or mine shafts, together with tunnels, are dug deep into the ground. Both miners and digging equipment can then get inside the ground to remove the coal.

Coal miner underground

Coal was the main fossil fuel up until the early 1900s. It was used to power steam engines and factories and to generate heat for making steel and iron. Today, coal is mostly used to generate electricity.

Although we have many uses for fossil fuels and have become dependent on them, in the process of burning, fossil fuels give off chemical by-products that can be harmful to the environment, and as fossil fuels are used, their potential energy is eventually converted to unusable energy. Fossil fuels are considered a nonrenewable energy source because they form so slowly that new fossil fuels won't be available to take the place of fossil fuels that have been mined. The supply of fossil fuels available today can be used up, and as the easily mined sources are removed from the Earth, fossil fuels become increasingly more difficult to mine. In addition, the mining, drilling, and processing of fossil fuels uses a great deal of energy.

There are energy sources other than fossil fuels that we can use for powering cars, for electricity in our homes, and for other uses. Two important sources of usable energy are wind and water, which are considered to be renewable energy sources. This means that, unlike coal and oil, wind and water are continuously circulating rather than being used up. Heat from the Sun creates more wind, and water circulates around the Earth in the water cycle. Renewable energy sources don't create the pollution problems that the burning of fossil fuels does, and they are not going to run out.

Windmills harvest energy from the wind and have been used for centuries to pump water from the ground. Even today, it is common for windmills to bring groundwater to the surface for crops on farms and for cattle on ranches. Today's large windmills are called wind turbines and are being used to generate electrical energy. Earth's atmosphere is heated unevenly by the Sun, creating the kinetic energy of winds as air moves from high pressure to low pressure areas. As the wind hits the blades of a wind turbine, the gravitational potential energy of the blades is converted to kinetic energy as the blades move. The kinetic energy of the blades is converted to mechanical energy in an attached generator. The spinning of the generator converts kinetic and mechanical energy to electricity.

Flowing water in rivers is used in many places as a source of energy. A dam is built in a river to create a large lake, or reservoir, behind the dam. The water in the reservoir is higher than that of the river, giving it gravitational potential energy. As the water falls down from the reservoir through a passageway in the dam, the water's gravitational potential energy is converted to kinetic energy and has enough force to turn a turbine, creating mechanical energy which in turn is used to generate electrical energy. The reservoir is refilled by rain or flowing rivers, making water a renewable energy source.

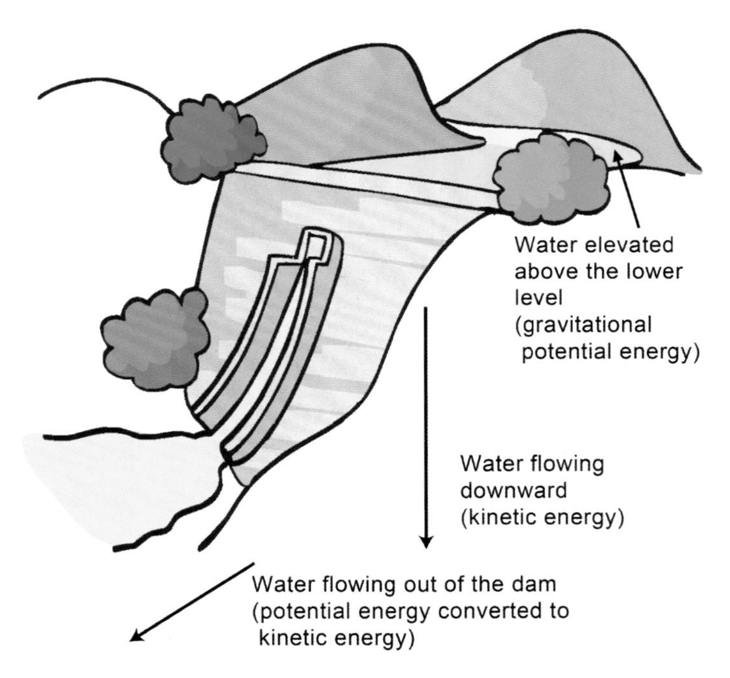

The Sun is a very important source of energy for plants. Ultimately, all the energy contained in fossil fuels came from energy from the Sun that was used by plants to make food. The Sun's energy, solar energy, can also be used directly to generate electricity. Solar energy can be harvested using solar panels which are made up of small units called photovoltaic cells. A photovoltaic cell works at the atomic level to convert light energy from the Sun directly into electrical energy. Materials used in photovoltaic cells have what is called a photoelectric effect. The photoelectric effect makes these materials able to absorb photons of light and release electrons. These released electrons are then captured, resulting in an electric current that can be used as electricity for power. Albert Einstein was granted a Nobel prize in physics in 1905 for describing the photoelectric effect.

Solar panels

Photo Credit: US Air Force, Nellis AFB, Nevada/ photo by Airman 1st Class Nadine Y. Barclay

Solar panels that convert the Sun's energy into electricity can be used in homes and are used to power spacecraft like satellites and the International Space Station. At present, solar power is relatively expensive, so it is less commonly used than energy from fossil fuels, flowing water, or wind. But as the technology for harvesting solar power improves, it will most likely become cheaper and more common.

Another way that solar energy can be used is called passive solar. Passive solar uses parts of a building itself to collect energy from the Sun. Materials that absorb heat can be selected for walls, floors, and other parts of buildings. Heat energy from the Sun is absorbed by these materials and released later, reducing the use of fossil fuels for heat. A greenhouse or large windows might be added to the south side of a building to allow for the collection of more solar energy. You may notice that when you get into a car that's been in the sun for a while, the air is warmer inside the car than outside. Your car can collect heat energy from the Sun, becoming a passive solar unit!

13.5 Summary

- Energy is converted from one form to another.
- Energy is conserved. This means that the total amount of energy does not change as energy is converted from one form to another.
- Usable energy can be lost when it is converted to unusable energy, such as light or heat, that is not captured and converted to another form of energy.
- Some of our energy comes from fossil fuels like oil, coal, and natural gas. These are forms of nonrenewable energy.
- Some of our energy is harvested from wind, flowing water, and the Sun. These are forms of renewable energy.

Chapter 14 What Is Geology?

14.1 Introduction 130

14.2 What Is Geology? 130

14.3 Interpreting Geological Data 131

14.4 Why Study Earth? 133

14.5 What Do Geologists Study? 133

14.6 Geology and the Scientific Method 135

14.7 Summary 136

14.1 Introduction

Most people probably don't often think about Earth being the place where they live. When you ask someone where they live, they might reply "on 4th Street" or "in Minneapolis," but rarely do you hear "on Earth." In fact, everyone lives on Earth, and as far as we know, there is no one living on any other planet. Most people don't often wonder about what the Earth is made of or think about Earth being only one of many planets in the universe.

So what is the Earth? What is it made of? Has it always been this way, or has it changed? Why can Earth support life and the Moon can't? What makes Earth special? Finding out about the Earth, what it is made of, and how it changes are inquiries into the scientific field of geology.

14.2 What Is Geology?

The word geology comes from the Greek root words *geo* which means "earth" and *logy* which means "the study of." So geology is "the study of Earth." Geology is a science that focuses on bringing about a better understanding of the structure and history of Earth, the planet we live on.

The field of geology is divided into two broad categories—physical geology and historical geology.

Physical geology examines the chemical and physical nature of Earth and also the processes that operate on and inside Earth. Physical geology explores the Earth's surface, the processes that form the Earth, and the heat energy that drives these processes.

Historical geology examines the origin of Earth and incorporates biology, chemistry, and physics in an attempt to create a chronological narrative, or story, about how the Earth came into being and how it has changed over time.

14.3 Interpreting Geological Data

Science has two parts. One part is collecting scientific data through observation and experimentation. The second part is to find out what the data mean, and this is called interpretation. Interpreting scientific data is the process that scientists use to draw conclusions, formulate theories, and develop scientific laws and principles.

Because science is a human endeavor, the interpretations of scientific data are subject to human bias and presupposition. In science a presupposition is an assumption about how something works and is usually based on preexisting beliefs and sometimes on previous experience. For example, because it is known that planes can fly, if a plane is seen in a hangar, the assumption may be that the plane will fly even if this particular plane has not been seen in the air.

It is not incorrect for presuppositions to be used in science, and scientists do use them all the time. However, scientists may begin research with differing presuppositions, and even though scientists use logic and strive to be objective, there is often disagreement about how scientific data should be interpreted.

Disagreements in science are a vital part of scientific investigation and should be encouraged because they can lead to new ideas and new ways of thinking about observations. However, many people, including scientists, are uncomfortable with arguing.

Many scientists see the world in a certain way, and since they are not open to other points of view, they insist that every other scientist see the world in the same way. The way someone "sees the world" is called their worldview. Someone's worldview is made up of the philosophies and beliefs that they use to understand the world around them. There are as many different worldviews as there are people because no two people see the world in exactly the same way. This difference between worldviews causes many arguments in the scientific community.

Geologists with different worldviews disagree about how the Earth came into being, how old it is, and how it has changed over time. Most of these disagreements occur in the area of historical geology and the historical narrative for Earth. But sometimes they also occur in the area of physical geology, especially if historical presuppositions are used to develop physical theories.

This text will focus on physical geology and will not discuss different historical narratives for Earth. However, it is important to keep in mind that interpreting geological data is an exciting and dynamic part of studying geology and that disagreements help advance our understanding of Earth.

14.4 Why Study Earth?

Have you ever wondered why mountains are very tall and oceans are deep? Have you ever wondered why a desert has very little rain but it rains all the time in a tropical forest? Have you ever wondered where earthquakes come from or why some mountains erupt as volcanoes and others don't? Have you ever thought about where we get iron, copper, and oil?

Earth is a unique planet in our solar system and provides the habitat for all living things including human beings! By studying Earth we begin to understand what makes Earth so special.

We can learn where to find natural resources that improve the quality of our lives. We can also learn what causes certain geological catastrophes, such as earthquakes and hurricanes so we can help people prepare for and protect against devastating losses. We can learn how beautiful landscapes or vast forests have developed and work to preserve Earth's geological features. By studying Earth we can both protect Earth's native beauty and resources and use them to provide a future for the next generation.

14.5 What Do Geologists Study?

If you've ever met a geologist, you might have noticed that they can spend a lot of time outdoors—hiking up mountains and walking through fields. They also tend to collect a lot of rocks!

Geologists study the Earth, and in order to do this they go outside to explore and observe what is on and in the Earth.

There is much to investigate since Earth is a complex planet that is changing every moment of every day—whether it's rocks falling in a landslide, the top of a mountain breaking apart as a volcano erupts, or the ground moving in an earthquake.

A geologist studies snow

Photo Credit: US Geological Survey/by Lyn Topinka

A geologist studies erosion near the Dead Sea, Israel

Photo Credit: Mark A. Wilson, The College of Wooster

There are many different branches of geology, and each focuses on different aspects of the Earth. One branch of geology is called geochemistry. Geochemistry is the study of the chemistry of Earth. The Earth is made of atoms and molecules, just like all matter, and geochemists study the specific types of atoms and molecules that form Earth. In order to study the chemistry of Earth, geochemists take samples of the rocks, minerals, soils, and other matter that Earth is made from and analyze the samples. In this book we will take a close look at the matter that makes up Earth.

Another branch of geology is called structural geology which deals with the internal structure, form, and arrangement of rocks. Structural geologists study how rocks deform to make mountains and valleys. Deformation occurs when the shape and size of rocks change due to bending, twisting, or fracturing.

Deformed rock near Barstow, California
Photo Credit: Mark A. Wilson, The College of Wooster

There are also geologists who look for energy resources like gas, oil, and coal. This branch of geology is called resource geology. Resource geologists look for the natural resources that humans need for living on Earth.

When humans interact with Earth, sometimes they modify or change the environment, which includes those factors that affect living organisms, such as landscape, water, and air quality. Geologists need to monitor changes to the environment to help protect and clean it up. Geologists who study environmental changes caused by human activities are called environmental geologists.

14.6 Geology and the Scientific Method

In the science of geology, Earth itself is often the laboratory. Because things can happen very slowly on Earth, designing experiments and collecting results can be difficult. For this reason, geologists address many questions about Earth by observing features in rocks or landscapes, collecting rock samples, and using electronic equipment, among other things. Geologists formulate hypotheses based on what they've observed and then test those hypotheses. The conclusions they draw may be modified if the hypotheses are found to be incorrect.

Because many of Earth's features are not as testable or as provable as experiments in chemistry or physics, there is often disagreement about what the data mean. Even so, general principles about Earth's features can be proposed. These principles can be thought of as "scientific maps," and it is useful to keep in mind that scientific maps can change with new data or revised hypotheses.

14.7 Summary

- Geology is the study of Earth.
- Geology is divided into two broad categories—physical geology and historical geology.
- Physical geology examines the chemistry and physics of Earth. Historical geology attempts to create a chronological and historical narrative about Earth's origins.
- A person's worldview is made up of the philosophies and beliefs they use to understand the world around them.
- Geologists study Earth to learn more about Earth's features, to protect Earth's environment, and to find Earth's resources.

Chapter 15 Rocks, Minerals, and Soils

15.1 Introduction 138

15.2 Minerals 139

15.3 Rocks 142

15.4 Testing Rocks and Minerals 146

15.5 Soils 148

15.6 Summary 151

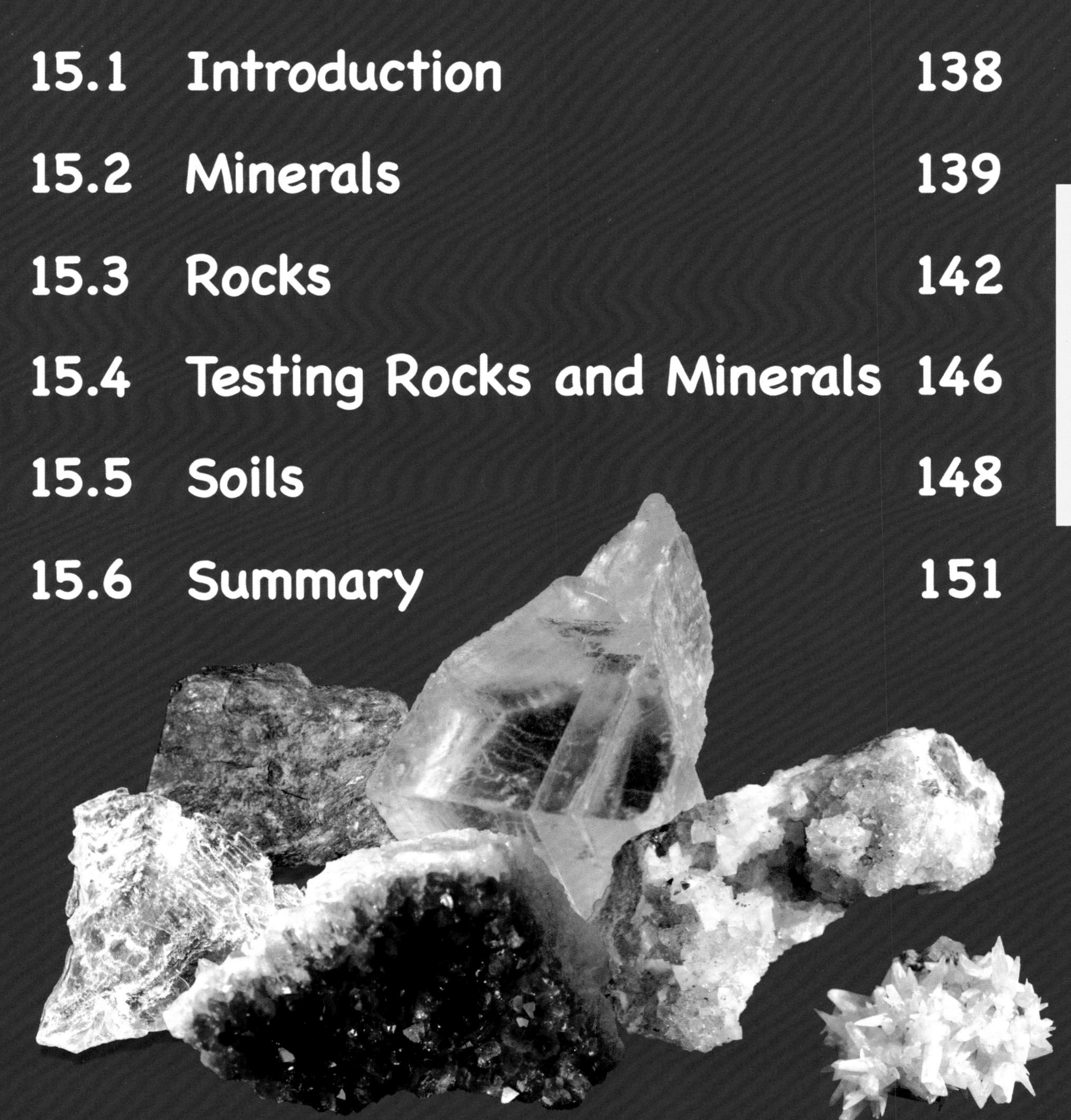

15.1 Introduction

When you walk outside or sit on the ground, you might wonder: What exactly is the Earth made of? If you dig your fingers into the ground you will discover that the ground is full of dirt (soil) and rocks. If you look under your house or under the library, you will find that rocks and dirt are also underneath the buildings. If you go to the tallest mountain or dive to the deepest part of the ocean, you will still find soil and rocks. In some places the soil is soft or sandy, and you can grab a handful of it and roll it around in your hand, letting it flow through your fingers. In other places the soil may be so full of big rocks that you cannot grab it with your fingers but instead need a jackhammer or drill to dig deeper.

The ground we walk on and build our houses and roads on is the outermost layer of the Earth and is called the crust. (We will learn more about the different layers of the Earth in Chapter 16.) The crust is composed of rocks and soils that are made of different chemical elements.

Different rocks are made from different minerals which are made from different chemical elements combined in a variety of ways. Different soils are made from different organic and inorganic materials. Both rocks and soils form the Earth.

15.2 Minerals

Minerals are the building blocks of rocks and soils. There are almost 4,000 different types of minerals. However, only a few dozen of those minerals are rock-forming minerals. There are eight chemical elements that make up the majority of rock-forming minerals: oxygen, silicon, aluminum, iron, calcium, sodium, potassium, and magnesium.

What is a mineral? If you look in your backyard and see plastic toys, trees, water, ice, and rocks, how can you tell which of these are minerals and which are not minerals? In geology, in order for a material to be considered a mineral it must meet the following criteria:

1) It must occur naturally.
2) It must be a solid.
3) It must be inorganic, meaning it does not contain the element carbon.
4) It must have an internal structure, or organization, of the atoms.

Plastic toys are not minerals because they are not naturally formed. Trees are not minerals because even though they are naturally formed, they contain carbon (are organic). Water is not a mineral because even though it is naturally formed and does not contain carbon, it is not a solid. Ice is not a mineral because even though it is naturally formed, a solid, and inorganic, it does not have an internal structure or organization of the atoms.

There are many different kinds of minerals found in rocks and soils; however, the majority of rock-forming minerals are silicates. Silicates contain the chemical compound silicate which is an oxgen-silicon compound that has four oxygens bonded to one silicon in a tetrahedral shape. (A tetrahedron is a solid geometric shape that has four sides.)

In a silicate molecule, the larger oxygen atoms surround the smaller central silicon atom to form a tetrahedral unit. These units join together to make single and double chains of molecules and also sheet structures.

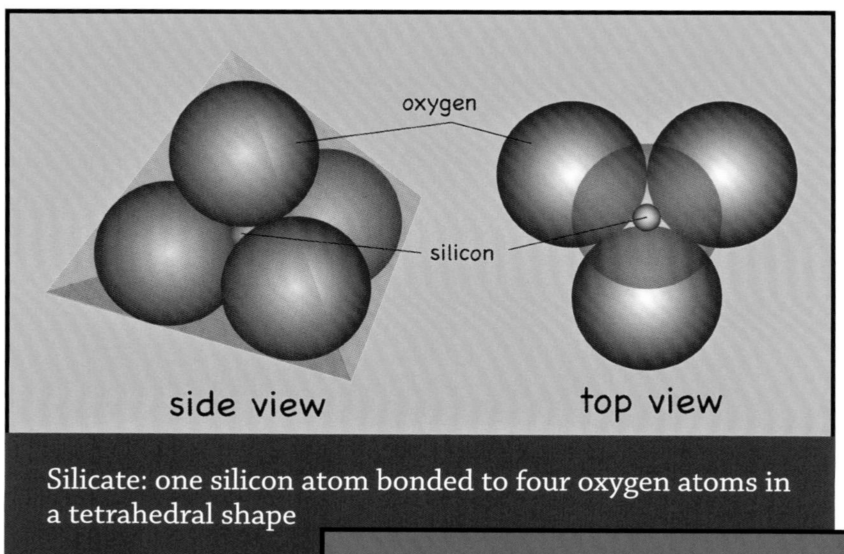

Silicate: one silicon atom bonded to four oxygen atoms in a tetrahedral shape

single chain

double chain

sheet structure

Chains of silicate molecules

Two common silicate minerals are quartz and feldspar. Quartz is made of silicon and oxygen and is found in many rocks and soils. Feldspar contains not only silicon and oxygen but also aluminum and either potassium, calcium, or sodium.

Silicate Minerals

Citrine quartz

Feldspar

Mica

Mica is another silicate and contains oxygen, silicon, and either potassium, magnesium, iron, or aluminum. Mica is very soft and comes apart in layered sheets.

Not all minerals found in rocks and soils are silicate minerals. Non-silicate minerals found in rocks and soils include calcite, dolomite, halite, and gypsum.

15.3 Rocks

Rocks are aggregates (mixtures) of different minerals glued together by the high heat and pressures found inside the Earth. There are three basic types of rocks called igneous, metamorphic, and sedimentary. Each of these rock types differ from one another based on their chemical makeup, how they were formed, and their texture.

Igneous rock makes up most of Earth's crust. Igneous rocks are formed from the molten (melted) magma deep within the Earth's core. Magma is made of rocks that have melted due to high temperatures within the Earth. Magma is mostly made of the chemical compound silicate which, as we now know, forms the silicate minerals.

Igneous rocks come in a variety of textures. Some igneous rocks are very coarse and contain large grains of silicates. Other igneous rocks are fine or even glassy, with small grains of silicates.

Granite

Granite is probably the best known igneous rock. Because granite has a natural beauty when it is cut and polished, it has been used as kitchen countertops in homes, for monuments, and as building stones. Granite is composed mainly of quartz and feldspar. The quartz particles are often clear and round in shape, and the feldspar is typically rectangular and pink. This combination of shapes and colors gives granite its beautiful texture.

Sedimentary rocks are made from particles of igneous and other rocks that have been weathered (worn away) by physical and chemical interactions. The word sediment comes from the Latin word *sedimentum* which means "to settle," so sedimentary rocks are those rocks formed from materials that are deposited by wind or water and then "settle." Sedimentary rocks are often layered.

There are two main types of sedimentary rocks: detrital sedimentary rocks and chemical sedimentary rocks. Detrital comes from the Latin word *detritus* which means "to wear away," so detrital sedimentary rocks are those rocks that have formed from layers of debris that has weathered, or been worn away, from

Sedimentary Rocks

Shale (detrital)

Limestone (chemical)

other rocks. Detrital sedimentary rocks may also contain other debris such as shells and plant matter. These layers of debris turn into rock as they are subjected to pressure from the weight of layers that form above them. Detrital sedimentary rocks include shales and sandstones.

Chemical sedimentary rock formations in a cave

Chemical sedimentary rocks are formed when minerals precipitate from the solution they are dissolved in. This means that the minerals separate out of the solution, most often from evaporation of the water. Limestone is a type of chemical sedimentary rock.

Metamorphic rocks are formed when one rock type transforms into another because of heat, pressure, or chemical reactions. *Meta* is a Greek prefix meaning "along, with, or between," and morph comes from the Greek word *morphe* and means "shape." Metamorphosis means "between shapes" and refers to the transformation or change of one thing into another. Metamorphic rocks are made from preexisting igneous rocks, sedimentary rocks, and even other metamorphic rocks.

Metamorphosis of rocks occurs in different ways depending on the environment they're in. Below the Earth's surface, rocks may be transformed by heat when they come in contact with magma. Rocks may also be exposed to hot iron-rich water or acids and bases, causing chemical changes. Mountains can form when rocks encounter extreme pressures.

Foliated metamorphic rock

Metamorphic rocks have different types of texture. Some metamorphic rocks are foliated, or layered. The word foliated comes from the Latin word *foliare* which means "leaf." As a verb, the word foliate means to divide into layers, like the "leaves of a book." The amount of foliation refers to how layered the texture of the metamorphic rock appears. Some rocks are highly foliated, and some are not foliated at all.

Marble statue of Socrates
Louvre Museum, Paris, France

Slate is a common metamorphic rock. The sedimentary rocks shale, mudstone, and siltstone, when exposed to high pressures, become slate. Because slate is a layered rock, it can be easily split into flat slabs. When slate splits, the flat slabs created can be used for patios and walkways and as a roofing material.

Marble is also a metamorphic rock. Marble is created when limestone is exposed to heat and pressure. Pure marble has a beautiful, naturally white color and has been used for monuments and by artists for sculptures.

Schist is a common metamorphic rock. Schist contains minerals such as mica and quartz. Schist is characterized as foliated because the individual minerals can split easily into flakes.

In summary, the three basic types of rock are igneous, sedimentary, and metamorphic. These rock types differ based on how they were formed and their texture.

<table>
<tr><th colspan="5">Three Basic Types of Rock</th></tr>
<tr><th>Rock Type</th><th>Igneous</th><th colspan="2">Sedimentary</th><th>Metamorphic</th></tr>
<tr><th>Formation</th><td>Formed from molten magma; made mostly of silicon and oxygen</td><td colspan="2">Formed from chemical and physical weathering processes</td><td>Formed from the transformation of one rock type to another</td></tr>
<tr><th rowspan="2">Textures</th><td rowspan="2">Fine
Coarse
Large crystals
Glassy</td><td>Detrital</td><td>Chemical</td><td rowspan="2">Foliated
Weakly foliated
Non-foliated</td></tr>
<tr><td colspan="2">Coarse
Medium
Fine</td></tr>
</table>

15.4 Testing Rocks and Minerals

A rock and mineral test kit can be used to help determine the type of mineral in a sample. A typical rock and mineral test kit contains a Mohs scale of mineral hardness, a penny, a nail, a streak plate, a dropper bottle, and a glass plate.

One identifying feature of minerals is how hard they are. Since a harder mineral will scratch a softer mineral, a scratch test can be used. In 1812 a German geologist named Friedrich Mohs developed the Mohs scale of mineral hardness which is a chart of the relative hardness of ten minerals. A rock or mineral sample can be tested by rubbing it with a known mineral to see if the known mineral will leave a scratch on the sample. The Mohs scale also assigns a hardness to objects such as a fingernail, a copper penny, a steel nail, window glass, and a steel file. Determining whether one of these objects will scratch the sample or whether the sample will scratch the object can help in identifying the mineral.

Mohs Scale of Mineral Hardness		
Hardness	**Mineral**	**Scratch Test**
1	Talc	can scratch with fingernail
2	Gypsum	can scratch with fingernail
3	Calcite	can scratch with copper penny
4	Fluorite	can scratch with steel nail and glass
5	Apatite	can scratch with steel nail and glass
6	Orthoclase	can scratch with steel file
7	Quartz	may scratch with steel file
8	Topaz	will scratch quartz
9	Corundum	will scratch topaz
10	Diamond	will scratch corundum

Mohs Scale: Hardness of Objects Used for Testing	
Hard-ness	**Test Object**
2.5	fingernail
3	copper penny
5.5	steel nail, window glass
6.5	streak plate
7	Steel file

A streak plate is an unglazed porcelain (white ceramic) tile used to show the actual color of the mineral sample. When an edge of the sample is rubbed across the streak plate, it leaves a colored streak. The colored streak left on the plate is actually the color of the powdered mineral which may be different from the appearance of the mineral sample as a whole. One example is hematite, an iron-containing mineral, which can have a gray color as a rock but when rubbed on a steak plate will leave a red mark. About 20% of minerals will leave a colored streak with about 80% leaving a white or clear streak.

Hematite rubbed on a streak plate
Hematite photo credit: NASA/JPL

A rock sample can also be tested to see if it will have a chemical reaction with acid. The acids most often used are dilute hydrochloric acid or acetic acid (vinegar). The dropper bottle in the test kit is used to apply the acid to the sample. For instance, when an acid is applied to rocks containing the mineral calcite, the chemical reaction can be observed by the formation of bubbles of carbon dioxide gas.

A rock and mineral test kit may also contain a sample of each of the ten minerals that appear on the Mohs scale of mineral hardness. These can be used for scratch testing unknown samples.

15.5 Soils

Soils are composed of different types of materials including weathered rocks and minerals and the remains of plants and animals. The source of the weathered matter from which soils develop is called the parent material.

The parent material affects the type of soil that is created. Some soils will support plant growth and some will not, according to the parent material from which they were formed. For example, soils developed from granite or sandstone do not support plant growth as well as do soils developed from limestone. Limestone is made of calcium carbonate, and calcium creates a nutrient-rich soil for plants to grow in.

Other factors that affect soils are climate, time, and topography. Topo comes from the Greek word *topos* and means "place." Graphy comes from the Greek word *graphe* which means "to write," so topography means the "description of the place." Topography describes the places where soils are developed (sloped mountain ranges, riverbeds, swamp beds, etc.) which also determine the type of soil formed.

In order to organize the different types of soils, scientists have created a soil classification system called soil taxonomy. The soil taxonomy system is similar in some ways to the taxonomy system used for living things. Both taxonomy systems attempt to organize a broad spectrum of characteristics into meaningful categories. Soil taxonomy categorizes the different types of soils found on Earth according to different soil properties, such as soils that provide nutrients for plant growth or soils that are made from volcanoes or clay.

World Soil Orders

Alfisols
high-nutrient soils

Andisols
volcanic soils

Aridisols
desert soils

Entisols
new soils

Gelisols
permafrost soils

Histosols
organic soils

Inceptisols
young soils

Mollisols
prairie soils

Oxisols
high nutrient soils

Spodosols
conifer forest soils

Ultisols
low-nutrient soils

Vertisols
swelling clay soils

The twelve main categories for soils are called soil orders. The names of soil orders are derived from Latin and Greek words, just like the names for biological organisms. For example, the order for dry soils is Aridisols which comes from the Latin words *aridus* which means "dry" and *solum* which means "soil." The order for prairie soils is called Mollisols which comes from the Latin word *molere* which means "to grind or crush." Mollisols are soils obtained from parent materials that have been ground or crushed, and these soils are loose and soft.

Global Soil Regions

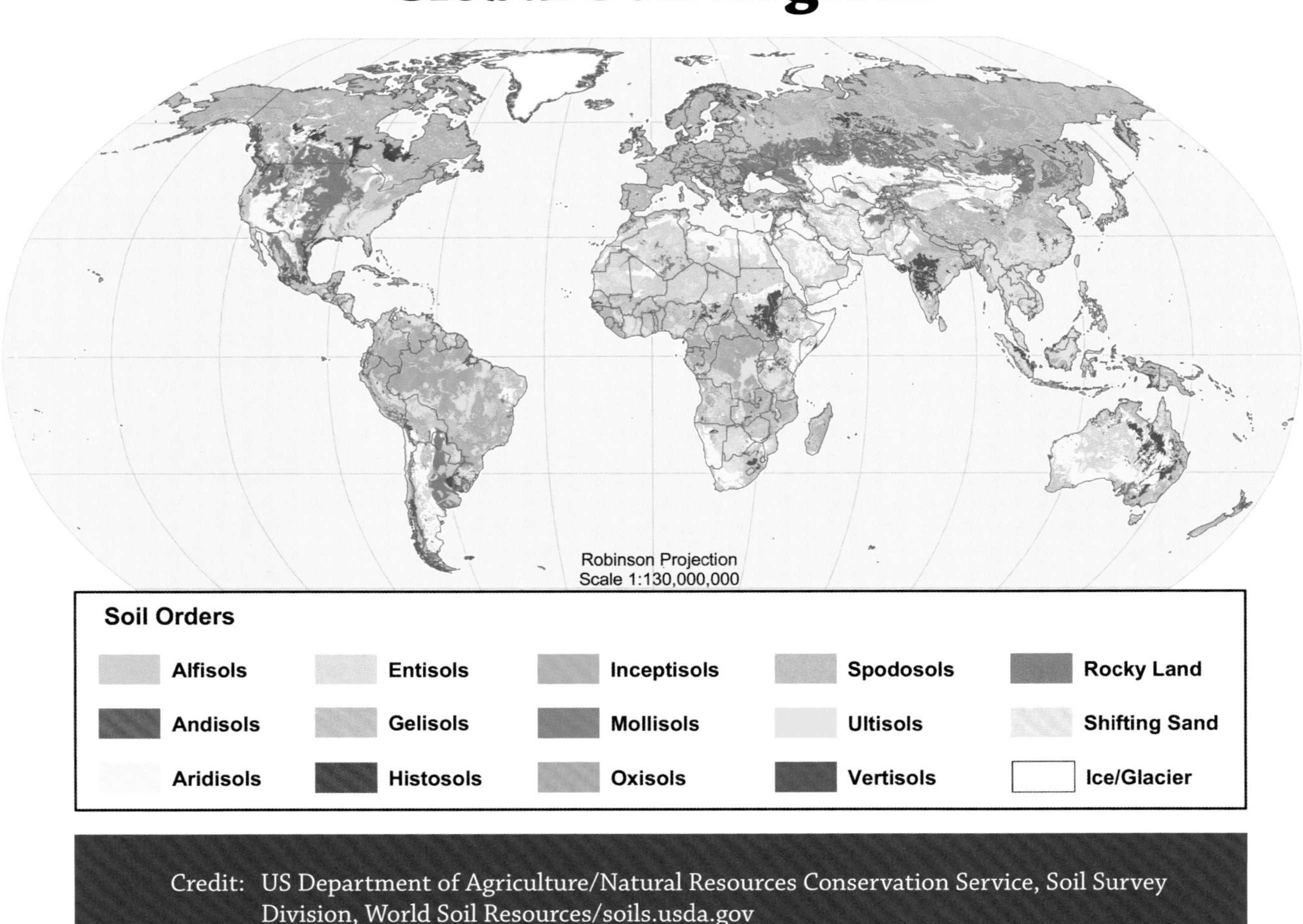

Credit: US Department of Agriculture/Natural Resources Conservation Service, Soil Survey Division, World Soil Resources/soils.usda.gov

15.6 Summary

- The surface of the Earth is made of rock, minerals, and soils.
- In order for a material to be considered a mineral it must meet the following criteria:

  1) It must occur naturally.
  2) It must be a solid.
  3) It must be inorganic.
  4) It must have an ordered arrangement of atoms.

- The eight elements that make up the majority of rock-forming minerals are: oxygen, silicon, aluminum, iron, calcium, potassium, sodium, and magnesium.
- The three basic types of rock are: igneous, metamorphic, and sedimentary.
- Soil taxonomy is a classification system that sorts different types of soils into categories according to their properties.

Chapter 16 Earth's Layers

16.1 Introduction 153

16.2 Inside the Earth 153

16.3 The Crust 154

16.4 The Mantle 155

16.5 The Lithosphere 156

16.6 The Asthenosphere 156

16.7 The Mesosphere 158

16.8 The Core 159

16.9 Summary 160

TO THE MIDDLE OF THE EARTH ↓

16.1 Introduction

We have seen that Earth is made of minerals, rocks, and soils, but how do they fit together to make a planet?

How far down do the rocks and soil go? Are there more rocks beneath the soil, or is there only empty space? What is in the middle of the Earth? Are rocks and soil all that make up the Earth, or is there more to the Earth? What about water, the air, and sky?

16.2 Inside the Earth

Scientific evidence suggests that Earth has layers, much like a golf ball. If you examine a golf ball sliced in half, you can see that the outer layer is different in texture and composition from the inner layers.

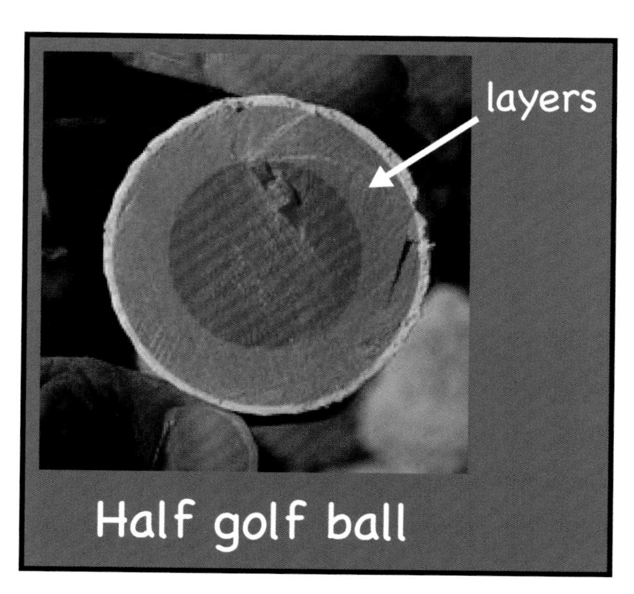

Half golf ball

Similarly, the Earth's layers are different from each other. The layers can be divided based on physical properties. The differences in physical properties include whether or not a layer is solid or liquid, how weak or how strong it is believed to be, and what it is made of. The Earth is considered by many scientists to consist of three distinct main layers—the crust, the mantle, and the core. The mantle and the core are further divided into layers.

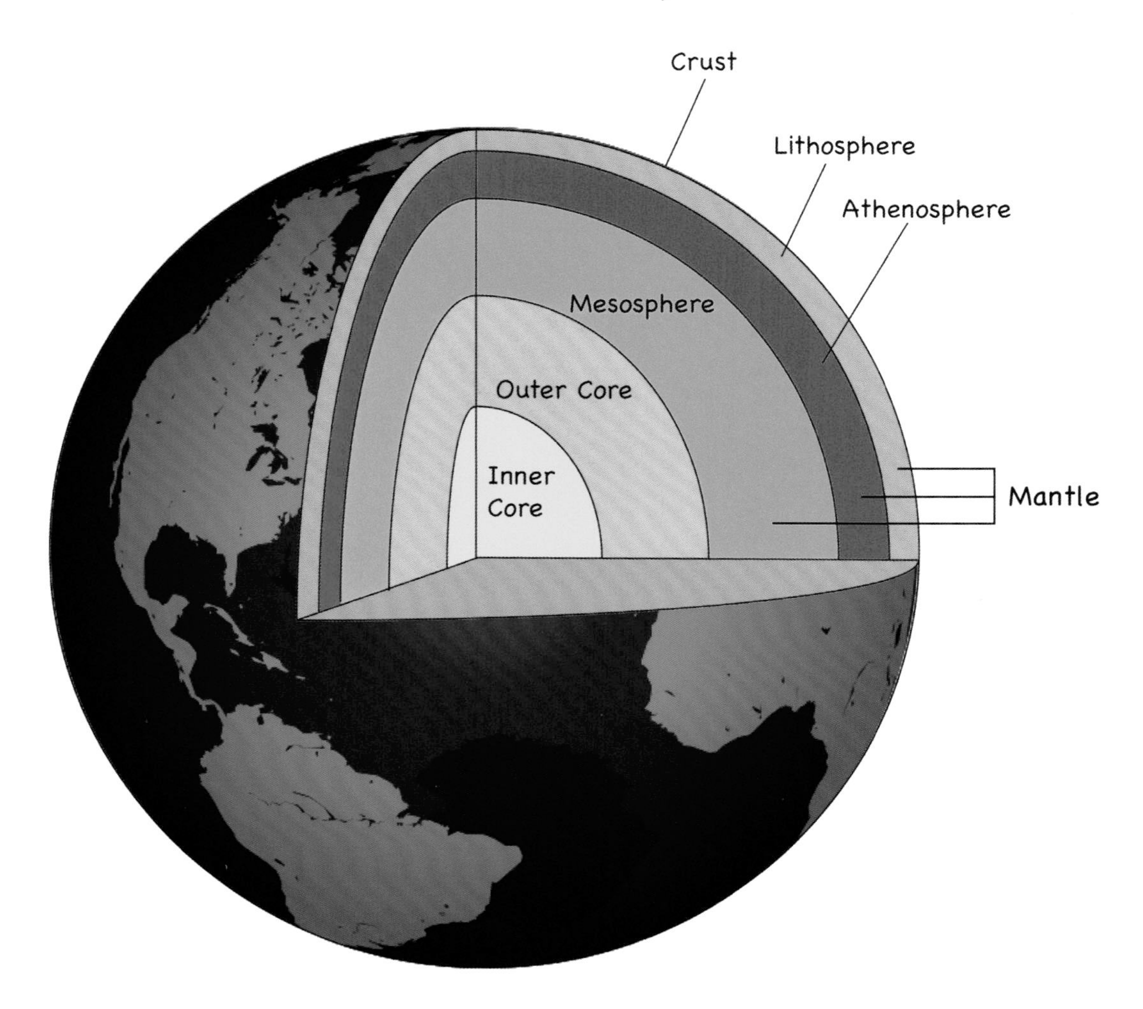

16.3 The Crust

Rocks and soil make up the Earth's surface, which is called the crust. The crust is often referred to as the outer shell of the Earth, just like the white layer surrounding a golf ball is its outer shell. Earth has two different types of crust—the continental crust and the oceanic crust.

The continental crust forms the continents, or land masses, on the surface of the Earth. The continental crust lies above sea level and is home to land-dwelling plants and animals. The continental crust averages about 35-45 kilometers (22-28 miles) in thickness and is composed mainly of granite but also includes other igneous rocks as well as sedimentary and metamorphic rocks.

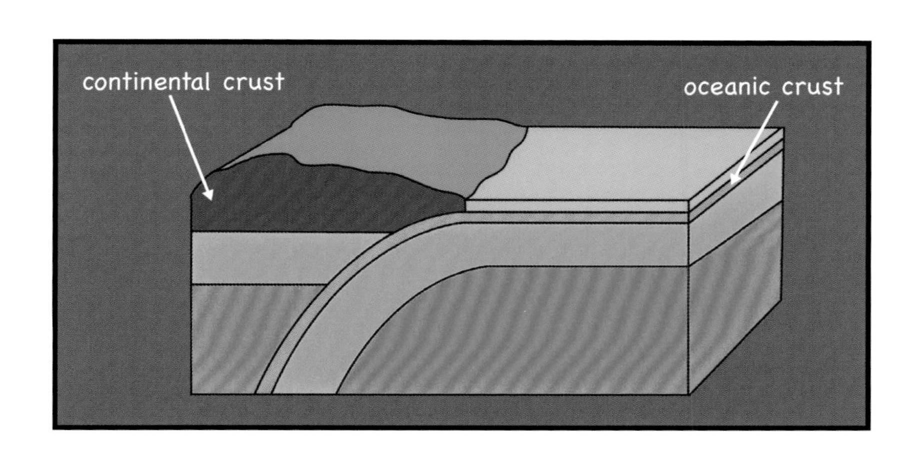

The oceanic crust is the part of the Earth's surface that lies below the oceans. The oceanic crust is much thinner than the continental crust—averaging about 7 kilometers (5 miles) thick—and is composed mainly of basaltic rock, an igneous rock formed from cooled magma. The oceanic crust has an upper layer of sediment that has been deposited on the basaltic rock layer.

16.4 The Mantle

The mantle is the layer of Earth just below the crust. The mantle is further divided into three layers which are called the lithosphere, asthenosphere, and mesosphere.

It's a little hard to know exactly what lies below the Earth's crust because no one has been able to drill deep enough to find out. The deepest land-based hole that has been drilled is on the Kola Peninsula in Russia and reaches a depth of about 12 kilometers (7 miles). There is also a research vessel named Chikyu that is designed to drill holes in the ocean floor where the crust is thinner, and the hope is that one day it can drill below the oceanic crust.

So far no one has been able to drill deep enough to directly sample Earth's inner layers. What we know of the material below the Earth's crust is based on data taken from a variety of observations including volcanoes, earthquakes, and seismic readings. By detecting vibrations caused by earthquakes, seismic readings record movements of materials within the Earth.

16.5 The Lithosphere

Just below the crust is the lithosphere which is the upper layer of the mantle. The prefix litho comes from the Greek word *lithos* and means "stone." Lithosphere literally means "stone sphere." The crust and lithosphere are sometimes considered together as one layer.

The lithosphere is believed to be a relatively cool, rigid shell about 100 kilometers (62 miles) thick. Scientists think that the lithosphere is divided into separate regions or plates. The crustal land masses sit on top of these plates, allowing the land masses to move.

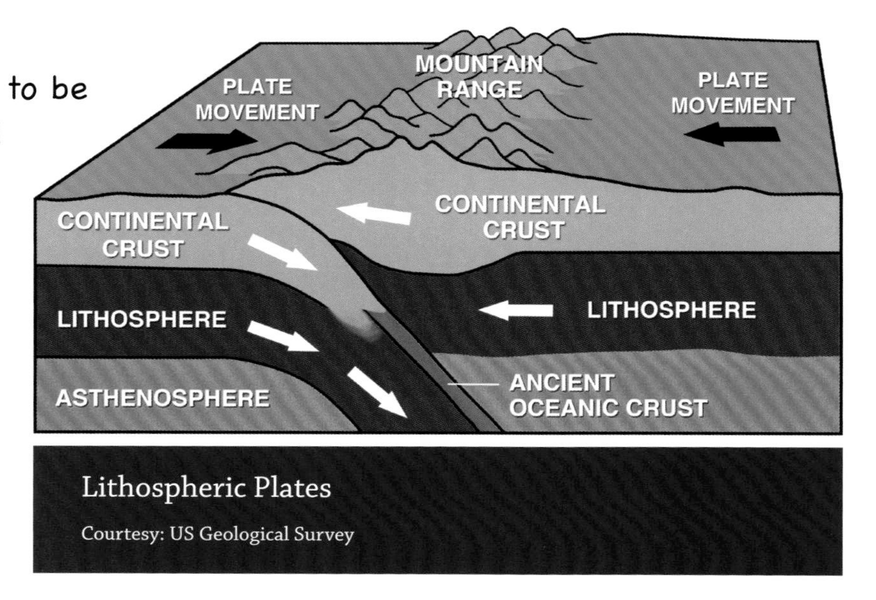

Lithospheric Plates

Courtesy: US Geological Survey

Although the lithosphere is believed to be made of different kinds of chemical materials, there is evidence to suggest that this layer is rigid and inflexible. For example, when different plates scrape against each other, the plates do not deform, or change shape, significantly. This would indicate that the plates are rigid. Also, volcanic activity tends to cluster at the edges of the plates with little or no activity occurring in the center. Again, this supports the theory that the plates are rigid enough to prevent the molten material below the lithosphere and crust from penetrating those layers and coming to the surface.

16.6 The Asthenosphere

The lithosphere sits on a softer layer called the asthenosphere. The prefix astheno comes from the Greek word *asthenes* which means "weak." Asthenosphere literally means "weak sphere."

The rock at the top part of the asthenosphere is under extreme pressure due to the weight of the lithosphere and crust above it. Scientists believe that this extreme pressure creates high heat and causes the minerals in the rock to melt. Because of the high heat and extreme pressure, the asthenosphere is believed to have a putty-like texture, allowing it to move around.

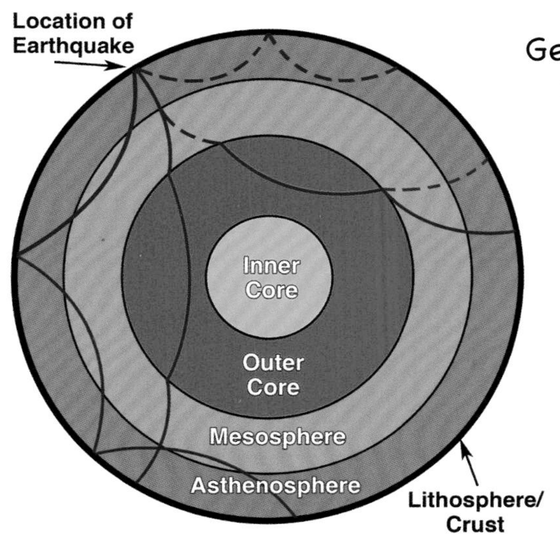

Seismic waves from an earthquake travel through Earth

Derived from US Geological Survey illustration

Geologists are unable to collect much information about the asthenosphere because, like the lithosphere, it is too deep to sample directly. However, the way seismic waves move through the various layers can be studied, and changes in the speed of seismic waves as they move through the Earth can be detected. This change in speed indicates a transition that suggests a boundary between layers. By observing how seismic waves travel and change their speed, geologists can get some idea of the type of material in the asthenosphere.

Based on seismic wave data, scientists believe that the asthenosphere may extend below the surface of the lithosphere as far as 700 kilometers (435 miles) and that the rigid lithospheric plates are able to move because they sit on top of the plastic, putty-like asthenosphere. It is also thought that currents in the Earth's inner layers cause these plates to move.

If you watch a pot of water come to a boil, you will observe the water moving and swirling just before it begins to boil. This moving and swirling occurs because of convection. Convection is the transfer of heat by the movement of molecules. When heat is applied to the water, energy is being added. However, water rarely heats uniformly, so some water molecules will be moving fast (have more energy) and other water molecules will be moving more slowly (have less energy). When this happens, energy is transferred from molecule to molecule as they bump into each other, causing the water to swirl. In a similar manner, convection occurs within the Earth's layers.

16.7 The Mesosphere

Below the asthenosphere lies the mesosphere. Meso comes from the Greek word *mesos* and means "middle" or "between." The mesosphere is the layer between the core and the outer layers of the Earth.

The mesosphere is believed to extend to a depth of 2900 kilometers (1800 miles). Many scientists believe that even though the temperatures are higher in the mesosphere than the asthenosphere, the rocks in the mesosphere are more solid due to higher pressures.

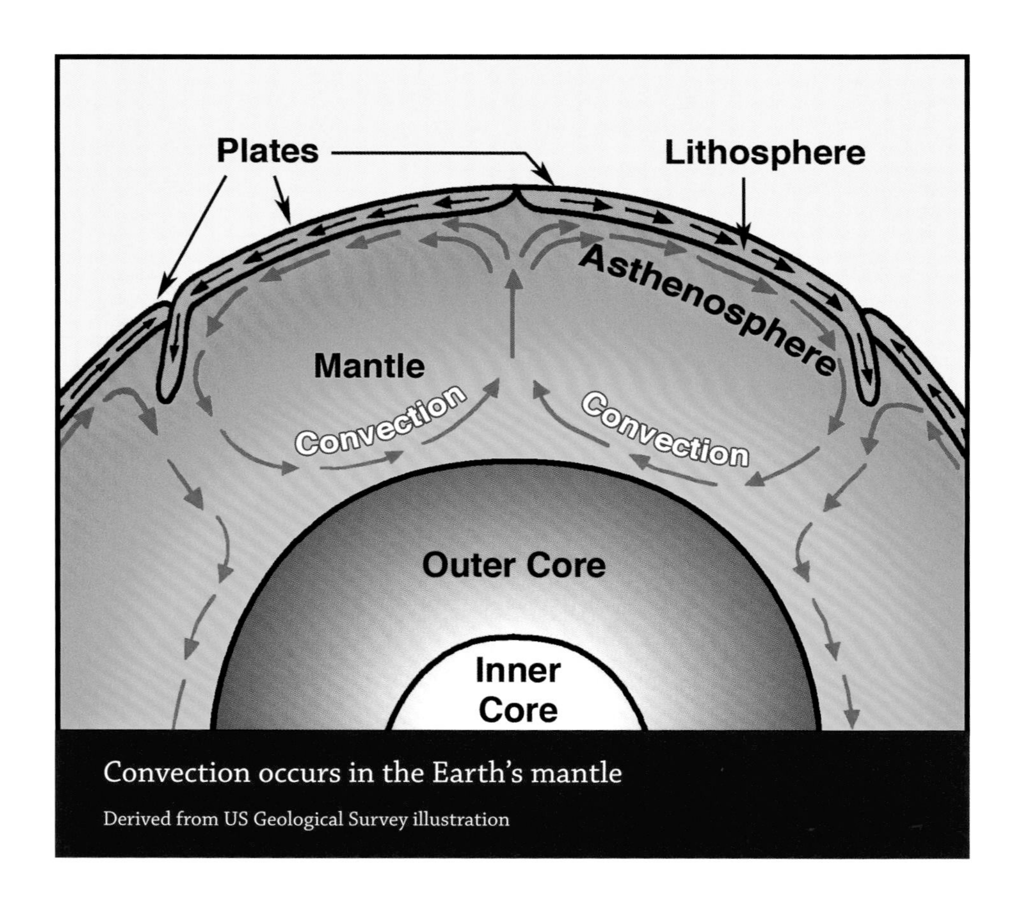

Convection occurs in the Earth's mantle

Derived from US Geological Survey illustration

16.8 The Core

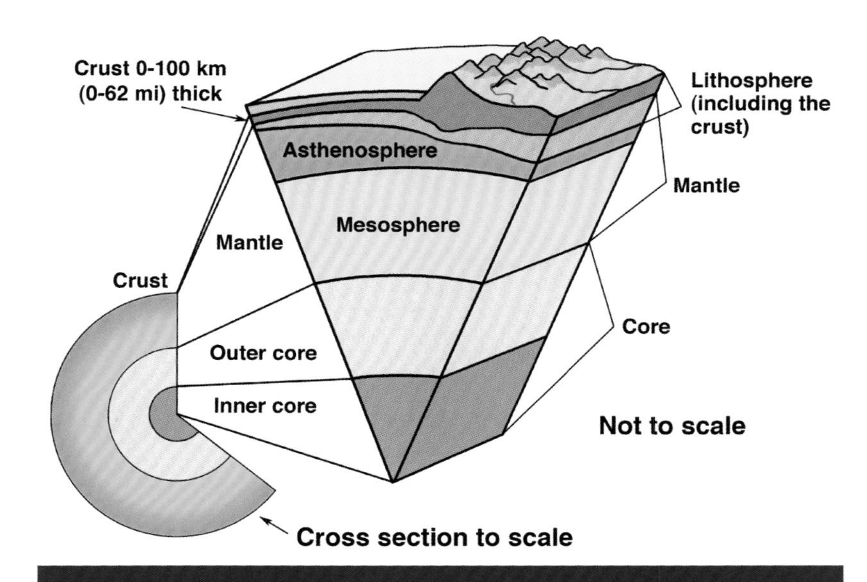

The structure of the interior of Earth

Credit: US Geological Survey

The core is at the center of the Earth and is divided into two layers—the outer core and the inner core. These two layers are believed to be composed of the elements iron and nickel.

The outer core seems to behave like a liquid layer and is thought to be about 2270 kilometers (1410 miles) thick. The inner core behaves more like a solid layer with a radius of about 1200 kilometers (745 miles). The inner and outer core layers together account for about one-sixth of Earth's volume and nearly one-third of its total mass. The density of the core is about 14 times the density of water. (Density is the amount of mass contained in a certain amount of three-dimensional space and is expressed mathematically as mass divided by volume.) This means that there is a large amount of matter packed very tightly into the core layers, making the core very dense.

It is thought that the temperature of the core can exceed 6700° C (12,092° F), and its pressure is millions of times greater than the pressure at the Earth's surface.

Convection occurs in the Earth's outer core. The hot liquid iron and nickel move and swirl because of convection. Many scientists think that heat convection happening in the outer core is responsible for many of the dynamic processes that occur on Earth's surface, such as earthquakes and volcanoes. Earth's core is also thought to create Earth's magnetic field.

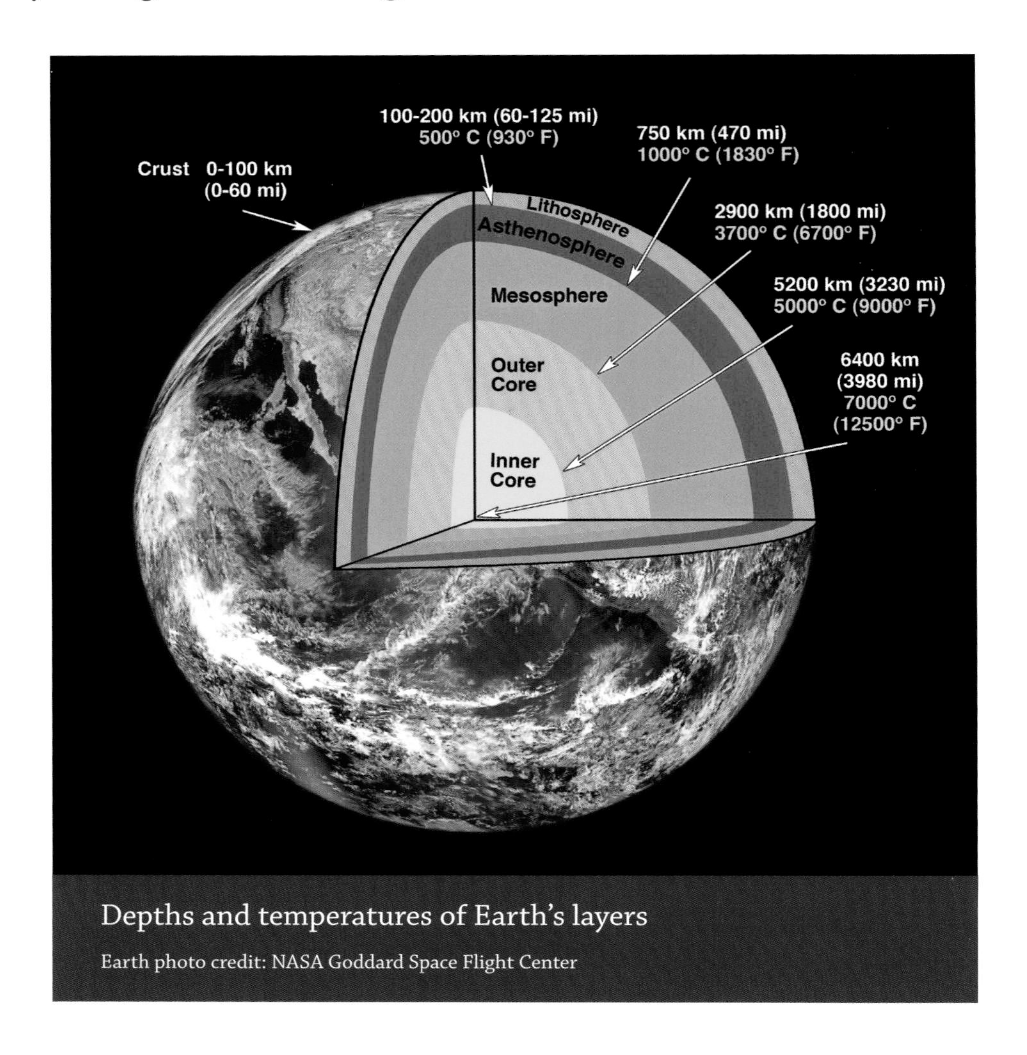

Depths and temperatures of Earth's layers

Earth photo credit: NASA Goddard Space Flight Center

16.9 Summary

- The Earth is thought to be made up of three main layers—the crust, the mantle, and the core.
- We live on the outer layer called the crust.
- The mantle is just below the crust and is made up of three layers—the lithosphere, the asthenosphere, and the mesosphere.
- The core is in the center of the Earth and has two layers which are called the outer core and the inner core.
- Geologists study volcanoes, earthquakes, and seismic readings to help them understand what lies below the Earth's surface.

Chapter 17 Earth's Dynamics

17.1 Introduction 162

17.2 Plate Tectonics 162

17.3 Mountains 165

17.4 Volcanoes 166

17.5 Earthquakes 169

17.6 Summary 171

17.1 Introduction

We know from experience that the Earth is dynamic and is constantly changing. Earthquakes, volcanoes, tsunamis, and other natural phenomena remind us that there is movement in the crust of the Earth and what is below it.

How do these changes occur? What causes earthquakes? During a volcano where does the hot molten rock come from? What happens during a tsunami? How do mountain ridges form? All of these questions address Earth's dynamics.

Geologists study the eruption of Mount St. Helens, Washington

Photo Credit: US Geological Survey

17.2 Plate Tectonics

Explaining what makes earthquakes, mountain ridges, and volcanoes occur can be a daunting task. But by analyzing data and observing changes on the Earth, scientists have developed the theory of plate tectonics to help them understand these events. In general, the theory of plate tectonics explains the movement of the lithosphere, and consequently, the movement of Earth's land masses, the formation of mountains, and earthquake and volcanic activity.

Scientists have found evidence to suggest that the lithosphere (the layer of the Earth just below the crust) is broken up into rigid plates. The crust sits on top of these plates which are "floating" on top of the softer, putty-like asthenosphere. These plates move very slowly as the material in the asthenosphere circulates due to convection.

According to plate tectonics, there are seven primary plates and several smaller secondary and tertiary plates that fit together like pieces of a jigsaw puzzle.

Heat convection from the core and lower mantle causes the plates to move very slowly at a rate of about 2 inches per year.

One line of evidence that supports the theory of plate tectonics is the observation that earthquakes and volcanoes congregate along certain regions of the globe. These regions are believed to be boundaries between the plates.

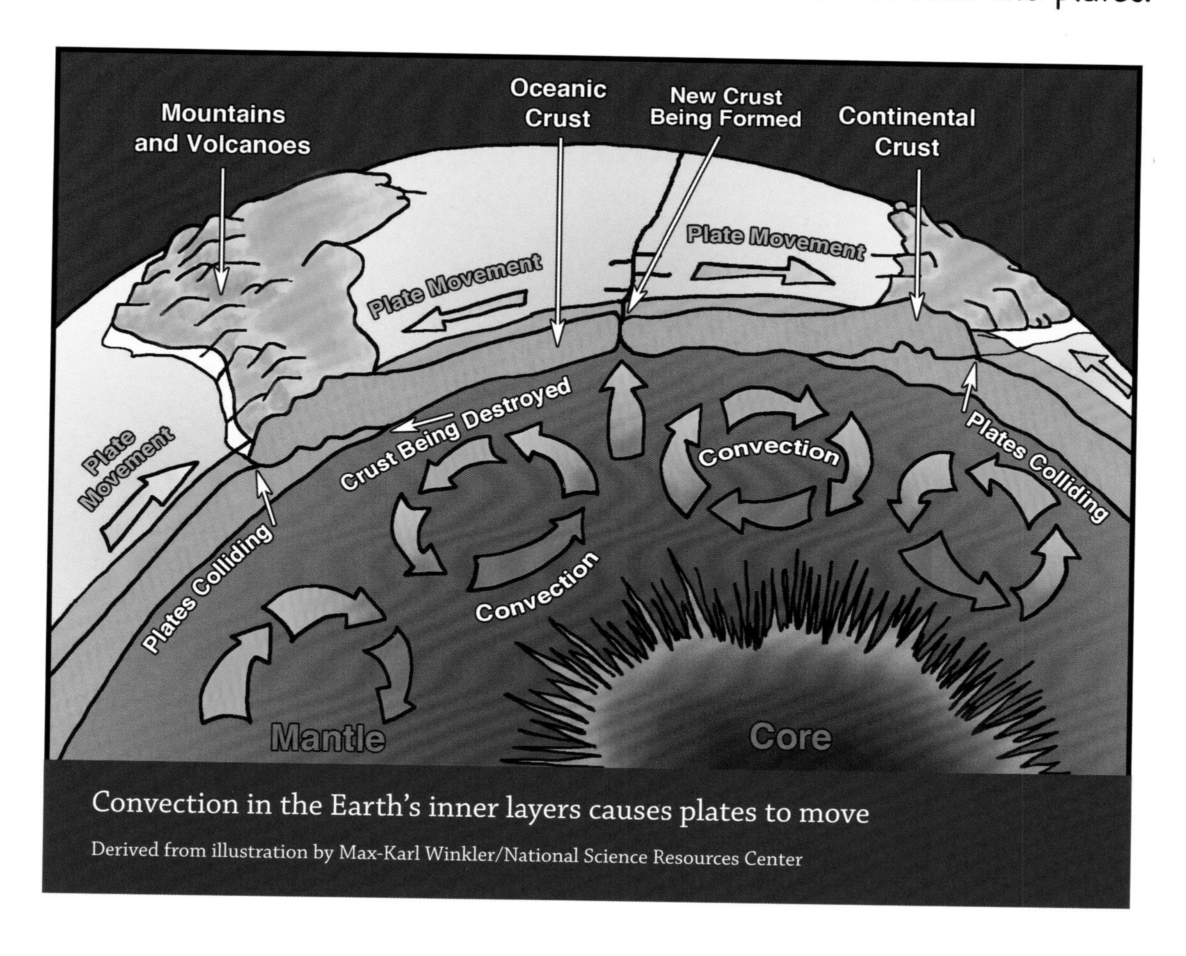

Convection in the Earth's inner layers causes plates to move

Derived from illustration by Max-Karl Winkler/National Science Resources Center

Curiously, much of the data supporting the theory of plate tectonics were collected shortly after World War II and during the Cold War. Countries, being suspicious of each other, developed worldwide seismograph networks to monitor underground nuclear testing. As a result, we now have a map of the areas of the globe that have the most earthquake activity.

Countries spent millions of dollars mapping the ocean floor to find safe ways to navigate and to discover ways to detect submarines. This research provided us with knowledge of the areas where volcanic activity dominates and where underwater mountain ridges associated with volcanic activity are located. Much of the data that was collected supports the theory of plate tectonics and the idea that Earth's land masses move on top of rigid lithospheric plates floating on the putty-like asthenosphere.

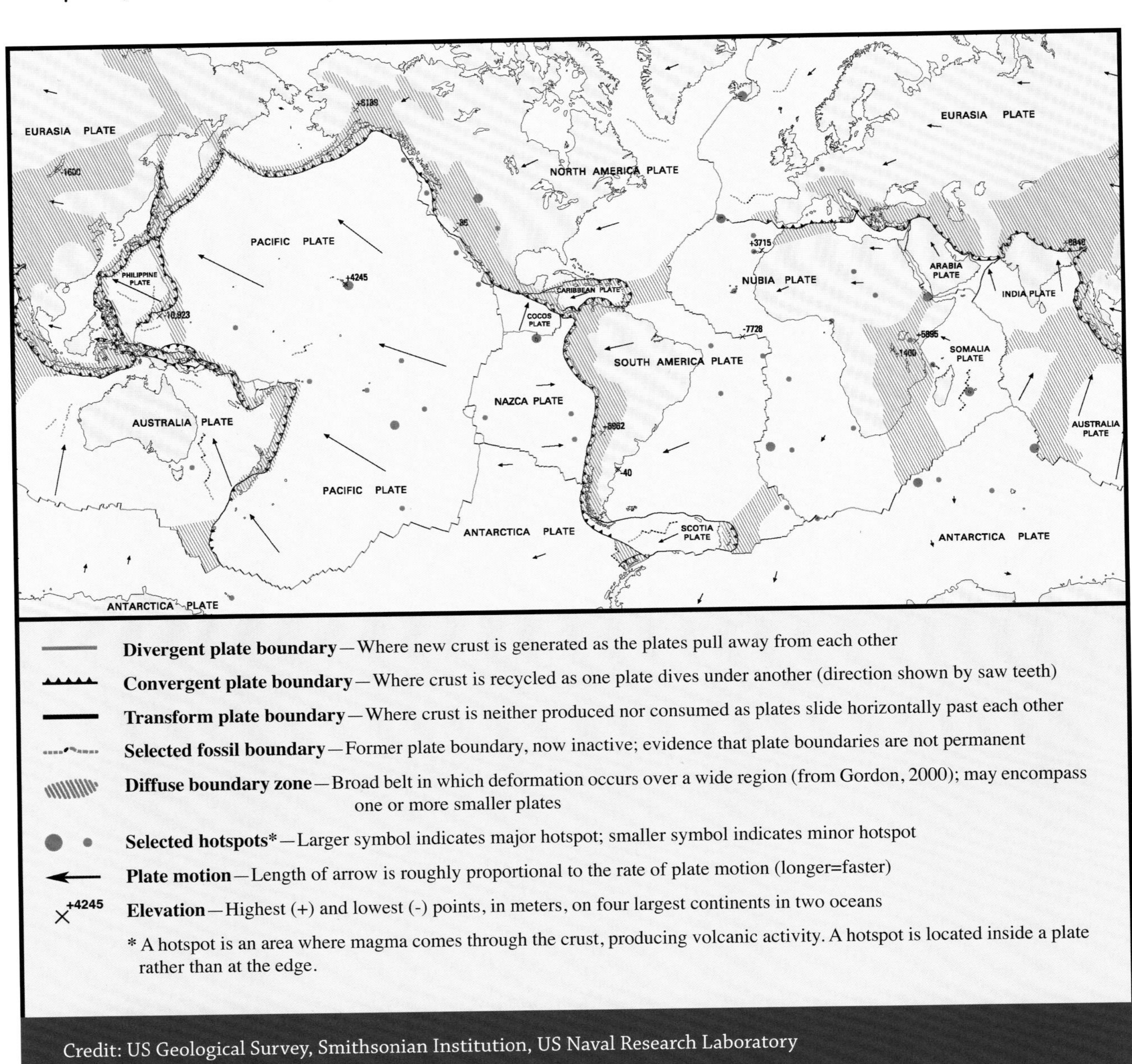

Credit: US Geological Survey, Smithsonian Institution, US Naval Research Laboratory

It should be noted that although this theory is useful in explaining many large-scale geological processes, plate tectonics is a theory that is still developing, and not everything is understood. As new data become available, the current theory will likely change and be refined.

17.3 Mountains

There are many different types of mountains. There are steep, jagged mountains and smooth, rounded mountains. There are mountains covered with lots of trees and mountains with rock alone and no vegetation.

How do mountains form? There are actually several different ways in which mountains are created. Mountains can form when land masses are pushed together and folded onto each other as a result of the movement of plates. These are called folded mountains. An anticline results when the land is folded in an arch shape. When land is folded in a trough shape, it is called a syncline.

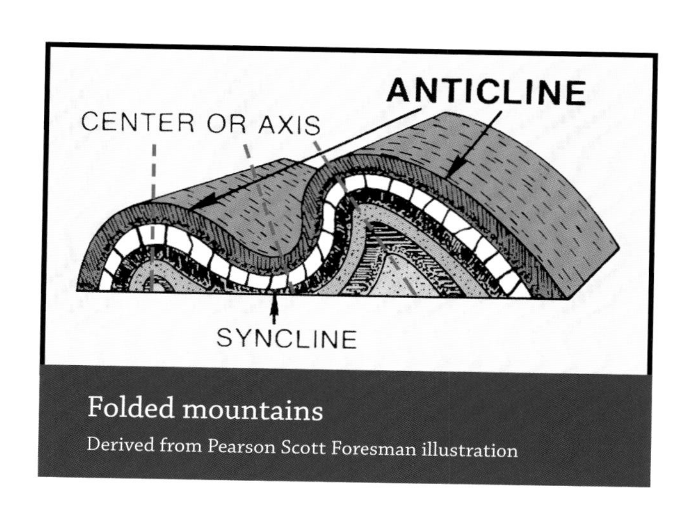

Folded mountains
Derived from Pearson Scott Foresman illustration

Fault-block mountains can form as a result of big blocks of land moving up and down. When plates slide up and down with respect to each other, a huge block of land is pushed upwards and another huge block of land is pushed downwards. The pushing up and down of these blocks can create fault-block mountains and also can cause earthquakes.

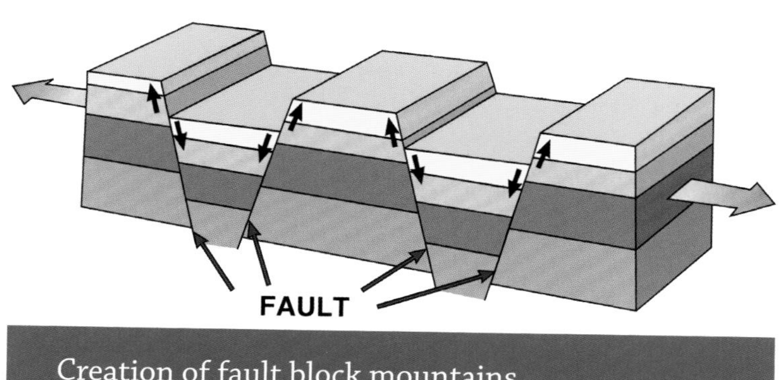

Creation of fault block mountains
Courtesy: US Geological Survey

Mountains can also form when molten rock, or magma, pushes up underneath the crust but doesn't break through the surface.

Instead, the force of the magma creates a large bump on the Earth's surface. The magma cools, leaving a smooth, rounded landform called a dome mountain.

Lava fountain and lava flows Kilauea Volcano, Hawaii Volcanoes National Park

Photo Credit: US Geological Survey/by J. D. Griggs

17.4 Volcanoes

Volcanoes are fascinating because we get to see the molten rock that comes from deep inside the Earth! We also get to witness the extreme pressures that force the molten material through the surface of the Earth. A volcano forms when a fracture, or break, in the upper mantle allows magma from below to be pushed through the surface of the Earth. When magma comes to the surface of the Earth, it is called lava.

Volcanic material, or magma, is mainly basaltic rock and is believed to come from the asthenosphere, the soft putty-like layer below the lithosphere. Some volcanic eruptions are "gentle," like the slow moving lava flows in Hawaii, and others are more violent, such as the eruption of Mount St. Helens in the state of Washington in 1980. The degree to which a volcano will erupt gently or

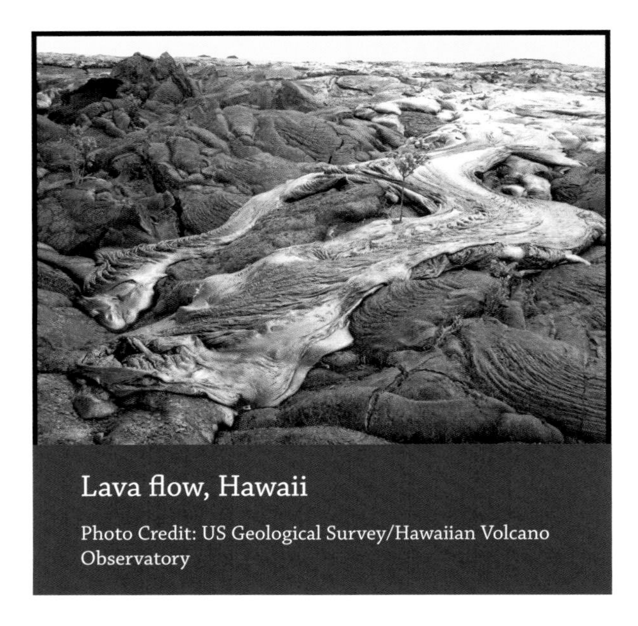

Lava flow, Hawaii

Photo Credit: US Geological Survey/Hawaiian Volcano Observatory violently depends on different properties of the magma, such as its viscosity (thickness or thinness), how much gas it contains, the minerals it is made of, and its temperature.

There are several different types of volcanoes. A cinder cone volcano is typically a small volcano that forms around a volcanic vent—the opening in the ground that the lava comes through. Cinder cones are formed as lava erupts from the vent in a fountain-like manner and quickly cools into basaltic fragments of rock called cinders.

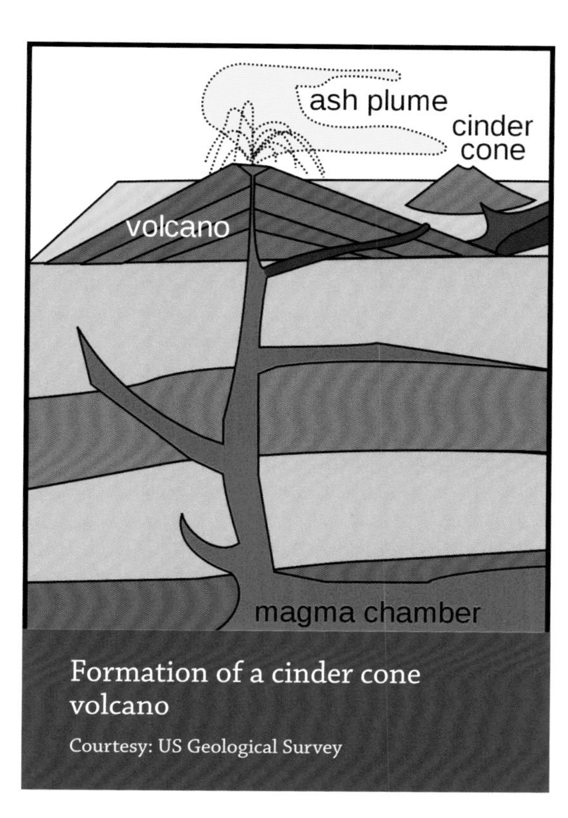

Formation of a cinder cone volcano

Courtesy: US Geological Survey

Cinder cone near Veyo, Utah

Photo Credit: Mark A. Wilson, The College of Wooster

Generally, cinder cones are less than 300 meters high (1,000 ft). The slope of the sides is very steep, and lava often oozes out from the base of the cone during the later part of the eruption.

Shield volcano
Mauna Loa Volcano, Hawaii
Photo Credit: US Geological Survey/by J. D. Griggs

A shield volcano is built up of layers of low viscosity (thin) lava that can flow over a long distance, resulting in the distinctively long, gentle, sloping sides seen in this type of volcano.

The eruptions that cause shield volcanoes to form are nonexplosive, and shield volcanoes can be extremely tall. The Mauna Loa Volcano in Hawaii is 4,169 meters (13,677 ft) above sea level and 8,534 meters (28,000 ft) above the ocean floor!

A composite volcano (also called a stratovolcano) has alternating layers of lava flow and lava flow rubble, such as volcanic ash and cinders. Composite volcanoes can be more than 3,000 meters (9,843 ft) high. Their sides are generally steep, and these volcanoes tend to erupt explosively.

Composite volcano, Mount St. Helens, Washington
Photo Credit: US Geological Survey/by Donald A. Swanson

17.5 Earthquakes

Have you ever been in a place where suddenly the ground began to move, the surface of the ground split, and buildings began to rumble and rock? If you have, you might have been in an earthquake.

San Francisco Earthquake, 1906
Photo Credit: H. D. Chadwick, NARA National Archives and Records

Earthquakes can be terrifying and many people have experienced their devastating effects. One of the most famous earthquakes to happen in the United States was on April 18, 1906 in San Francisco. In 1906 scientists didn't yet know why earthquakes happen.

When this big earthquake hit, large sections of land became displaced, or moved from their former positions. Fences were moved, homes were ripped apart, and land permanently shifted. This earthquake gave scientists some very important clues to help them understand why earthquakes occur.

Using the theory of plate tectonics, we now suspect that earthquakes occur as a result of neighboring plates colliding, pushing on, or sliding against each other. These plate movements create force, pressure, and stress along the edges of the plates and within them. This causes fractures, or cracks, in the rocks of the Earth's crust. These fractures are called faults. The term fault line is used to describe the area where the two sides of a fracture meet.

Observations show that earthquakes are caused by movement along the faults in the Earth's crust. Since the faults have rough rather than smooth surfaces, the two sides of a fault get stuck together instead of sliding past each other. As the tectonic plates move, stress (a force resulting from pressure or tension) is created along a fault line. This happens because the two sides of a fault are being pushed on but don't move because they are stuck together. As the plates continue to move, stress builds up along the fault line. When the stress, or stored energy, in the rocks gets too big for the sides of the fault to remain stuck together, the stored energy is suddenly released and the rocks lurch, causing the Earth to shake. The strength of earthquakes can vary from mild to violent depending on the amount of stress that was built up and then released.

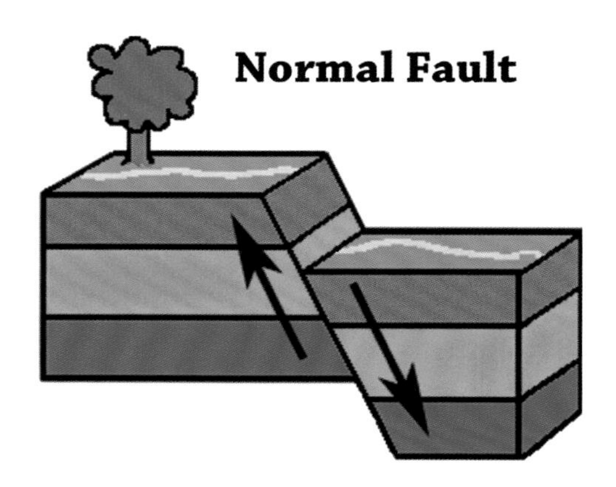

Millions of fault lines crisscross the Earth's crust. Some of these fault lines coincide with tectonic plate boundaries, but many fault lines are only a few kilometers (miles) long and are not located at plate boundaries. Most faults are inactive and don't change very much over time, thus causing little or no earthquake activity. However, some faults are quite active, with earthquakes occurring frequently. This is especially true of faults occurring along tectonic plate boundaries.

Earthquake at Loma Prieta, California, 1989

Photo Credit: US Geological Survey

Volcanic activity can also cause earthquakes, and large earthquakes can lead to increased volcanic activity.

17.6 Summary

- The Earth is dynamic and constantly changing.
- Plate tectonics is a theory that helps explain Earth's dynamics.
- Mountains can form when land is pushed together (folded mountains), as the result of earthquakes (fault-block mountains), or by pressure created from molten magma (dome mountains).
- Volcanoes occur when magma is pushed through the Earth's surface. Three types of common volcanoes are cinder cone volcanoes, shield volcanoes, and composite volcanoes (stratovolcanoes).
- Earthquakes occur along fault lines due to stresses within the Earth's crust caused by different areas of land moving differently with respect to each other.

Chapter 18 What Is Astronomy?

18.1	Introduction	173
18.2	Early Astronomers	173
18.3	Modern Astronomers	175
18.4	Changing View of the Cosmos	175
18.5	Summary	178

18.1 Introduction

Astronomy is considered by many to be the oldest science. Since long before the invention of the telescope, human beings have been looking at the stars. The word astronomy comes from the Greek words *aster* which means "star" and *nomas* which means "to assign, distribute, or arrange." The word astronomy literally means "to assign or arrange the stars." Astronomers are scientists who assign names to all the celestial bodies in space, including stars, and study how they exist and move in space.

18.2 Early Astronomers

The earliest recorded history reveals an interest in the stars. Cave drawings show primitive humans recording observations from the skies, and later the Babylonians recorded detailed planetary positions, eclipses, and other astronomical observations. Egyptian and Greek observers expanded on the information collected by the Babylonians. Some people think that the pyramids in Egypt align with the stars of Orion and this suggests that the Egyptians acquired sophisticated abilities to observe the sky. The Ancient Greeks were the first astronomers to add mathematics to astronomy.

Many early civilizations used the stars and the movements of celestial bodies as tools to measure time. The Sumerians of Babylonia used the phases of the Moon to create the first lunar calendar, and the Egyptians, Greeks, and Romans copied and revised this calendar. Today our calendar is derived directly from the Sumerian calendar and is connected to the monthly and yearly orbits of the Moon and

Earth. On the other side of the ocean, the Incan and Mayan civilizations created sophisticated calendars by observing the planetary cycles. The Mayan calendar is circular and has aspects that relate the movement of the Sun, Moon, and planets.

Early astronomers named individual stars as well as groups of stars that form constellations. A constellation is any group of stars that fit together to form a pattern in the night sky. Some of the major constellations that come from Greek mythology are familiar to many people. Orion the Hunter is a constellation of stars that can be seen from the Northern Hemisphere from December through March. Orion has a "belt" of three bright stars in a straight row. Once the "belt" is located, it is easy to find the "club" and "shield" by looking for neighboring stars.

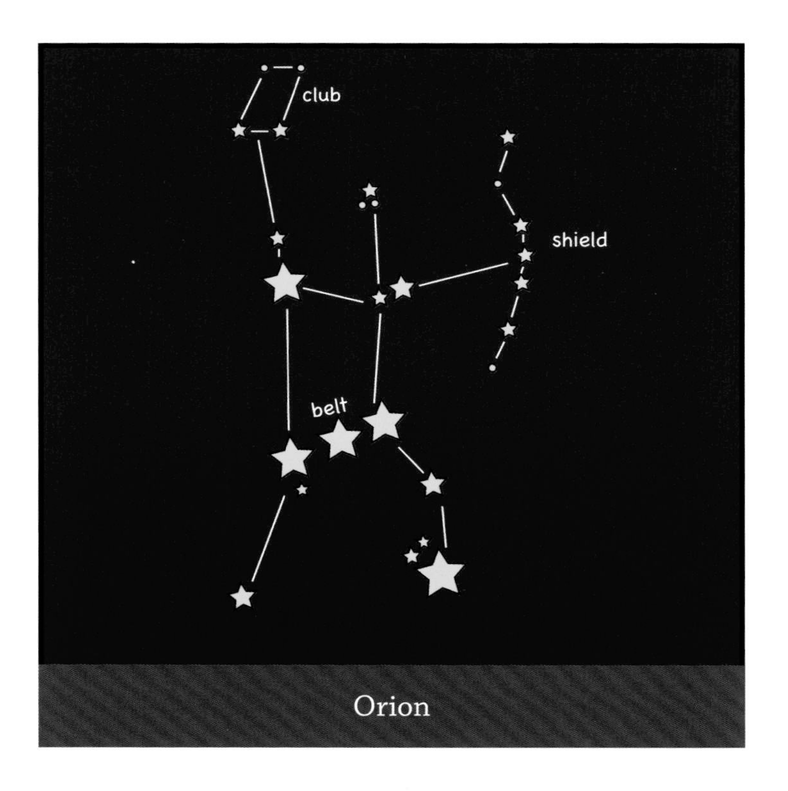

Orion

The constellation names derived from Greek mythology have changed very little since 1000 BCE. There are currently 88 constellations that are recognized by the International Astronomical Union (IAU), and over half of those were observed by the ancient Greeks!

18.3 Modern Astronomers

Today, astronomers can see many more stars than their ancient predecessors could. Modern astronomers can also see details about the planets and stars that were not visible in ancient times.

Telescopes, radios, and cameras are just some of the tools astronomers use when studying the planets and stars. Modern astronomers also use chemistry and physics to understand astronomical data. Understanding how planets move requires knowing the physics behind gravity, inertia, and mass. Understanding how stars give off heat and light energy requires knowing the chemistry behind nuclear reactions. And understanding how the Sun affects our weather requires knowledge of magnetic and electric fields. Modern astronomers not only have sophisticated tools to explore the universe, they also have centuries of complicated mathematics, chemistry, and physics to help them understand how the universe works.

18.4 Changing Views of the Cosmos

The practice of astronomy changed dramatically after the invention of the telescope, a scientific tool that uses lenses to magnify distant objects. In the 1600's Galileo Galilei, an Italian scientist considered to be the first modern astronomer, used the telescope to look at the planets. Galileo was also able to see the moons of Jupiter and the rotation of the Sun. Based on his observations, Galileo confirmed a radical new view of the cosmos. The cosmos, or solar system, includes our Sun and the planets around it.

In ancient times most people believed that the Earth was the center of the universe. These ancients believed that the planets and the Sun moved in a circular orbit, or path, around the Earth. This view of the world is called geocentric. Geo comes from the Greek word *ge* which means "earth" or "land"and centric comes from the Greek word *kentron* which means "point" or "center." A geocentric view is one that considers the Earth as the true center of the universe.

Geocentric Cosmos

It is not hard to understand why this view was held. Stepping outside at any given time of the day and observing the motion of the Sun, it looks like the Sun rotates around the Earth. A geocentric view of the universe was first proposed by Aristotle (384-322 BCE) and was the dominant belief held by most people for many centuries.

However, not everyone agreed with Aristotle. Aristarchus of Samos, who lived from 310-230 BCE, was an expert Greek astronomer and mathematician who did not believe that the Sun and planets revolved around the Earth. He was the first to propose a heliocentric cosmos. The word heliocentric comes from the Greek word *helios* which means "sun." A heliocentric cosmos is a view of the universe with the Sun as the central point and the Earth and planets orbiting the Sun.

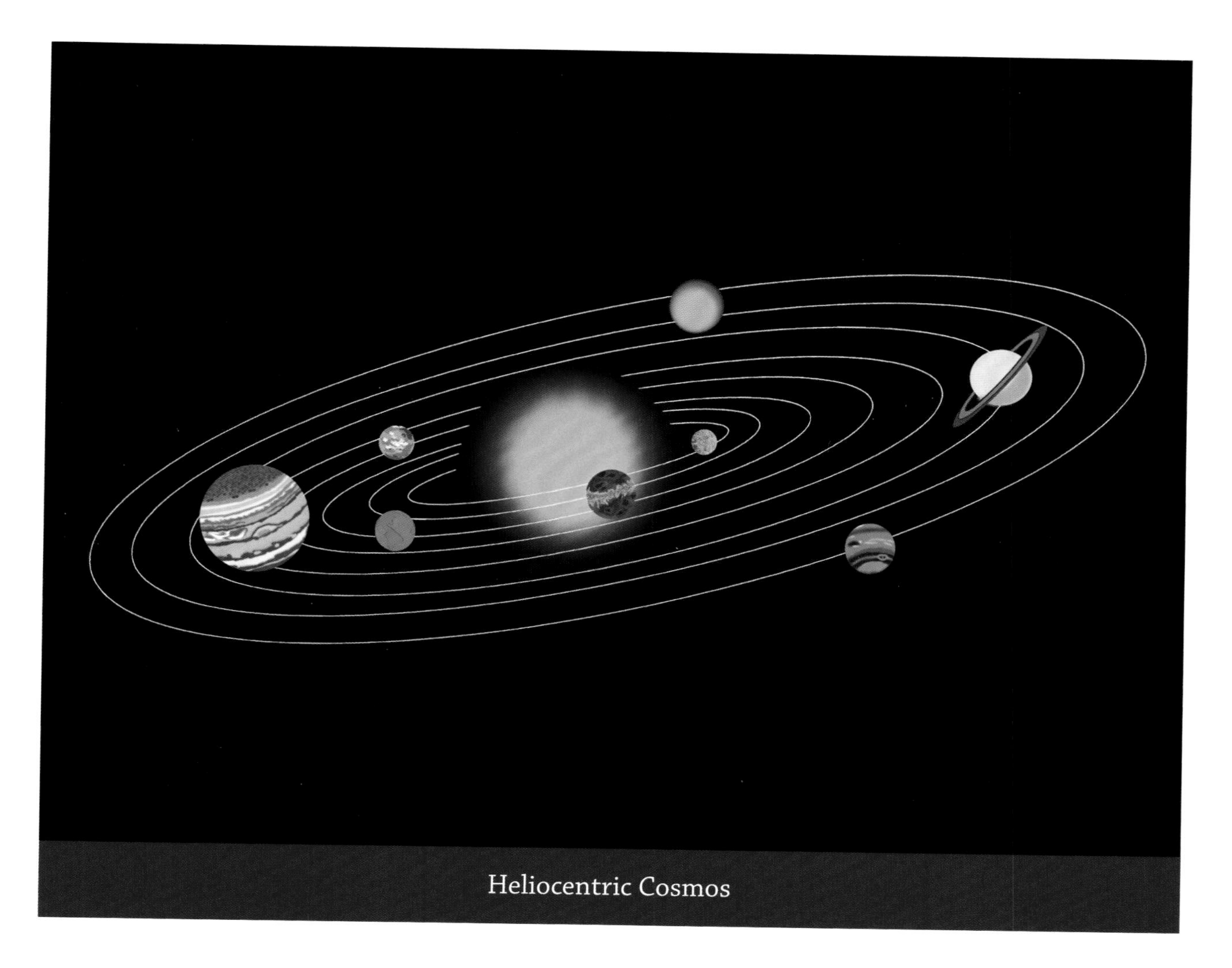

Heliocentric Cosmos

Although today we know that Aristarchus was right, his proposal was rejected by his colleagues because it seemed to contradict everyday observation. If the Earth was not stable (central and not moving), how did everything not bolted down keep from flying off the Earth as it rotated around the Sun?

The physics of Aristotle was the scientific consensus view during Aristarchus' lifetime and that meant that a heliocentric cosmos would have violated the laws of physics! It was almost 2000 years before the idea of a heliocentric cosmos was reintroduced by Nicolaus Copernicus (1473-1543 CE) and confirmed by the scientific observations of Galileo.

Today, astronomers do not believe in a geocentric cosmos and know that our Earth orbits the Sun and that we live in a heliocentric solar system. Modern technologies, a deeper understanding of physics, and a willingness to challenge prevailing scientific theories were needed before the geocentric view could be replaced by the more accurate heliocentric view of the cosmos.

18.5 Summary

- Astronomy is the field of science that studies celestial bodies and how they exist and move in space.
- Early astronomers were able to map the movements of the planets and stars and used celestial motions to create calendars.
- Modern astronomers use chemistry and physics together with modern technologies to study the universe.
- Ancient peoples once believed in a geocentric cosmos, or Earth-centered universe. Today we know that we live in a heliocentric solar system with the Sun at the center.

Chapter 19 Earth in Space

19.1	Introduction	180
19.2	The Earth in Space	180
19.3	The Earth and the Moon	183
19.4	The Earth and the Sun	186
19.5	Eclipses	188
19.6	Summary	189

Astronomy

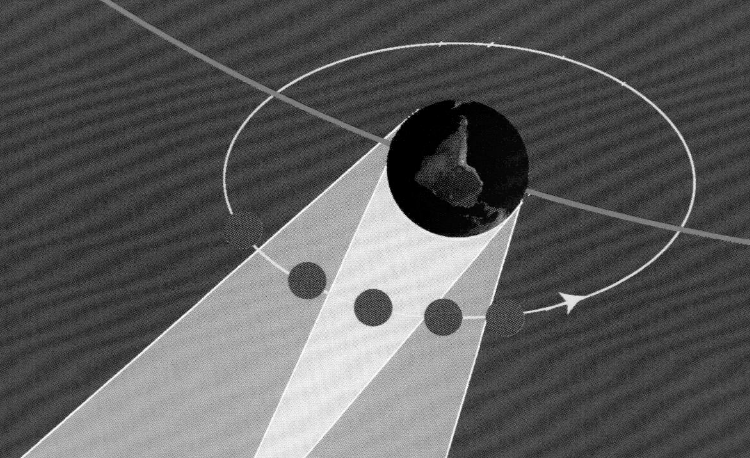

19.1 Introduction

In this chapter we will start looking at celestial objects in space. The first object in space that we will explore is Earth itself.

What is the shape of the Earth? Is it flat, round, elliptical? Where does the Earth sit with respect to the larger universe? Is it in the middle, off to the side, on the outer edge? In this chapter we will explore these questions and others as we examine the Earth in space.

19.2 The Earth in Space

The ancient Greeks understood that the Earth is a ball, or spherical mass. The best evidence in ancient times for the Earth being spherical came from the observation that a circular shadow is cast during a lunar eclipse. The ancient Greeks could see the curvature of Earth from its shadow on the Moon.

However, it was only within the last 100 years that we have been able to photograph the Earth in space. The very first pictures of Earth as seen from space were taken in 1946 by a group of scientists in New Mexico. These scientists attached a 35 millimeter camera to a missile and launched the missile 65 miles into space. The missile came crashing down, but the camera was protected in a tough metal container. The crude black and white photos showed the curvature of the Earth and marked a new era of space exploration.

Earth is a planet. The word planet comes from the Greek word *planetai* which means "wanderer." A planet is a large spherical object or celestial body that "wanders" in space. To qualify as a planet, a celestial body must orbit a sun, must have enough mass to have its own gravity, and must have cleared its orbit of other celestial bodies (in other words, a planet can't have other celestial bodies with it in the same orbit around the Sun). Because Earth "wanders," or moves in space, around the Sun, is massive enough to have its own gravity, and also has cleared its orbit, Earth qualifies as a planet.

At the equator, Earth is 12,756 kilometers (7,926 miles) in diameter. Between the North Pole and the South Pole Earth's diameter is 12,714 kilometers (7,900 miles). You can see that Earth is not a perfect sphere but is slightly larger in one dimension.

Earth sits on a tilted axis, which is the imaginary line around which the Earth rotates. Having a tilted axis means that the North and South Poles are not straight up and down in relation to the Earth's orbit around the Sun. If you were to look at the planetary axis, you would see that the poles are tilted about 23 degrees from center. This deviation from perpendicular is called orbital obliquity. Orbital obliquity, the tilt of Earth's axis, gives us the seasons.

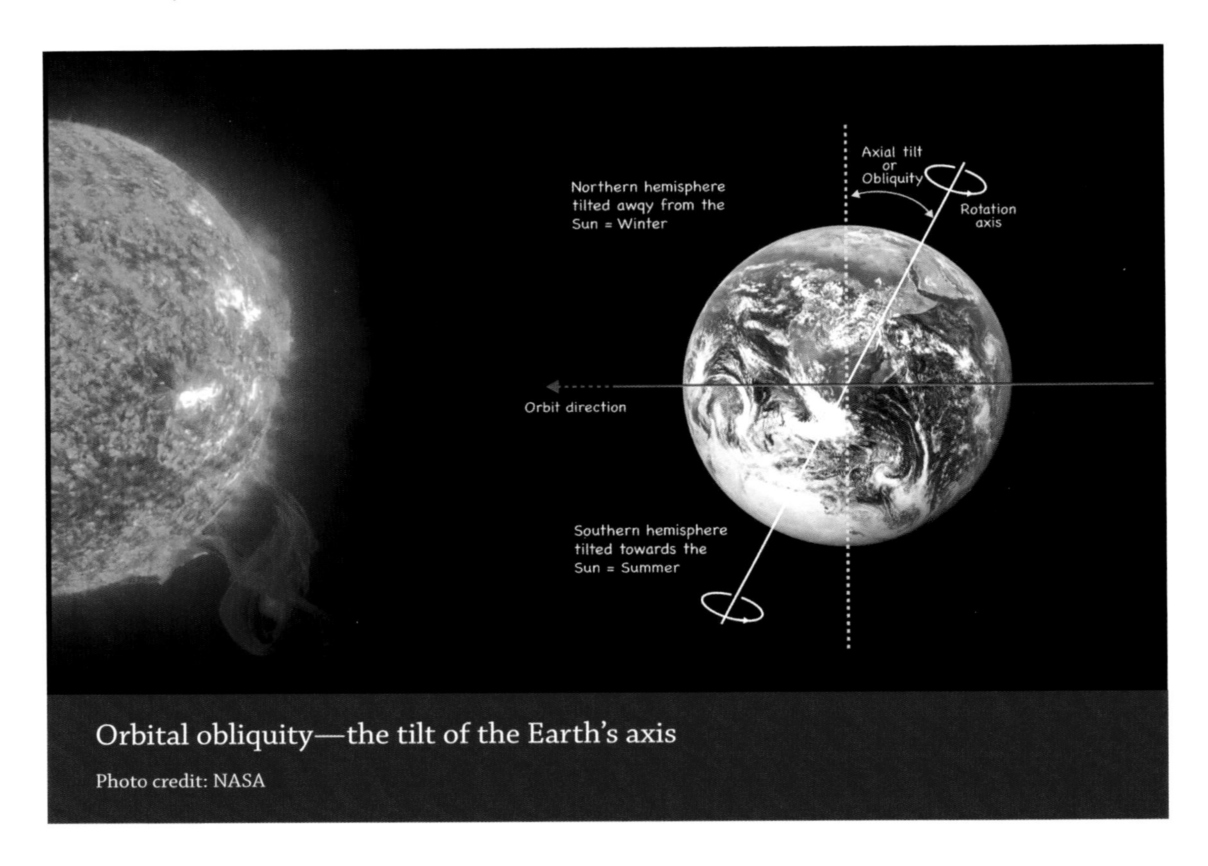

Orbital obliquity—the tilt of the Earth's axis

Photo credit: NASA

As the Earth spins, or rotates, on its axis, different parts of the Earth face toward or away from the Sun. The Earth actually makes one full rotation around its axis in slightly less than 24 hours, at 23.93 hours. This rotation on a roughly 24 hour cycle gives us our days and nights.

During different seasons of the year, the North and South Poles get more sunlight or less sunlight than the areas around the equator because the tilt of the axis points a pole toward or away from the Sun. Because of this, the poles can have nearly 24 hours of sunlight or 24 hours of darkness. So, not all days and nights are equal everywhere on the planet.

19.3 The Earth and the Moon

The Earth has one moon. A moon is any celestial body that orbits a planet. A moon is also called a natural satellite. The word moon comes from the Greek word *menas* which means month. The Moon orbits the Earth and completes one orbit every 27 days (roughly one month), hence its name—the "Moon."

Phases of the Moon
Image credit: NASA/nasaimages.org

The Moon can be seen from Earth because the Moon reflects light from the Sun. As the Moon orbits the Earth and as both the Earth and the Moon orbit the Sun, the appearance of the Moon changes. We call these changes phases.

In the first phase, on Day 0, the Moon is called a new moon. The new moon occurs when the Moon is between the Earth and the Sun. Only the back side of the Moon is illuminated by the Sun, so from Earth the Moon looks dark.

As the Moon continues to orbit the Earth, by Day 4 it enters the next phase called the waxing crescent moon. From Earth, only a small portion of the Moon appears illuminated and is crescent shaped. By Day 7 the Moon moves to the next phase and appears half-illuminated, This is called the first quarter moon, or half-moon. A few days later, on Day 10, the Moon moves to the waxing gibbous phase. A gibbous moon is between a full moon and a quarter moon. The word gibbous means "marked by convexity or swelling," so a gibbous moon is a moon that looks "swollen."

By Day 14, the Moon enters the full moon phase. The Moon is now on the opposite side of the Earth from the Sun and is seen with full illumination. A few days later, by Day 18, the Moon becomes a waning gibbous moon. Then, by Day

22, it enters the next to last phase, the last quarter moon, when the Moon is again half-illuminated, but now the illumination appears on the opposite side from the first quarter moon. Finally, by Day 26 the Moon enters the last phase, becoming a waning crescent moon. By Day 30 the Moon is back to being a new moon and the cycle repeats.

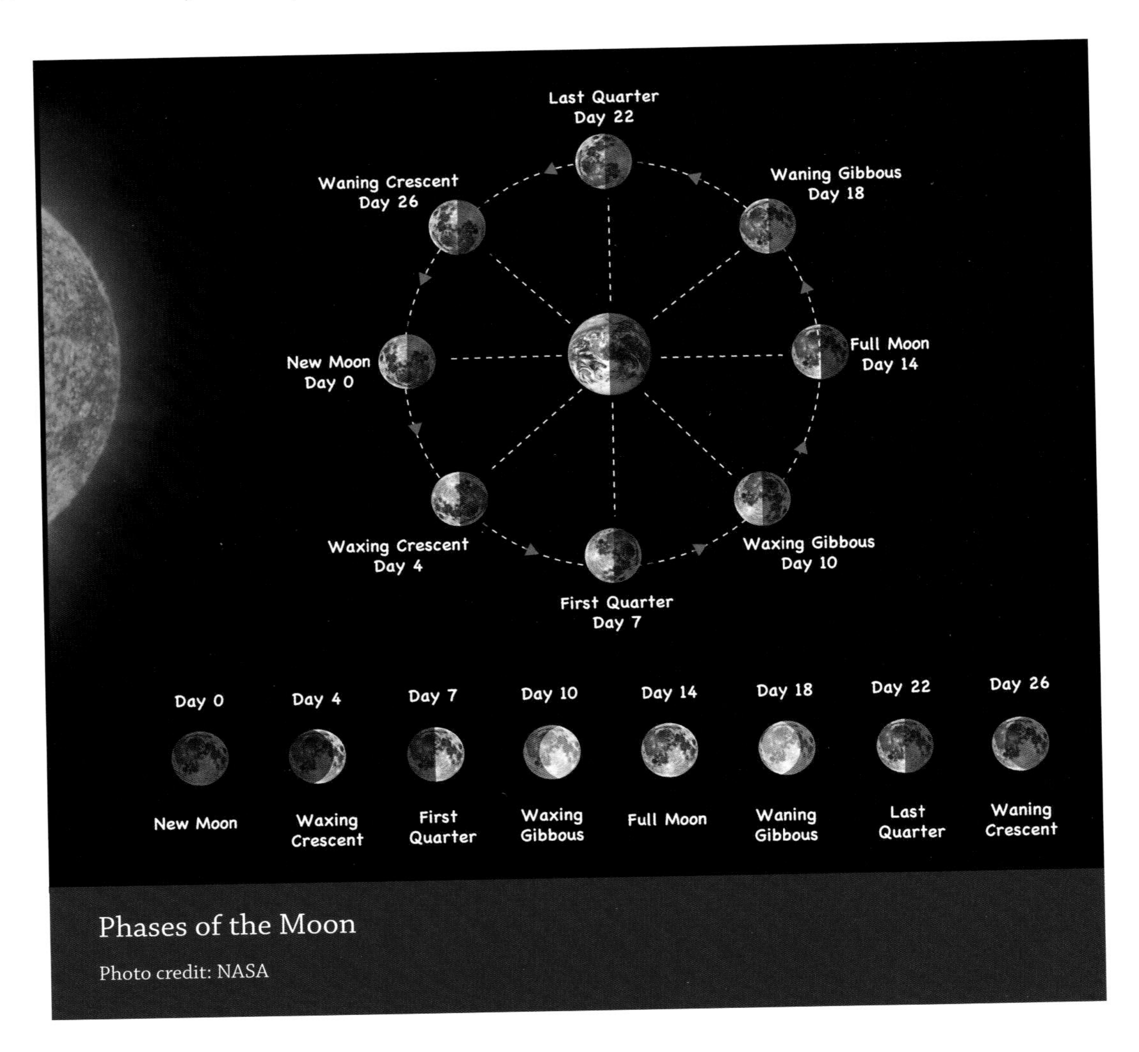

Phases of the Moon

Photo credit: NASA

The Moon and the Earth interact with each other through long range gravitational forces. Any object that has mass (the property that makes matter resist being moved) also has gravitational force (the force exerted by objects on one another). Your body has mass and also a small amount of gravitational force. But because you are very small compared to the Earth, your gravitational force does not affect the Earth.

The Moon is much bigger than you. But it has much less mass than the Earth and therefore has less gravitational force. However, the Moon has enough mass to create a gravitational pull on the Earth.

The Moon has dramatic effects on Earth. For example, the Moon is believed to stabilize Earth's rotation and the tilt of its axis. Without a moon, the Earth might swing more dramatically between degrees of obliquity, unable to maintain an average tilt of 23 degrees. If the Earth tilted more or less dramatically, this could result in extreme or even catastrophic changes in the seasons.

The Moon also contributes to the rise and fall of ocean tides. Ocean tides on Earth are created in part by the gravitational forces exerted by the Moon. The Moon (together with the Sun) pulls on the Earth's center, which creates two tidal bulges. As the Earth rotates on its own axis, these bulges are dragged along the Earth's surface, causing the sea level to rise and fall, thus creating tides.

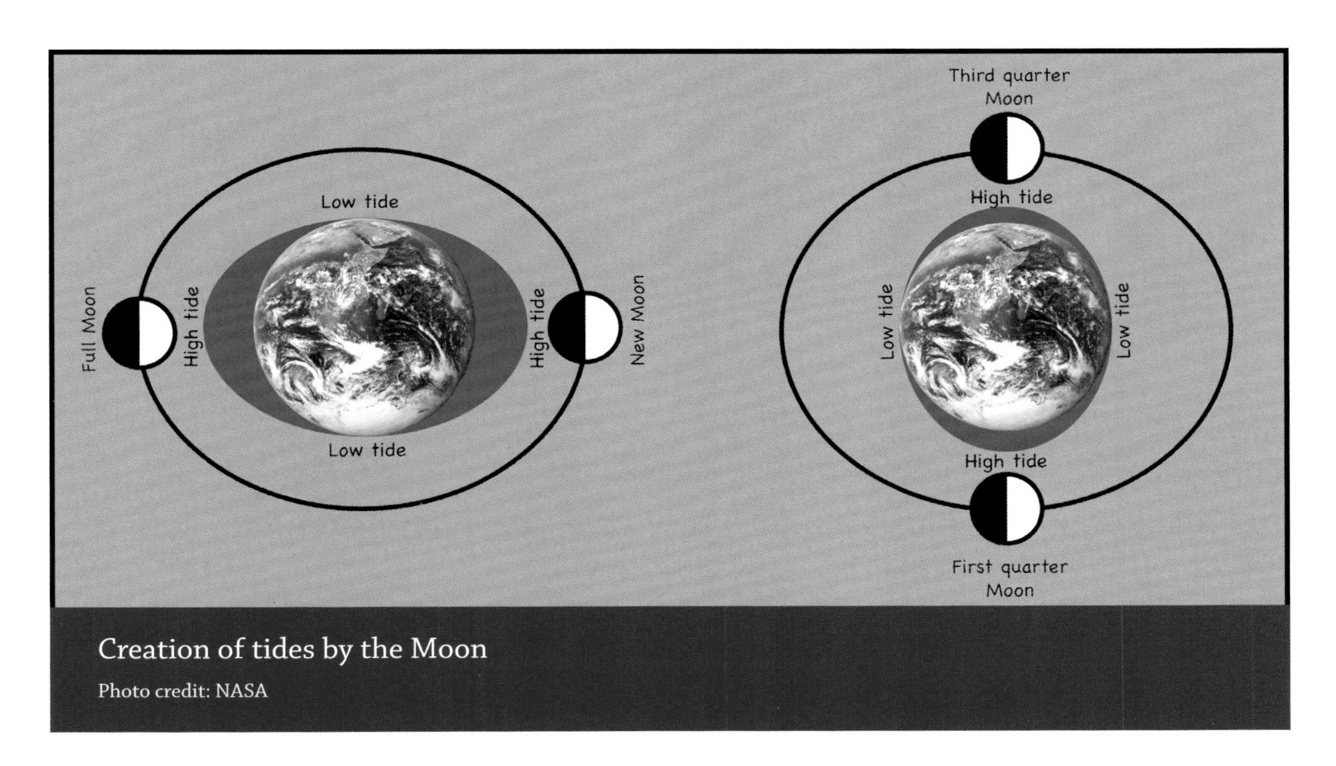

Creation of tides by the Moon

Photo credit: NASA

19.4 The Earth and the Sun

The Sun is a celestial body in space. It provides the Earth with power. The Sun is like a big battery that never runs out, continuously giving us energy in the form of light and heat. From this energy, life is possible. Without the Sun there would be no plants, animals, reptiles, fish, or even microbes. All of life requires energy in order to move, grow, eat, and reproduce. Every chemical reaction in your body requires energy, and it is ultimately the Sun's energy that powers the chemical reactions in your body.

Not only does the Sun power our planet, it also interacts with Earth, affecting tides, weather, and even our magnetic field. We saw in the last section how the Moon pulls on the Earth causing tides in our oceans. The Sun also pulls on the Earth causing tidal activity.

Did you know that "space weather" affects our own weather on Earth? It's easy to forget that Earth is not a closed system. We are a blue ball in space, interacting with other space objects like planets and the Sun. The Sun affects our planet in major ways, and one way is the weather.

Weather can be tough to predict on Earth. You might not think that a solar storm on the Sun could cause a storm on our planet, yet this is exactly what happens. Earth's weather is caused by temperature and moisture variations in different places. When the Sun has a solar storm and a burst of heat escapes, we get a rise in temperature on Earth, which can then create storms.

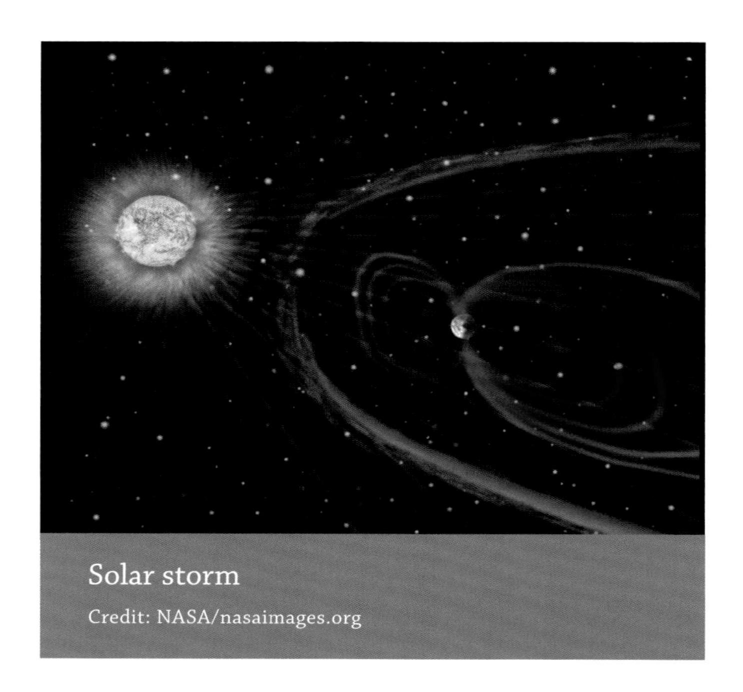

Solar storm

Credit: NASA/nasaimages.org

The Sun also interacts with Earth's atmosphere causing auroras, which are sometimes called northern lights and southern lights. Auroras are caused by solar storms that charge particles in space. These charged particles get trapped by Earth's magnetic field. When this happens, they pass through our atmosphere and give off light as they release energy.

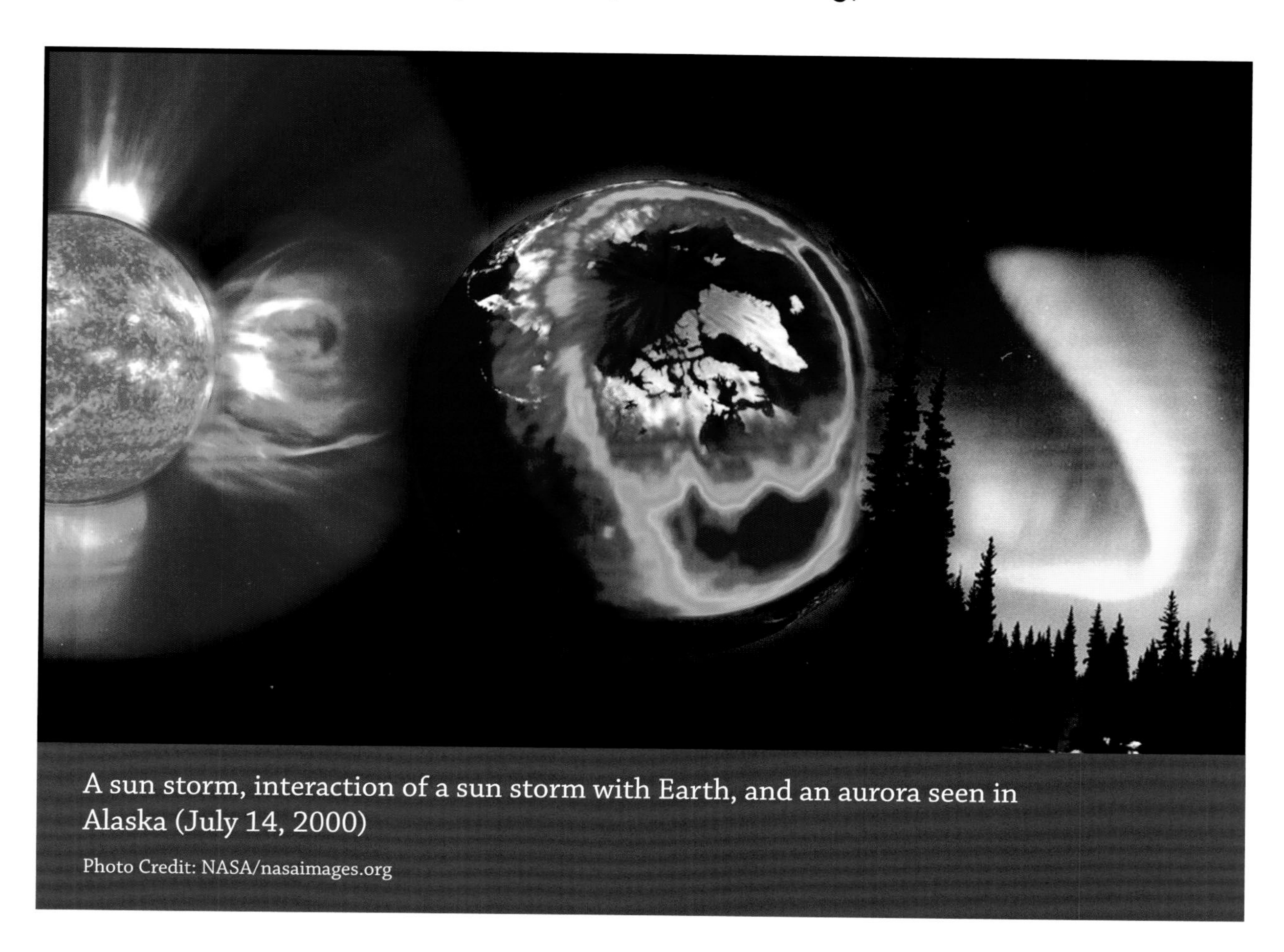

A sun storm, interaction of a sun storm with Earth, and an aurora seen in Alaska (July 14, 2000)

Photo Credit: NASA/nasaimages.org

19.5 Eclipses

There are two types of eclipses that occur. A lunar eclipse occurs when the Moon passes directly behind the Earth and the Earth blocks the Sun's rays from illuminating the Moon. The Moon is darkened as the Sun's rays are blocked and the Earth's shadow passes across the Moon.

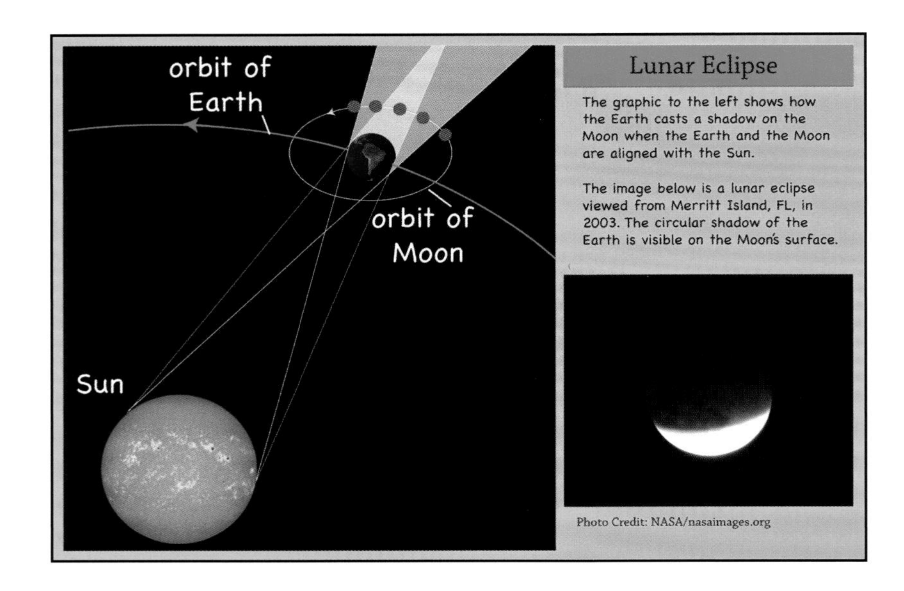

The other type of eclipse is called a solar eclipse. A solar eclipse occurs when the Moon passes between the Sun and the Earth, blocking the Sun's rays from reaching some location on Earth.

It is tempting to look at a solar eclipse with your naked eye. However, it is very dangerous to look at the eclipse directly. Special glasses or projection techniques must always be used to view a solar eclipse.

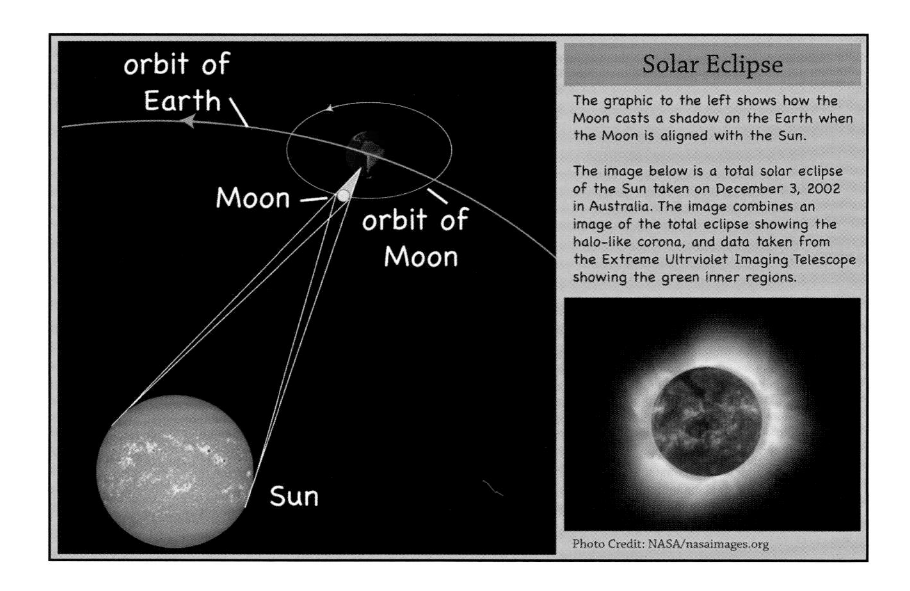

19.6 Summary

- Earth is classified as a planet because it rotates around the Sun, has enough mass to have its own gravity, and has cleared its orbit.
- Earth rotates on a tilted axis. This tilt is called orbital obliquity. The rotation of Earth on its axis gives us night and day, and orbital obliquity creates the different seasons.
- The Earth has one moon orbiting it. The Moon stabilizes the tilt and rotation of Earth and contributes to the activity of the tides.
- The Earth orbits the Sun. The Sun provides Earth with energy and contributes to Earth's weather and tidal activity.

Chapter 20 The Moon and the Sun

20.1 Introduction 191

20.2 The Moon 191

20.3 The Sun 194

20.4 Chemistry and Physics of Stars 195

20.5 Summary 197

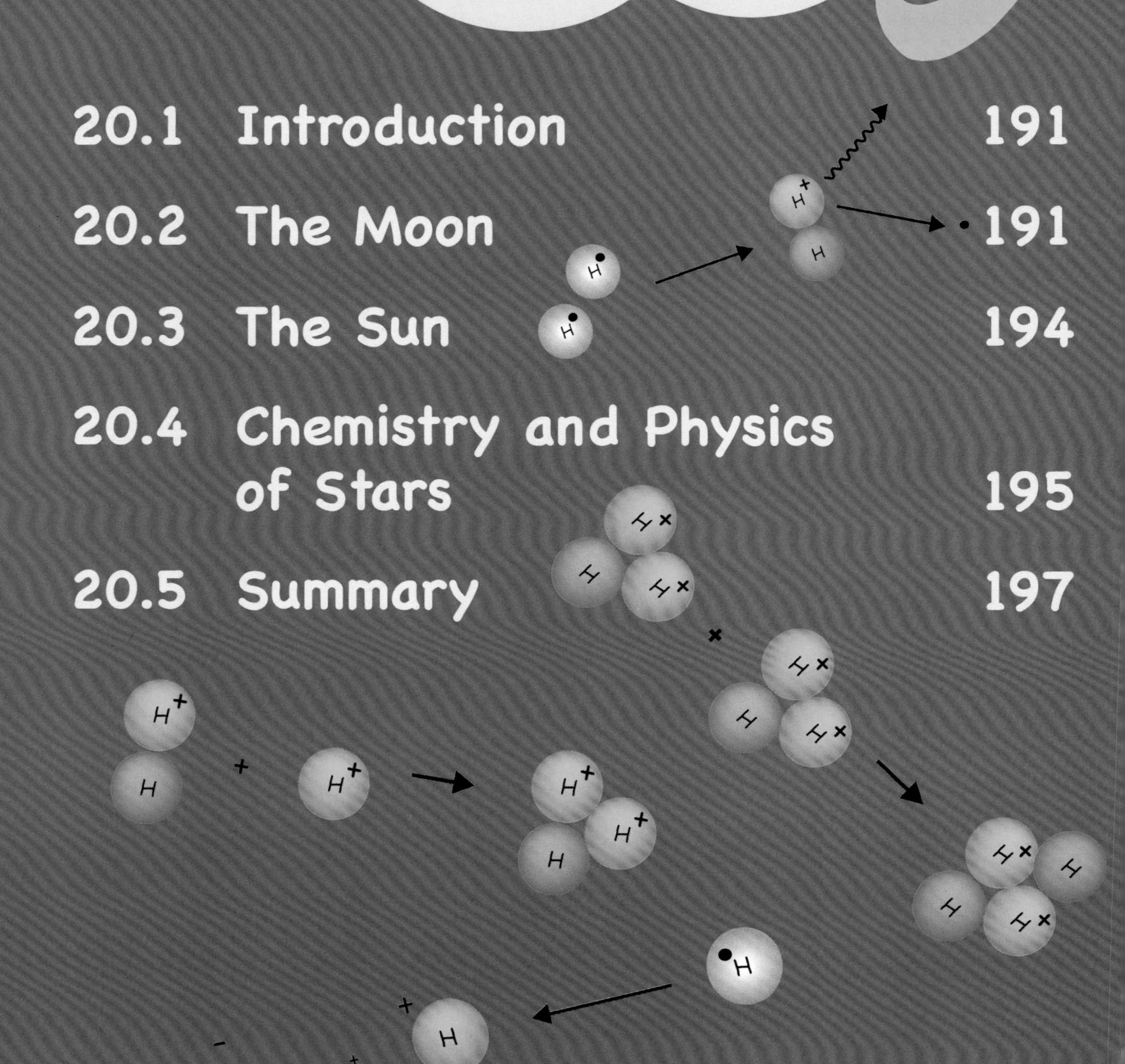

20.1 Introduction

As we saw in Chapter 19, the Moon and the Sun play an important role in many of Earth's properties, including the Earth's stability, rotation, weather, and tidal actions. In this chapter, as we move away from the Earth and start exploring space, we will take a closer look at the Moon and the Sun.

20.2 The Moon

The Moon Photo Credit: NASA/nasaimages.org

Recall that the word "moon" comes from the Greek word *menas* which means month. We call our moon "the Moon" because it orbits the Earth in a monthly cycle, but not all moons orbit their planets in a monthly cycle.

The adjective lunar is also used to refer to the Moon. Lunar comes from the Latin word *luceo* which means "to shine bright." Although the Moon does not create its own light, it reflects the Sun's light and is the brightest object in the evening sky.

The Moon is not made of green cheese. In fact, the Moon is made of elements and minerals, just like Earth. We know that the surface of the Moon is made of elements and minerals because Moon samples were collected by the Apollo astronauts between 1969 and 1972. Moon soil contains aluminum, calcium, iron, magnesium, silicon, and titanium.

There are at least two different types of Moon rocks, basaltic rocks and breccia. Basaltic rocks were formed by the hardening of lava that came from lunar volcanoes and from lava that flowed through cracks that occurred in the Moon's surface when meteorites struck it. A meteorite is a rocky object in space that has hit the surface of another object in space. Rocks called breccia were formed from soil and pieces of rock that were squeezed and melted by the extreme pressure created when objects such as meteorites hit the Moon.

The Moon has little or no atmosphere, and in fact, the space around the Moon is close to being a vacuum. A vacuum is an area that contains no matter. The result of the lack of atmosphere is that there is no weather on the Moon. There are no clouds, rain, or wind. However, water in the form of ice has been discovered below the surface of the Moon.

The Earth and the Moon

Photo Credit: NASA

The Moon is about 3.5 times smaller than the Earth, with a diameter of 3475 kilometers (2158 miles). However, in our solar system it is relatively the largest moon compared to the size of the planet orbited.

Because the Moon has less mass than Earth, it also has less gravity. The gravitational force on the Moon is about one sixth the gravitational force on Earth.

It takes the Moon the same number of days to complete one rotation on its axis as it takes the Moon to make one orbit around the Earth. This means that as the Moon is going around the Earth, the side of the Moon that faces the Earth is slowly rotating at exactly the same rate that the Moon is orbiting the Earth. Therefore, the Moon always has the same side facing Earth.

The temperature on the Moon varies wildly because it has no atmosphere to hold onto the heat from the Sun. During the day, temperatures can be as high as 173 degrees Celsius (280 degrees Fahrenheit). At night, the temperature can dip to as low as -240 degrees C (-400 degrees F).

If you look up at the Moon, you will see both light and dark areas on the surface. The light areas are known as terrae. The word *terrae* is Latin and means "lands." These light areas are rugged with craters that can exceed 40 kilometers (25 miles) in diameter.

The dark areas on the Moon are known as maria. The word maria comes from the Latin word *marinus* which means "sea." When 17th century astronomers were looking at the Moon through their telescopes, they thought that the large dark areas were bodies of water, or seas.

The early astronomers gave the maria fun names such as Mare Tranquillitatis, meaning "The Sea of Tranquility," and Mare Nectaris, meaning "The Sea of Nectar." Modern astronomers still use these names but know that the dark areas of the Moon are not seas. Instead, these dark areas are lava flows.

Like Earth, the Moon is thought to be made of a crust (an outer, rocky shell), a mantle (the layer below the crust), and an iron-rich core. However, the Moon now has no magnetic field. By studying rocks brought back from the Moon by the Apollo astronauts, scientists have discovered that the Moon had a strong magnetic field in the far distant past. Scientists don't know for sure why the Moon lost its magnetic field, but they are exploring different theories to discover the cause.

The Moon—crust and interior
Photo credit: NASA

The Apollo astronauts placed seismometers on the Moon's surface. Seismometers are instruments that detect motion or vibration in the ground. By using these seismometers, scientists found that the Moon is seismically active and can have earthquakes that last longer than 10 minutes—much longer than those on Earth. It is thought that the Moon does not have moving tectonic plates like Earth but that earthquakes may be caused by events such as meteorites striking the Moon's surface and the sides of craters collapsing, among other things.

20.3 The Sun

As we saw in Chapter 19, the Sun affects Earth's tides, weather, stability and rotation. But what is the Sun?

The Sun is different from both the Earth and Moon. The sun is a star. A star is a celestial body that generates light and heat energy. Our star, the Sun, is composed mainly of hydrogen and helium. Hydrogen and helium are the lightest elements known and are gases. Hence, one way to think about the Sun is to imagine it as a hot ball of gas.

The Sun and the Earth

Photo Credit: NASA/nasaimages.org

Although the Sun is made of lightweight gases, the Sun's diameter is about 100 times the diameter of the Earth, and the Sun is over three hundred thousand times as massive as the Earth.

Mass of Sun/Mass of Earth = 332,840

To get an idea of just how large the Sun is compared to the Earth, know that about 1 million Earths would fit inside the Sun!

The Sun's temperature is extremely hot, averaging 5800 degrees kelvin (5510° Celsius or 9900° Fahrenheit) with some regions exceeding tens of thousands or even millions of degrees kelvin. Life on Earth is made possible by the extreme temperatures on the Sun that radiate into space. But how does the Sun generate so much energy?

20.4 Chemistry and Physics of Stars

To understand how the Sun can provide the energy to fuel our planet, it is important to look at the chemistry and physics of stars.

As we saw in Section 20.3, the Sun is composed largely of hydrogen and helium, two lightweight gases. When gases are compressed (squeezed into a smaller space), their temperature increases. If you hold your hand on a tire tube as you pump air into it, you will find that the tube gets warm. This heat is generated by the increasing pressure imposed on the gas (air) as more gas molecules are forced into the tube.

The Sun is a huge ball of compressed gases and has extremely high temperatures at its center. It is believed that these temperatures are so high that the hydrogen atoms become ionized. Ionization is a process where the electrons and nucleus of an atom become separated. Since a hydrogen atom is made of one proton, one electron, and no neutrons, when hydrogen ionizes, it is converted to a free proton (the nucleus) and a free electron. The proton is positively charged and the electron is negatively charged.

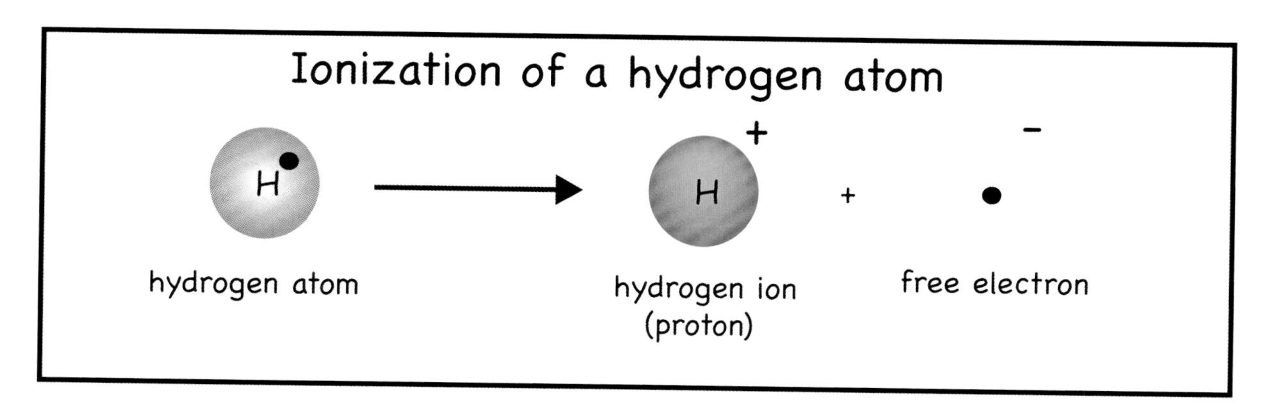

What happens when free hydrogen protons meet? We know that when two like charges meet they will repel each other. However, at the extreme pressure and temperature that exist at the center of the Sun, when two hydrogen protons meet, they combine, or fuse, together. This process is called hydrogen fusion. The fusing together of two protons is also called thermonuclear fusion because it can take place only at extremely high temperatures.

However, not only do the two hydrogen protons fuse, but one of the two is converted into a neutron. Eventually, four hydrogen protons (nuclei) will fuse to make a single helium atom.

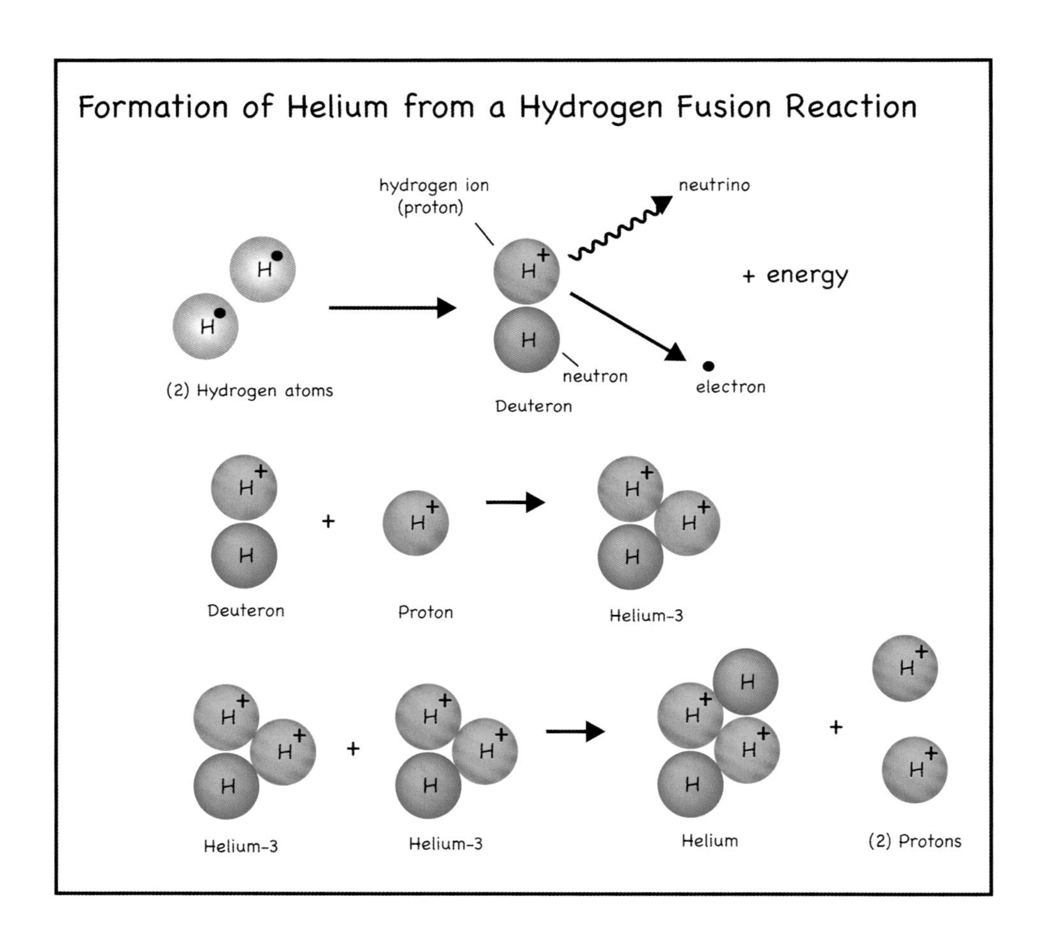

Thermonuclear fusion is a nuclear reaction that releases massive amounts of energy. In 1905 Albert Einstein showed that mass can be converted to energy with his elegantly simple equation:

$$E = mc^2$$

The symbol "E" represents "energy," the symbol "m" represents "mass," and the symbol "c" represents "the speed of light." Because the speed of light is a very large number (c = 299,792,458 x meters/seconds) and is multiplied times itself ("c^2") and then multiplied times the mass ("m"), only a small amount of mass is needed to create large amounts of energy.

For example, if you had a mass ("m") of one gram of hydrogen, using the formula $E=mc^2$ you would get a result of 21,480,248,771,809 calories of energy ("E"), with calorie being the unit of measurement of energy. This means that one small gram of hydrogen would give 21 trillion units of energy!

A chocolate chip cookie contains 227 calories. If you eat a chocolate chip cookie, your body gets 227 units of energy. Your body needs energy to do things like ride a bike or row a boat. To get 21 trillion units of energy you would need to eat about 94 billion chocolate chip cookies!

Thermonuclear fusion is the process the Sun uses to convert hydrogen into helium and energy. With the tremendous amounts of energy thermonuclear fusion creates, the Sun can fuel our entire planet!

20.5 Summary

- The Moon is made of the same elements found on Earth.
- The Moon is smaller than the Earth and has little or no atmosphere and no liquid water.
- The light areas of the Moon are called terrae and the dark areas are called maria.
- The Sun is a large celestial body composed mainly of the two gases, hydrogen and helium.
- The Sun converts hydrogen to helium and generates energy using thermonuclear fusion.

Chapter 21 Planets

21.1 Introduction 199

21.2 Types of Planets 199

21.3 Earth-like Planets 200

21.4 Jupiter-like Planets 202

21.5 What Happened to Pluto? 205

21.6 Summary 207

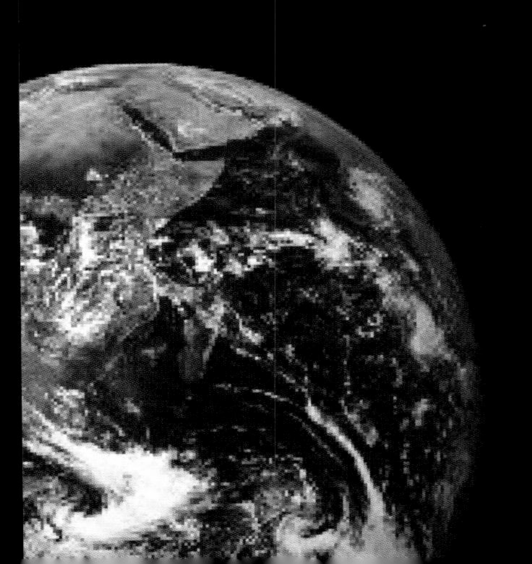

21.1 Introduction

Up to this point we have been introduced to the Earth, the Moon, and the Sun. Although all of these celestial bodies are made of the same elements as those found on Earth, they also differ from each other in significant ways. We discovered that the Earth is a planet, the Moon is a moon, and the Sun is a star. In this chapter we will take a look at different types of planets.

21.2 Types of Planets

Each of the planets that orbits the Sun is unique. Earth is the only planet that has liquid water and an atmosphere that is breathable by humans. Jupiter is the only planet where immense storm systems last for centuries, and Venus has a cloud layer made of sulfuric acid.

In our solar system there are officially eight planets (Pluto lost its status as a planet, and we'll find out why in Section 21.5). The names of the eight planets that orbit our Sun are Mercury, Venus, Earth, Mars, Jupiter, Saturn, Uranus, and Neptune.

The Planets

Image Credit: NASA/nasaimages.org

Although the planets differ greatly from one another, they can be placed into two broad categories: the terrestrial planets (Earth-like) and the Jovian planets (Jupiter-like).

The terrestrial planets differ from the Jovian planets in their physical properties and distance from the Sun. The terrestrial planets are all made of rocky materials and are relatively close to the Sun compared to the Jovian planets. The Jovian planets are made primarily of helium and hydrogen and are at greater distances from the Sun.

21.3 Earth-like Planets

The terrestrial planets include Mercury, Venus, Earth, and Mars. The word terrestrial comes from the Latin word *terra* which means "earth."

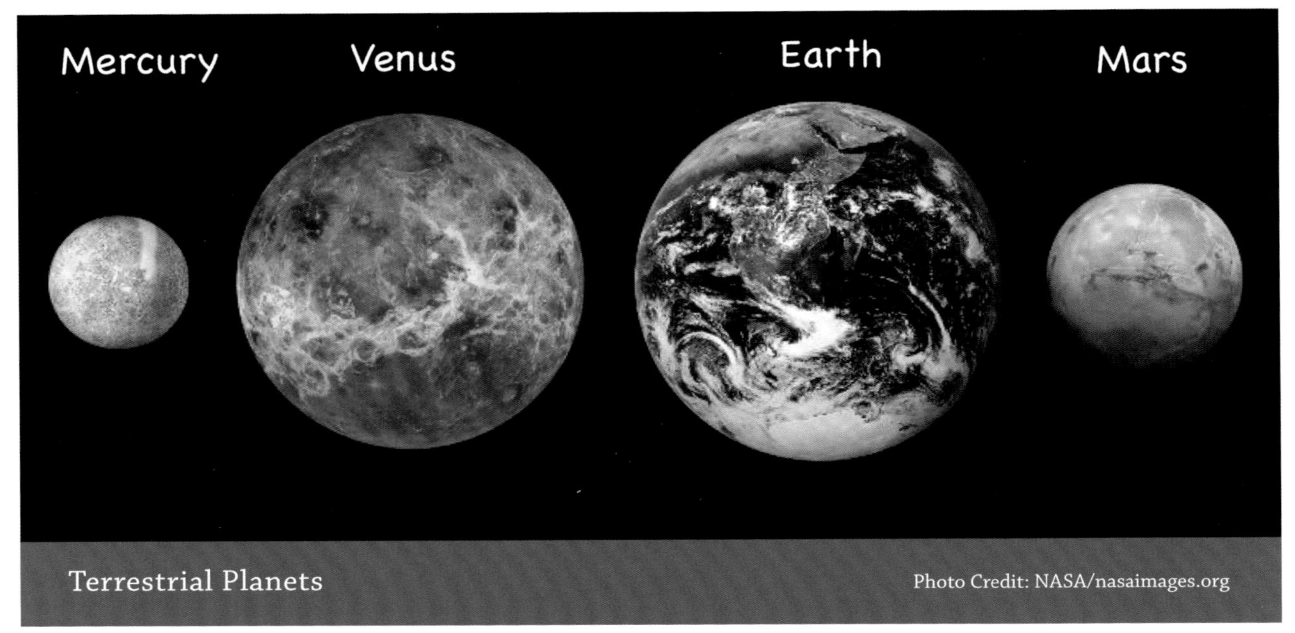

Terrestrial Planets Photo Credit: NASA/nasaimages.org

All of the terrestrial planets resemble Earth in some ways. The terrestrial planets have hard, rocky surfaces with mountains, craters, and volcanoes.

Mercury
Photo Credit: NASA/nasaimages.org

Mercury is the terrestrial planet closest to the Sun. Because it is so close to the Sun, it is difficult to get images of it from Earth. However, in 1974 and 1975 an unmanned spacecraft called Mariner 10 got close enough to Mercury to take photographs. The Mariner 10 space probe revealed Mercury's rough, cratered surface. Although Mercury looks similar to the Moon, Mercury does not have the light and dark areas (terrae and maria) seen on the surface of the Moon.

Venus is the next closest planet to orbit the Sun. Venus looks deceptively like Earth in size and shape. For years scientists thought Venus might be a warm jungle version of Earth with teeming life. But modern technologies have given us more information about Venus, and today we know that Venus is inhospitable for life as we know it.

Venus Photo Credit: NASA/nasaimages.org

The atmosphere on Venus is composed almost entirely of carbon dioxide. The high level of carbon dioxide creates a surface temperature of 460 degrees Celsius (860 degrees Fahrenheit). The clouds that cover Venus contain corrosive sulfuric acid.

Earth is the third terrestrial planet from the Sun.

The fourth terrestrial planet from the Sun is Mars. People have been fascinated by Mars and have long speculated that life on Mars exists. "Martians" are a favorite character in many science fiction novels and films. Early astronomers even suggested that features on Mars included linear canals, denoting intelligent life and liquid water. Today we have found that Mars has water in the form of ice, and some scientists think they may find bacteria on Mars, but there are no advanced forms of life.

Mars Photo Credit: NASA/nasaimages.org

Mars is about half the diameter of Earth [6794 km (4220 mi)] with a relatively thin, almost cloudless atmosphere. Mars appears bright red to Earth observers, but the surface of Mars is actually reddish-brown. In the late 1960s several unmanned spacecraft flew past the surface of Mars and sent back the first close-up pictures of the Martian surface, showing that it is covered with craters. More recently, rovers have landed on Mars and sent back to Earth photos and much data about Mars.

21.4 Jupiter-like Planets

The Jupiter-like, or Jovian, planets include Jupiter, Saturn, Uranus, and Neptune. The term Jovian comes from Roman mythological stories about Jove, who was the god of the sky. The Jovian planets are those planets that resemble Jupiter in their physical properties and distance from the Sun.

Jovian planets Photo Credit: NASA/nasaimages.org

Jupiter is the largest of the Jovian planets, with a diameter about 11 times larger than that of the Earth. It is also about 318 times more massive. Jupiter orbits the Sun very slowly, taking almost 12 Earth years to make one orbit.

Looking at Jupiter through an Earth-based telescope, you can see light and dark bands circling the planetary surface. The light bands are called zones, and the dark bands are called belts. The zones and belts are parallel to Jupiter's equator and are colored red, orange, yellow, and brown. The zones and belts are gases at various temperatures. Scientists believe that the zones appear lighter because the clouds are higher and colder in this region, and the belts appear darker because the clouds are lower and warmer.

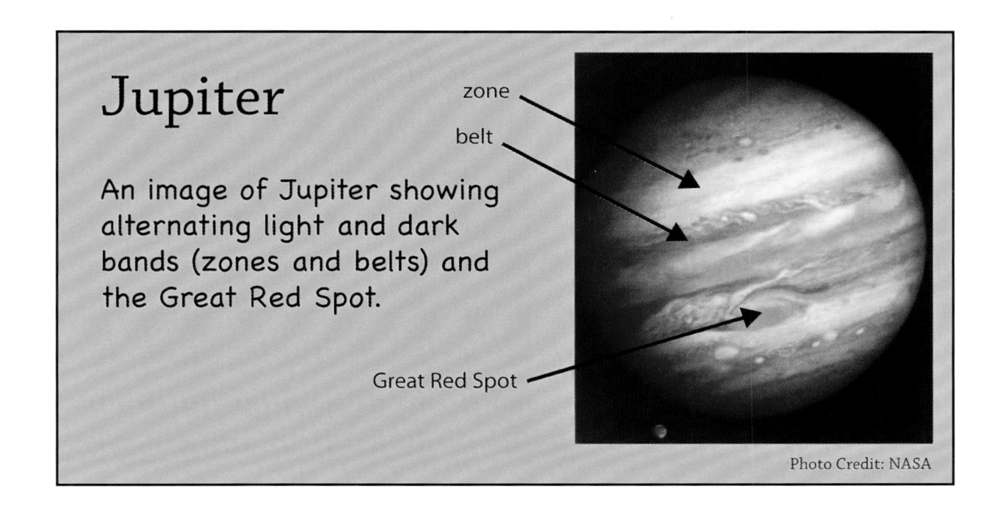

Jupiter

An image of Jupiter showing alternating light and dark bands (zones and belts) and the Great Red Spot.

Photo Credit: NASA

The Great Red Spot appears to be a huge long-lived storm where clouds complete a counterclockwise rotation about every six days. Jupiter is composed primarily of hydrogen and helium and has no rocky surface to break up the storm which has lasted for centuries.

Saturn is the next largest Jovian planet. With a diameter nearly 9 times that of Earth, it is about 95 times more massive than Earth. Saturn, like Jupiter, is a mostly gaseous planet that slowly obits the Sun, taking 29 Earth years to make one orbit.

Saturn Photo Credit: NASA/nasaimages.org

Like Jupiter, Saturn has belts and zones resulting from different gas clouds at different heights and temperatures. In addition to the belts and zones, Saturn has many colored rings extending laterally from the equator. Saturn's rings are believed to be made of many millions of icy fragments that are not connected but uniformly circle the planet. These icy fragments reflect the Sun's light, causing them to illuminate brightly.

The last of the Jovian planets are Uranus and Neptune. Uranus and Neptune extend to the darkest edge of our solar system and are many millions of miles away from the Sun.

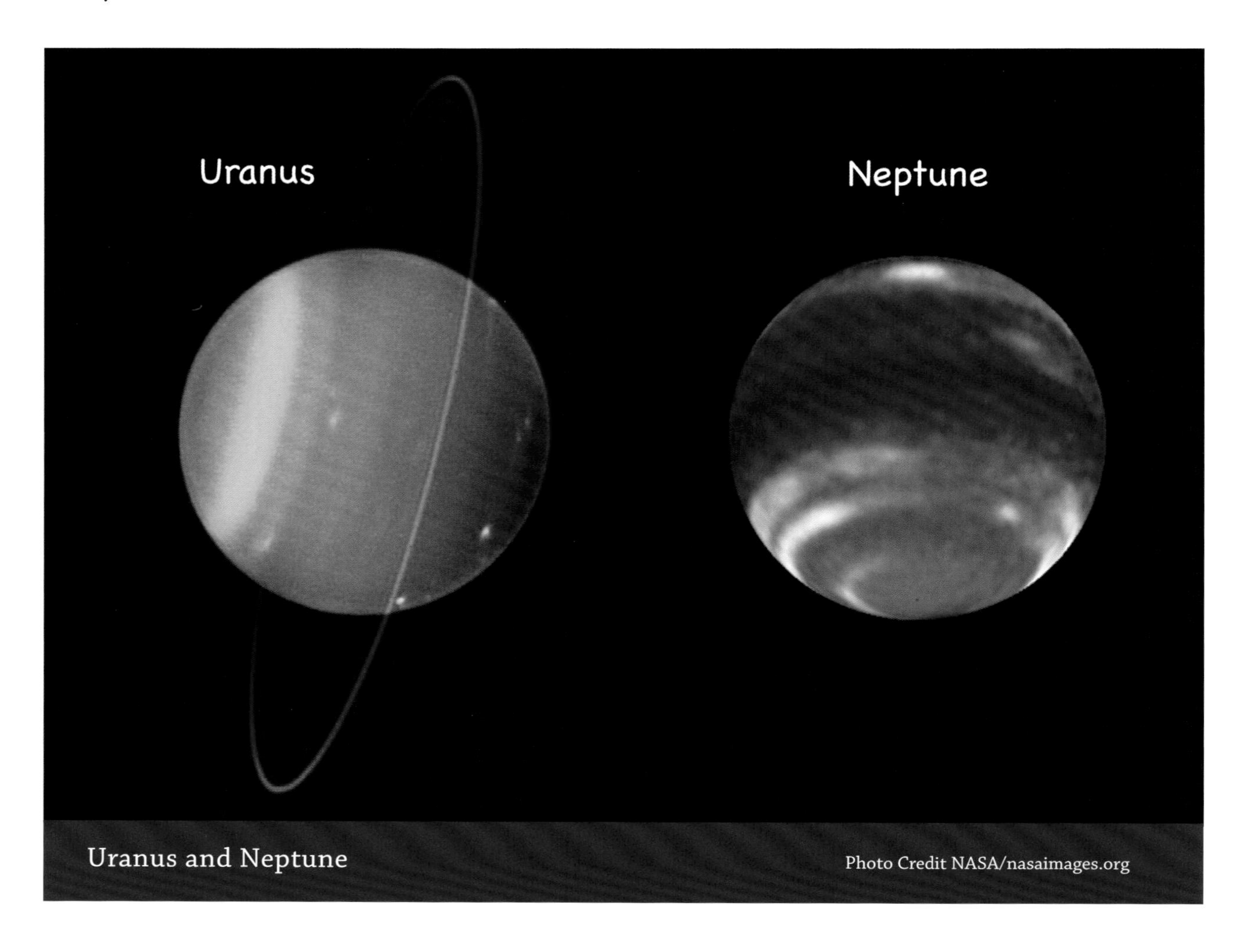

Uranus and Neptune

Photo Credit NASA/nasaimages.org

Uranus rotates around the Sun every 84 Earth years, is just over 4 times the diameter of Earth, and is 14 times as massive. Uranus has an almost featureless surface without zones and belts. Uranus is made up of mostly hydrogen and helium, like Jupiter and Saturn, but also contains a significant amount of methane. The presence of methane gives Uranus a distinctive bluish color. Computer imaging shows some very faint banding which is thought to be the result of sunlight breaking down the methane gas on the planet's surface. Uranus sits on its side as it orbits the Sun and, like Saturn, it is circled by several rings.

Uranus is colder than either Jupiter or Saturn. Because of its low temperature, Uranus does not have dense clouds like those of Jupiter and Saturn, and this may explain its very bland, featureless surface.

Neptune rotates around the Sun every 164 Earth years and like Uranus is about 4 times the diameter of Earth. But Neptune differs from Uranus in that it is 17 times more massive than Earth and has Jupiter-like atmospheric clouds, belts, and zones. In 1989 the unmanned spacecraft Voyager 2 flew past Neptune and captured images of a giant storm called the Great Dark Spot. The Great Dark Spot was similar in many ways to Jupiter's Great Red Spot but was not as long-lived. In 1994 telescope images revealed that the storm had disappeared.

21.5 What Happened to Pluto?

Until recently Pluto was a favorite planet for many celestial enthusiasts, both young and old. Until August 2006 Pluto, at the far outer edge of our solar system, was considered the tiniest of the planets.

Pluto—size comparison (diam.)
Image Credit: NASA/JPL-Caltech/R. Hurt (SSC)

Pluto was discovered by Clyde Tombaugh on January 23, 1930. Tombaugh was curious about what appeared to be irregularities in the orbits of both Uranus and Neptune. Many astronomers of Tombaugh's day were troubled by the fact that Uranus and Neptune did not orbit the Sun as the astronomers thought they should. Tombaugh, knowing that neighboring planets can disturb planetary motions, found Pluto as a dim speck among the stars. Pluto was immediately given the title of the 9th planet in our solar system.

But, as it turns out, the naming of Pluto as a planet was a mistake. It was later determined that Pluto is too small to disturb the orbits of Uranus and Neptune. Also, astronomers decided there was nothing wrong with their orbits in the first place.

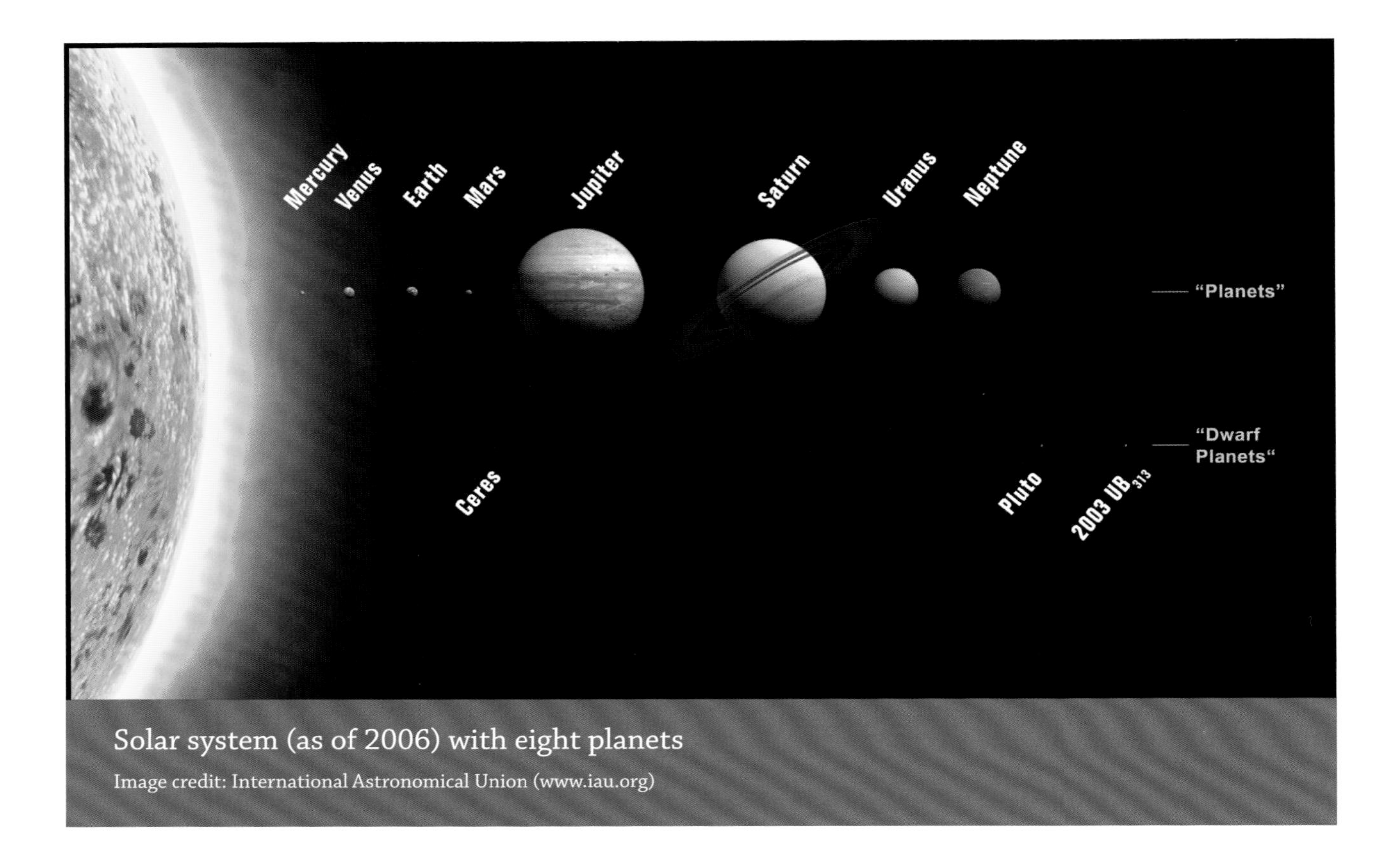

Solar system (as of 2006) with eight planets
Image credit: International Astronomical Union (www.iau.org)

In 2006 the International Astronomers Union (IAU) had a meeting to discuss the definition of a planet. At this meeting it was decided that in order to qualify as a planet, a celestial body must have "cleared the neighborhood around its orbit." In other words, it can't have other celestial bodies orbiting the Sun with it. Pluto is actually in a belt of other celestial bodies called the Kuiper Belt. So the IAU reclassified Pluto as a dwarf planet rather than a true planet. A dwarf planet has not cleared its orbit but does have enough gravity to have formed a spherical shape like a true planet.

However, as is typical in science, the debate continues. As of the writing of this text, the IAU has come up with a new classification for Pluto called a plutoid. A plutoid is like a dwarf planet but its orbit is beyond that of Neptune. Other scientists don't accept the IAU's definitions and would like to have Pluto reinstated as a planet. Who knows—a future young astronomer may help Pluto regain its planetary status!

21.6 Summary

- There are officially eight planets in our solar system: Mercury, Venus, Earth, Mars, Jupiter, Saturn, Uranus, and Neptune.
- The terrestrial planets are "earth-like" (made up of mostly rock) and are Mercury, Venus, Earth, and Mars.
- The Jovian planets are "Jupiter-like" (made up of mostly hydrogen and helium) and are Jupiter, Saturn, Uranus, and Neptune.
- Pluto was considered the 9th planet in the solar system, but lost its planetary status in 2006. It is now considered a dwarf planet or a plutoid.

Chapter 22 Putting It All Together

22.1 Science 209

22.2 Science and the Public 210

22.3 Science in the Movies 212

22.4 Real Scientists 213

22.5 Summary 214

22.1 Science

In this text we explored what science is, how science works, how science was developed, and how people think about science in different ways. We explored the five main branches of science—chemistry, biology, physics, geology, and astronomy. It is important to remember that science continues to change as new ideas and new technologies are discovered.

Science has shaped modern life, and without science we would not be able to cure diseases, fly across the ocean, or put a man on the Moon.

In this text we saw how chemistry developed and how chemists proved the existence of atoms, discovered oxygen, found out how molecules are formed and changed, and today have even turned lead into gold!

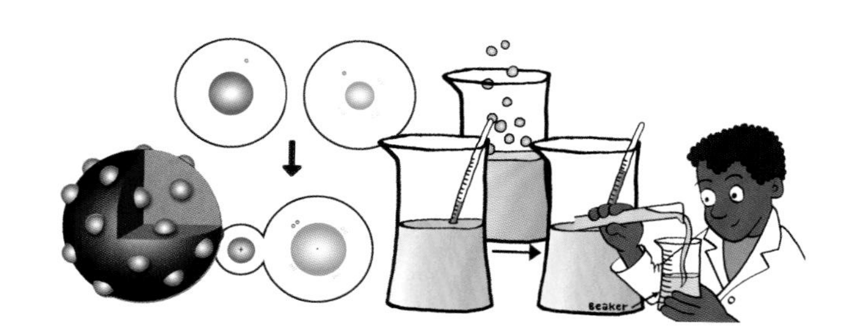

We saw how biologists have sought to understand what life is and how to define, name, and catalog living things. We've also seen how chemistry and biology fit together and how atoms and molecules make up the machinery, structure, and code that makes life possible.

In physics we saw how matter and energy obey physical laws and how physics and math connect to provide

an understanding of how the world works. We explored how mathematics can exactly describe the way physical laws work.

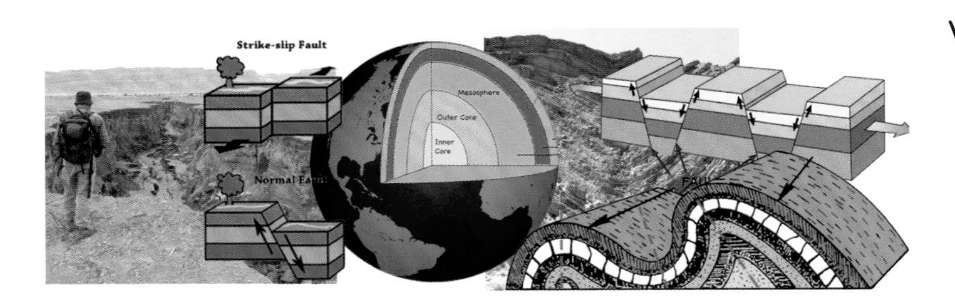

We saw how geologists study Earth, how chemistry is needed for understanding rocks, minerals, and soils, and how some geologists also study biology. We saw how geologists use technology to develop theories about how the deep layers of Earth may work.

And finally, we saw how astronomers study the cosmos, how chemistry is important for understanding how stars generate energy and how physics helps astronomers understand stars and planets and make spacecraft to explore the universe.

Science is a large and complex blend of ideas and facts and covers everything from how an ant moves a grain of sand to how a galaxy is formed. Because science covers so many diverse, complicated topics, most scientists specialize in a particular subject and typically work in only a very small area of science. In order for scientists to have a broader view of how their specialty fits into the workings of the world and the universe as a whole, it is important for them to have an overall understanding of all the areas of science and an appreciation for how they are put together.

22.2 Science and the Public

Many people don't study science in school, and science is often presented to kids in a way that is confusing and difficult to understand. As a result, many people don't really know very much about science, what questions science can answer, and what questions science can't answer. This lack of understanding can create problems for both scientists and the general public.

The confusion around what science is, what it can answer and what it can't answer opens the door for non-scientifically based ideas, products, and policies to be accepted. Some of these ideas, products, and policies can harm people and the environment.

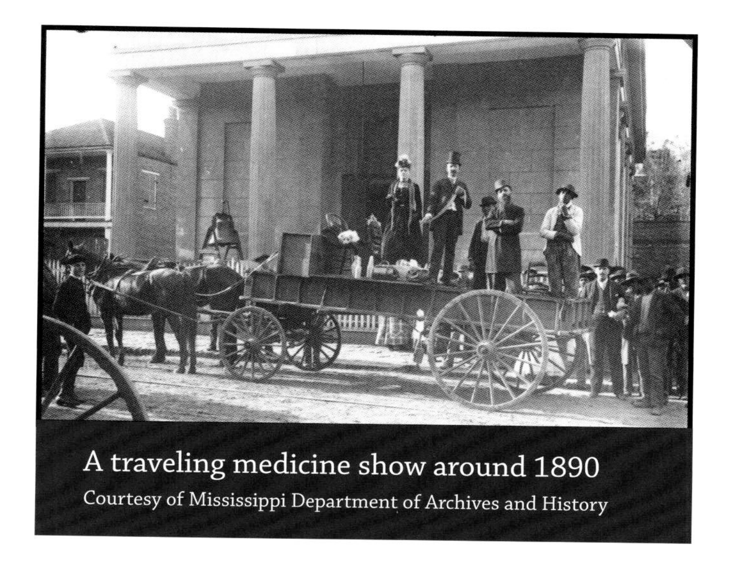

A traveling medicine show around 1890
Courtesy of Mississippi Department of Archives and History

For example, around the turn of the 20th century, showmen traveled around the United States by horse and wagon performing medicine shows and selling miracle cures to the uniformed public. Many of these miracle cures were harmless, but some were very dangerous.

One popular miracle cure of the early 20th century was Kopp's Baby Friend. This product promised desperate parents a cure for whatever was ailing a crying baby. However, it contained large amounts of alcohol and some opium which today we know are addictive and harmful, especially to children. Another product with similar ingredients was Mrs. Winslow's Soothing Syrup which was sold for many years.

A medicine for children that contained opium and alcohol. It was sold from 1845-1930.

Another popular miracle cure was radioactive baths. In the early 1900's some naturally occurring mineral springs were found to contain small amounts of radioactive water. Medical journals at the time claimed that radium, a radioactive element, slowed aging and as a result "radium spas" where people could bathe in radioactive water became popular. Radioactive beauty cream, toothpaste, and ear plugs were also sold. It was only after chemists and physicists began to understand the real effects of radiation that these products finally disappeared.

People need to have a basic understanding of chemistry, biology, physics, geology, and astronomy and how they fit together. By learning the basic building blocks of science, people can make more informed decisions about what they buy and what ideas and policies they support.

22.3 Science in the Movies

Science themes are a favorite in the movies. The mad or crazy scientist is a common character in many movies. There are both the mad scientist determined to end the world and the fun loving scientist who invents ways to leap over buildings, shrink his kids, or travel back in time. There are also serious scientists who solve world problems, caution eager businessmen about the dangers of untested ideas, and solve criminal cases.

The movies can be a great way for the general public to explore scientific ideas, products, and problems. Although the movies rarely portray how real science works and how real scientists do science, a well-informed and well-researched movie can give people some idea about the nature of science and scientific language and investigation.

Because movies can reach an audience much larger than scientific journals can, the movies can be used to help educate people. However, movies can also be used to distort information, represent science inaccurately, and draw false conclusions. Movie directors and screen writers who have a basic understanding of what science is, how it works, and how it is put together, can more accurately portray scientific endeavors.

22.4 Real Scientists

Although there are many fun and quirky scientists who have made important discoveries, scientists are just regular people. Real scientists are not "mad" or "crazy" but instead are people who have an intense curiosity about how the world works and an interest in solving real world problems.

Scientists spend many years studying a particular area of science and often work in research labs at universities, industrial companies, hospitals, and even as advisors to presidents! Scientists are valued in a variety of industries because while studying and doing science they have learned how to think critically and solve problems.

Scientists are ordinary men and women who, like other ordinary people, make mistakes, get into disagreements, and sometimes even cheat or falsify data. Scientists who are given money to perform research need to prove that they are getting results from their research in order to keep getting money, and many scientists also need to show that they are making new discoveries in order to keep their jobs. This can put a lot of pressure on scientists to "prove" something true or false even if the data don't support a conclusion. Sometimes scientists will be in such a hurry to publish results that they will skip doing an essential experiment or draw an inaccurate conclusion in order to meet a deadline or satisfy the group that has given them money.

It is helpful that scientists are constantly examining the work of each other and challenging conclusions that may not be correct. Scientists go to conferences to present their data to other scientists, and scientific papers are reviewed by several scientists and sometimes not published if there are too many mistakes or if the papers are lacking key experiments. Although this form of "peer-review" does not catch all the errors, it does help scientists put it all together and present their very best work. Maybe even more importantly, conferences and peer reviews allow scientists to share ideas and research findings. This sharing leads to new ideas for further research. The more that is discovered and the more that ideas and findings are shared, the faster scientific discovery can advance.

22.5 Summary

- Science combines chemistry, biology, physics, geology, and astronomy.
- Because the public is sometimes uniformed about science, people can be sold harmful products and made to believe ideas that are harmful to them and to the planet.
- Movies can help represent science accurately if writers and directors know some basic science.
- Scientists work hard to understand how the world works and to solve problems, but they do sometimes make mistakes.

More REAL SCIENCE-4-KIDS Books
by Rebecca W. Keller, PhD

Building Blocks Series yearlong study program — each Student Textbook has accompanying Laboratory Notebook, Teacher's Manual, Lesson Plan, Study Notebook, Quizzes, and Graphics Package

Exploring Science Book K (Activity Book)
Exploring Science Book 1
Exploring Science Book 2
Exploring Science Book 3
Exploring Science Book 4
Exploring Science Book 5
Exploring Science Book 6
Exploring Science Book 7
Exploring Science Book 8

Focus On Series unit study program — each title has a Student Textbook with accompanying Laboratory Notebook, Teacher's Manual, Lesson Plan, Study Notebook, Quizzes, and Graphics Package

Focus On Elementary Chemistry
Focus On Elementary Biology
Focus On Elementary Physics
Focus On Elementary Geology
Focus On Elementary Astronomy

Focus On Middle School Chemistry
Focus On Middle School Biology
Focus On Middle School Physics
Focus On Middle School Geology
Focus On Middle School Astronomy

Focus On High School Chemistry

Super Simple Science Experiments

21 Super Simple Chemistry Experiments
21 Super Simple Biology Experiments
21 Super Simple Physics Experiments
21 Super Simple Geology Experiments
21 Super Simple Astronomy Experiments
101 Super Simple Science Experiments

Note: A few titles may still be in production.

Gravitas Publications Inc.
www.gravitaspublications.com
www.realscience4kids.com